Palgrave Debates in Business and Management

Series Editor
Anders Örtenblad, Department of Working Life and Innovation, School of Business and Law, University of Agder, Grimstad, Norway

This series takes a refreshing and creative approach to business management research, showcasing diverse opinions and angles on some of the major debates in Business and Management. Each title examines one specific topic and includes a number of chapters from authors around the world, presenting their differing points of view on the question in hand. Without taking an editorial stance on the issues, this series takes stock of controversial and complicated topics of debate within Business and Management, and clearly presents the variety of positions within it.

Silvia Cinque · Daniel Ericsson
Editors

Debating 'Homo Academicus' in Management and Organization

Ontological Assumptions and Practical Implications

palgrave
macmillan

Editors
Silvia Cinque
University of Liverpool Management School
Liverpool, UK

Daniel Ericsson
School of Business and Economics
Linnaeus University
Växjö, Sweden

ISSN 2524-5082 ISSN 2524-5090 (electronic)
Palgrave Debates in Business and Management
ISBN 978-3-031-58194-6 ISBN 978-3-031-58195-3 (eBook)
https://doi.org/10.1007/978-3-031-58195-3

This Palgrave Macmillan imprint is published by the registered company Springer Nature Switzerland AG
The registered company address is: Gewerbestrasse 11, 6330 Cham, Switzerland

Contents

Notes on Contributors

Maira Babri currently holds a position as Associate Senior Lecturer in the intersection between Circular Economy Studies and Organization Studies at Mälardalen University. She received her Ph.D. in Organization Studies from Umeå University in 2017. Between 2018 and 2023, Maira worked as Senior Lecturer and Head of Division at the department of Business Administration at Örebro School of Business where she still teaches a course in Business and Society. Her research covers questions of glocal relevance, with a specific interest in the entanglements of the human and material world and the consequent possibilities for organizing. She also has an interest in methodology and particularly ways of reconciling the self and body in scientific work. Her theoretical inspiration in interdisciplinary and her empirical focus has ranged between organizing multinational corporations, SMEs, academia-industry collaborations, and the researcher herself.

Martin Blom is Associate Professor in Business Administration (Strategic Management) at Lund University School of Economics and Management (LUSEM), Sweden. His research interests cover topics such as leadership/followership, strategy, and corporate governance. Currently he also serves as Director of International Affairs at LUSEM. Blom has been a guest researcher at HEC Montreal, Canada. His research has recently been published in journals such as *Human Relations, Leadership and Corporate Governance: An International Review*, and with publishers such as *Cambridge University Press, Edward Elgar Publishing, Palgrave Macmillan, Routledge* and *SAGE*.

Kate Black is Professor of Management Learning and Education at Newcastle Business School, Northumbria University, where she is Head of Education and is founding convenor for the "Professional Learning and Management Education" research group. Kate's research interests lie in examining learning, as a process of 'being' and 'becoming'—that is, of identity formation. Much of her work examines such identity formation for professionals within the contemporary knowledge economy. This understanding also underpins her academic practice and informs her pedagogic research and education scholarship activity. Kate typically adopts a qualitative approach to research data generation with particular emphasis upon visual methods including artifactual conversations and the use of participant-generated imagery. Kate is Vice Chair for *the British Academy of Management* with responsibility for the Management Knowledge and Education portfolio. She is also Associate Editor for *Human Resource Development Quarterly* and an Editorial Board Member for *British Journal of Management*.

Malgorzata Ciesielska is Professor of Management and Organisation Studies at Sheffield Business School, Sheffield Hallam University where she leads a research group on Responsible Leadership & Socially Sustainable Organisations. In 2010 she received her Ph.D. in Organisation & Management Studies from Copenhagen Business School and subsequently moved to work in the UK higher education. Her research interests range from organizational justice to methodological innovations in coaching and team facilitation, supporting EDI agenda and HR Development practices. She has been working with a range of organizations in the healthcare, sport, and tech sectors as well as local authorities. In 2022 she received Praxis Auril Knowledge Exchange Strategic Partnership award for the project on restorative just culture with NHS. Gosia is specializing in qualitative research methods, especially interviewing, organizational ethnography and case studies. She is also Associate Editor of *Journal of Organizational Change Management, Tamara Journal for Critical Organization Inquiry* and *Culture and Organisation.*

Silvia Cinque is Lecturer in Organisation and Management at the University of Liverpool Management School, and Fellow at SDA Bocconi School of Management. She conducts research across the areas of organisation and management theory, business and society, and social theory. Her main interests involve identity, meaningful work and work as a calling, power and resistance, gender, and the creative industries.

Daniel Ericsson earned his Ph.D. from the Stockholm School of Economics in 2001. Currently, he is a Professor of Organization and Management at Linnaeus University and a visiting professor of Cultural Entrepreneurship at Lund University. He is particularly interested in understanding how creativity is constructed in society, and in exploring different ways of writing within the social sciences, drawing inspiration from, among others, Umberto Eco's semiotics, Erich Auerbach's ideas on narrative styles, and Raymond Queneau's playful poetry. His research has recently been published in journals such as *Culture and Organization, Gender, Work & Organization,* and *Journal of Organizational Change Management*. He is the founding editor of Art, Culture & Entrepreneurship (Linnaeus University Press), an online, open access, peer-reviewed journal and platform devoted to the study of initiatives within the art and cultural sector to establish new forms of organized practices. He also serves as an associate editor for *Culture and Organization* (Taylor & Francis).

Anna M. Górska Ph.D. is Assistant Professor at Kozminski University and a director of Women and Diversity in Organizations Research Center. She studies higher education institutions from the perspective of management, communication, and diversity. Her works have been published in international academic journals such as *Gender, Work and Organization, Gender in Management,* and *Information & Management.* Her recent book *Gender and Academic Career Development in Central and Eastern Europe* was published by Routledge. Anna has participated as a principal investigator and researcher in multiple research grants funded by the Polish National Center of Science, EU funds, and Norwegian Funds. She has also been awarded scholarships and awards, including the Fulbright Junior Research Award. She has gained international experience as a visiting scholar at Columbia Business School and ESCP Business School. Anna is also involved in organizational work at KU as an Impact Manager, part of the international accreditations office, an expert on antidiscrimination initiatives, and a head of Students Association Women in Organizations. She is responsible for KU's Gender Equality Plan, Sustainable Transition Strategy, and Business School Impact System.

Martin Holgersson is Assistant Professor in business administration at Linnaeus University. His research interests include a broad range of topics, such as the financialization of everyday life, academic writing, the relationship between science and art, entrepreneurship, and social aspects of management accounting. A recurring theme in his research is that he draws inspiration from diverse scientific fields, including sociology, philosophy, and literature, to gain insights into economic and business phenomena. Currently, he primarily teaches courses in management accounting at both undergraduate and master's levels. However, he possesses experience in teaching across various subfields of business administration, such as management, finance, and corporate governance, as well as research methodology.

Mattias Jacobsson, Ph.D., is Associate Professor of Management and Organization at Umeå School of Business, Economics and Statistics, Umeå University, Sweden. Currently, he is also working part-time at the School of Engineering, Jönköping University, Sweden. His main research interests are in projects, practice, and temporary organizations, and, on four occasions, he has been a prizewinner at the Emerald Literati Network Awards for Excellence. Jacobsson has also been a guest researcher at RMIT University in Melbourne, Australia, and at Virginia Tech in the States. His work has been published in a large number of journals, including *Business Horizons, European Management Journal, Management Decision, Project Management Journal®, International Journal of Project Management, the International Journal* *of Managing Projects in Business*, and *Construction Management and Economics*. For more information, see http://mattiasjacobsson.me.

Mikael Lundgren is Senior Lecturer in Business Administration (Organization) at Linnaeus University School of Business and Economics, Sweden. His research interests are within the areas of leadership/followership, strategy, and qualitative methodology. Lately, Lundgren has worked extensively with developing and executing leadership development programs based on interactive and collaborative methods. Lundgren is a regular guest lecturer at Universidad de Valladolid, Spain. His research has been published in journals such as *International Business Review, Leadership*, and *Journal of Change Management*.

Carmelo Mazza is Ph.D. in Business Economics from IESE-Universidad de Navarra (Spain). His main research interests have focused on institutionalization processes and on creative industries. He has published in leading academic journals on several contexts such like creative industries, higher education institutions, media companies, consulting firms, and has taught Organization Theory and Organizational behavior in several leading universities and business schools throughout Europe. Recent research projects focus on the current transformation of management education and on the interplay of tradition and innovation within creative settings. His most recent research is published in *Managing Cultural Festivals between Tradition and Innovation* (2022, Routledge) and *New Themes in Institutional Analysis: Topics and Issues from European Research* (2017, Edward Elgar Publishing). Along with these academic activities, Carmelo Mazza holds a relevant experience in consulting and management, assisting/sitting in Boards of Directors.

Pernilla Nilsson has extensive experience as Lecturer in management, organization and strategic change at Umeå School of Business, Växjö University and Linnaeus University. In her research, she has focused on organizational identity construction in local business counselling services. She has also conducted processual evaluation studies for national and regional authorities. Currently, she has an interest in issues of academic integrity on the virgule between the individual and research community.

Anders Örtenblad is both a human and an academic. He works as Professor of Working Life Science at the University of Agder, Norway. He is a big fan of research as open, academic debate, and is the editing founder of the book series *Palgrave Debates in Business and Management*. Among other collections, he has edited many books, *The Oxford Handbook of Metaphor in Organization Studies* and *Making Sense of the Learning Turn: Why and In What Sense Toys, Organizations, Economies, and Cities are "Learning"* both published by Oxford University Press.

Anders Söderholm, Ph.D. is the president of KTH, Royal Institute of Technology, in Stockholm. He is also the former Director General of the Swedish Higher Education Authority (UKÄ) and former Vice-Chancellor and professor at the Mid Sweden University. Söderholm obtained his Ph.D. from Umeå University in 1991 and became a professor of Business Administration in 2005. His main research interest is in projects and temporary organizations. Söderholm has also been a guest researcher at Stanford University, Royal Institute of Technology, and Åbo Akademi University.

Pär Vasko, Ph.D. is working as Senior Lecturer at the School of Business and Economics at Linnaeus University. He defended his dissertation, *Moving Beyond Stewards versus Agents,* in December 2022. The dissertation explores the dichotomies in the discourse of stewardship theory and agency theory, with the aim of illustrating an alternative understanding of the theoretical ideals underpinning the two theoretical positions. Currently, he is working in a research project *Cultural Entrepreneurship in the field of music* that aims to contribute to, and develop the local culture scene of music—in the broad sense of the word. In many ways, music has been, and still is, a source of inspiration for his life in academia when engaging in writing, reflecting and reading.

Alf Westelius is Professor at Linköping University, specializing in how new and mature organizations navigate and function in the ever-more digitized and dynamic world. People build, manage/control and shape organizations. Therefore, a cornerstone of his research and consulting is Perspectives Management, identifying and paying heed to perspective differences among people. The role of universities in societies, including knowledge and skill development and branding processes, has always been one of his interests.

Dr. Dawn Whitton is Associate Professor (Education) at Durham University Business School, where she is the Deputy Director of Education for Management and Marketing. Dawn's research interests focus on pedagogic research, relating to employability and career development, enhancing the student experience and widening access to Higher Education. Her professional doctorate focused on employability and career development but more recently, and since joining Durham University, Dawn has developed her research and teaching interests in Corporate Responsibility and Sustainability. Dawn undertakes both quantitative and qualitative approaches to research and adopts a pragmatic approach to research data collection and analysis. Dawn is a Certified Management and Business Educator and strives to create and develop opportunities for students to achieve and succeed in Higher Education. She has recently started a project which evaluates decolonizing the curriculum and the impact on international postgraduate students' career preparedness. Dawn strives to support all students to support their individual development.

List of Figures

1

Debating *Homo Academicus*: A Maieutic Quest for Self-Reflexivity

Daniel Ericsson and Silvia Cinque

Instigating a Debate on *Homo Academicus*

The fields of management and organization have long been permeated by the ontological and normative assumption that people are—and should be—maximizers of utility, a *Homo oeconomicus*. Facing a decision between alternatives, each of which is likely to give different outcomes, people in organizations, especially those that occupy managerial positions, should calculate the pros and cons of each of their alternatives, and choose the one that maximizes the outcome in terms of utility.

This assumption was established by early economic philosophers such as Adam Smith (1776/2012) and John Stuart Mill (1863/1962), and

D. Ericsson (✉)
School of Business and Economics, Linnaeus University, Växjö, Sweden
e-mail: daniel.ericsson@lnu.se

Department of Arts and Cultural Sciences, Lund University, Lund, Sweden

S. Cinque
University of Liverpool Management School, Liverpool, UK
e-mail: silvia.cinque@liverpool.ac.uk

S. Cinque and D. Ericsson (eds.), *Debating 'Homo Academicus' in Management and Organization*, Palgrave Debates in Business and Management,
https://doi.org/10.1007/978-3-031-58195-3_1

popularized by scholars ranging from Frederic Winslow Taylor (1911/1913) to Michael Jensen and William Meckling (1976), and is still feverishly reproduced and embraced, not the least by practitioners within certain walks of organizational life such as New Public Management and Corporate Governance. As an assemblage of different ideas such as (perfect) rationality, opportunism, and managerial agency, it is however something that has been heavily debated throughout the years. For example, the laureate of the Nobel Memorial Prize in Economic Sciences, Herbert Simon (1957) contested the notion of "maximizing man" by introducing the notion of "satisficing man"; Nils Brunsson (1982), one of the progenitors of Scandinavian institutionalism, questioned the rationality of being rational, and argued for the rationality of acting irrationally; the well-known economists Lex Donaldson and James H. Davis (1991) pleaded for replacing opportunistic agents with benevolent stewards in both theory and practice; and more recently, Peter Fleming pronounced the death of the notorious character in his *The death of Homo economicus* (2017).

Today there is an abundance of both different ontological assumptions about people and normative stories on how to act and think in accordance with these different assumptions in the fields of management and organization. Scholars have widely confronted the ontology of *Homo oeconomicus* by presenting empirical evidence or theoretical and philosophical arguments in favor of alternative assumptions, replacing *Homo oeconomicus* as the protagonist of management and organization theory and practice with among (many) others *Homo faber* (Arendt, 1958, 2018), *Homo ludens* (Haustein, 1981), *Homo narrans* (Vasquez, 1993), *Homo politicus* (Nyborg, 2000), *Homo creativus* (Kakko & Inkinen, 2009), *Homo heuristics and Homo duplex* (Kluver et al., 2014), *Homo sustainabiliticus* (Russ, 2014), *Homo dialogicus* (Kent & Taylor, 2016), *Homo entrepreneurus* (Lounsbury et al., 2019), *Homo sacer* (Redmalm & Skoglund, 2020), and *Homo projecticus* (Jacobsson & Söderholm, 2021).

In this book, we would like to advance the debate about different assumptions about people in and around organizations, as well as their consequences, but in a self-reflexive direction: What ontological assumptions about themselves do scholars in the fields of management and organization live by? Do they think they are something "special", distinctively separated from the life-world of managers and employees but linked with other academics such as, say, philosophers and sociologists? If so, what do they have in common? And what are the consequences and implications of the assumptions made?

Initially, the working title for our project was "Who do we think we are?" Being an intertextual allusion to Deep Purple's album from 1973 with the very same title, it is intended to convey a satirical twist on the Jante law's moralist expression "Who do you think you are?" (see Chapter 2 in this volume, Ericsson and Nilsson [2024]), and as such point to what we were looking for in a clear-cut manner: an unpretentious and productive debate about the ontological assumptions scholars in the fields of management and organization make about themselves—and that might result in unintended consequences. As an informative book title, however, it was severely underdeveloped, not to say "fraught with background" (to use Auerbach's [1953/1974] famous concept), in acute need of explication. Neither did it point to the "empirical" context we envisioned in terms of the fields of management and organization, nor did it signify the relation between ontological assumption and practical implications that we wished to scrutinize. In addition (and perhaps most troublesome): our working title kept quiet about our desire to stir a debate.

Soon enough, the working title for our project was to be abandoned in favor of the title that now graces the cover: "Debating *Homo academicus* in Management and Organization: Ontological Assumptions and Practical Implications". Albeit this title, in many respects, is straighter to the point, it does not present the intention and meaning of our project in "full light". It is still in need of contextualization and explication. Therefore, before we present the book's narrative structure and the different contributions, we believe it to be fruitful to pay some attention to each of the words in the title to inculcate even further the nuances that we ascribe to our project, and at the same time confront some of the troublesome issues that surfaced in the process of writing, reviewing, and editing the book.

Prior that, however, we would like to position our project in relation to what appears to be one of the major conversation topics within the fields of management and organization: self-fulfilling prophecies, i.e., the phenomena in which unsubstantiated, unethical, or dysfunctional assumptions about humans can lead to adverse practical consequences (see, for instance, Eden, 1992; Felin & Foss, 2009; Kierein & Gold, 2000; McGregor, 1960; Merton, 1948; Meyers & Van Woerkom, 2014). It is in light of such dangers, we argue, that management and organization scholars need to reflect upon the taken-for-granted assumptions they make of themselves, and to interrogate what consequences these assumptions bring to the research they conduct, the knowledge they produce, and the practical implications they advocate. As we see it, it is in relation to such a need for reflexivity that this book acquires both its meaning and its relevance.

On Self-Fulfilling Prophecies

The phenomenon of self-fulfilling prophecy has been problematized throughout history, in its many different shapes and contexts. Perhaps one of the oldest and most known representations of it, the *Pygmalion effect*, stems from Greek mythology and tells the story of the sculptor Pygmalion who takes such a liking to his statue, Galatea, that it eventually comes to life. Throughout history, this myth has acquired a strong positive meaning, not the least in educational settings where it has come to represent the idea that a teacher's expectations of students have a positive impact on their performances (see Rosenthal & Jacobson, 1968). Galatea, in turn, has come to name the phenomenon where the self-fulfilling prophecy is not dependent on a relation, but generated within the individual, i.e., the *Galatea effect* refers to a situation in which one's beliefs in one's own abilities affect one's performance in a positive manner (see Eden, 1992). Where the self-fulfilling prophecy has a reversed outcome, i.e., when low expectations on individuals cause them to perform poorly, educational scholars often refer to it as the *Golem effect* (Babad et al., 1982). This effect also has deep cultural roots, as its name is taken from a legend within Jewish mythology. According to this legend, Golem was a clay creature brought to life by Rabbi Loew in Prague in the sixteenth century with the intention of protecting the Jews from anti-Semitic persecution. However, Golem goes astray in a spiral of violence, and has to be put to sleep.

As cultural memes, the Pygmalion, Galatea, and Golem effects, each individually or taken together, permeate not only popular culture—from Frankenstein's monster and Pinocchio to My Fair Lady and Pretty Woman—but also the fields of management and organization. For instance, just to name some of the different theories and concepts that are impregnated with ideas on self-fulfilling prophecies: the Golem effect echoes in McGregor's (1960) Theory X, whereas the Pygmalion effect echoes in Theory Y; the conversation on transformational leadership (Bass, 1985) takes the Pygmalion effect for granted; and Vroom's (1964) expectancy theory of motivation assumes the workings of the Galatea effect. According to Eden (1992), even Management by Objectives might set the stage for self-fulfilling prophecies; when successfully implemented, Management by Objectives creates "a double expectation effects, i.e., a Pygmalion effect on the part of the manager and a Galatea effect on the subordinate's part" (p. 297).

On an overall level, it seems as if scholars in the fields of management and organization tend to overtly reflect upon self-fulfilling prophecies as a central empirical aspect of work organizations (see Kierein & Gold, 2000) and of the empirical relation between leaders and followers (see Whiteley et al., 2012). Occasionally, they also turn their empirical attention to management and organizational development consultants, who are seen as prophets (or Messiahs) that unwittingly fulfill their own prophecies (Eden, 1986). Self-fulfilling theories in use by the scholars themselves have also been a conversation topic even if most attention has been paid to theories within economics and their supposedly negative effect on management and organization practices (see Felin & Foss, 2009; Ferraro et al., 2005). Problematizing self-fulfilling prophecies at work within management and organization research is, however, rarer—besides an overarching methodological awareness of experimenter or observer effects and interpretative biases (see, for instance, Bell et al., 2022). There are however three different strands of research that address and problematize how management and organization researchers' assumptions, in one way or the other, influence research outcomes in a self-fulfilling manner.

The first of these strands acknowledges the paradigmatic aspects of research. With reference to Burrell and Morgan's (1979) seminal *Sociological Paradigms and Organisational Analysis*, it is here argued that researchers' assumptions about the nature of, on the one hand, social science and, on the other hand, society are ordered in four distinct paradigms: the radical humanist paradigm, the radical structuralist paradigm, the interpretative paradigm, and the functionalist paradigm. These paradigms, it is further argued, encompass different assumptions about ontology, epistemology, human nature, and methodology, and they are mutually exclusive—or incommensurable—due to their inherent differences. All in all, these differences boil down to two major incommensurable set of assumptions: (1) the ontological assumptions on whether reality is "out there", external to the researcher, or "in there", a product of individual consciousness—which in turn is inextricably intertwined with the epistemological assumption whether it is possible to obtain either objective knowledge or subjective knowledge; and (2) the assumptions on whether research should concern societal regulation or radical change. Burrell and Morgan (1979) do not explicitly deal with self-fulfilling prophecies, but clearly the idea about incommensurable paradigms fosters research that is consistent with the underlying assumptions of the paradigms. If not, then the research would be a troublesome case of "mixed discourse" (Giorgi, 1994), that is, mixing incommensurable assumptions.

The second strand of research that problematizes management and organization researchers' assumptions in relation to the research outcome in terms of self-fulfilling prophecies is the metaphorical approach. Most vividly, this approach has been brought forward by Gareth Morgan, who in his *Images of Organization* (1986) presents eight different ways of thinking about and seeing organizations—as machines, organisms, brains, cultures, political systems, psychic prisons, flux and transformation, and instruments of domination. Thinking about and seeing something *as* something is metaphorical in character, and metaphors, Morgan argues (p. 13), not only frame and limit our understanding of the world, they are also powerful devices to reproduce taken-for-granted assumptions. That is, if researchers in the fields of management and organization only talk about, say, organizations as if they were machines, then we will most likely end up advocating managerial practices adapted to running the machine in a smooth but mechanistic manner. In this regard, Morgan speaks in favor of the use of many different metaphors to grapple with the complexities and ambiguities of organizations, but his book has also prompted a self-reflexive turn toward the (root) metaphors that researchers themselves live by (see Jermier & Forbes, 2011; Norén, 1995; Örtenblad, 2024).

The third strand, attentive to self-fulfilling prophecies among researchers, is constructionist in character, with a slight postmodern twist. Within this strand, management and organization researchers acknowledge on the one hand the constructionist bridging of the chasm between subjectivism and objectivism as conveyed by the Thomas theorem, "If men define situations as real, they are real in their consequences" (see Berger & Luckmann, 1966/1991; Merton, 1948), and on the other hand the hermeneutic idea of preunderstanding (see Alvesson & Sandberg, 2022). The resulting positioning is a self-reflexive one, which highlights the researcher's subjective (dis)position to the phenomenon at hand—and to the knowledge produced.

As we see it, all three of these strands have had considerable impact within the fields of management and organization, heightening both theoretical and methodological awareness. However, in none of these strands has attention specifically been directed to the assumptions scholars make of themselves and how these assumptions might turn into troublesome self-fulfilling prophecies.

On "Debating *Homo Academicus* in Management and Organization"

Although we have carefully weighed our words in the title, each and every one of them is in need of some explication and contextualization to understand the nuances that we ascribe to our project. To start with "debating", the book is published in Palgrave's book series *Debates in Business and Management*, which has the explicit intention to present a variety of positions given a specific topic/debate. That is, we are acknowledging both the notion that there are specific topics/debates in business and management *and* the possibility of a neighborly debate between researchers of different positions. At the same time, we are well aware of the different debating traditions in academia. On the one hand, there is the *eristic* tradition in which debate is perceived of as a struggle to defeat the opponent, not for the sake of good arguments, but for the sake of the victory in itself (as sarcastically outlined by Arthur Schopenhauer) (see Rankin, 1983). On the other hand, there is Socrates' somewhat forgotten *maieutic* tradition in which debates are seen as vehicles for advancing—or rather: *delivering*—the speaking partner's arguments (Rankin, 1983). Reflecting upon the different implications these two traditions have for life in academia in general, and in terms of self-fulfilling prophecies specifically, we have taken an ethical stand in favor of the latter: instead of approaching our book project as an eristic struggle with the final and absolute outcome of crowning the best ontological assumptions scholars in the fields of management and organization could make about themselves, we have approached it as a maieutic quest, as an ongoing conversation through which discursive positions on the subject are made visible, reflected upon, and (perhaps could be) altered. Hopefully, this ethical stance of ours enables us to challenge the assumption of *Homo academicus* as a "winner of debates"—and to refrain from partaking in the constructions of eristic scholar identities in the fields of management and organization. In our opinion, there are already too many of them out there.

Closely connected to the issue of "debating" is the issue of constructing solid and compelling arguments. In this regard, the eristic tradition is typically characterized by "rhetoric devices" whose sole purpose is to win over the opponent by ontologically distinguishing "what is" from "what is not" (see Potter, 1996). Most often, these rhetoric devices come in the form of "theoretical rigor", "empirical evidence", and "analytic statistics". By contrast, scholars engaging in the maieutic tradition are typically trying to probe what potentially "could be" together with the opponent in an emancipatory manner—which is an endeavor characterized by a completely different type of rhetoric, as we see it. Instead of hitting their opponent in the head with hard, cold, and objective facts, maieutics typically deliver arguments from a subjective (dis)position characterized by (a mutual) respect and empathy for the opponent paired with a playful openness for the unknown. Their arguments are typically sprung from their subjective and historically mediated experiences, mobilized in unforeseen ways, and the rhetorical power of their arguments depend on their ability to resonate or fuse with the opponent's subjective and historically mediated experience (see Gadamer, 1979). Consequently, the eristic weaponry of validity, reliability, and generalizability is typically downplayed in favor of plausibility, intelligibility, and promises; deduction and induction are typically overtaken by hermeneutic abduction (see Alvesson & Sköldberg, 2009); and traditional scientific writing, in accordance with the so-called IMRAD-model (Introduction, Methods, Results, and Discussion), is typically replaced by essayistic forms of writing. As we see it, this typical maieutic (dis)position has much in common with the type of academic craftsmanship that Charles Wright Mills (1959) advocated for in terms of *sociological imagination*: to see beyond what is "here and now", to question the taken-for-granted aspects of everyday life, to focus upon the greater picture and problematize how seemingly small things in life fit into this picture, and, above all, to shift perspectives (see also Ericsson & Kostera, 2022).

In the process of writing, reviewing, and editing this volume, all of the above typical characteristics of majestic argumentation and imagination have been encouraged in different ways and to different extents. As editors we, however, have taken into consideration that scholars within the fields of management and organization not only are brought up and trained in different scientific traditions but also to varying degrees have to face the hegemony of scientific writing. In this regard, one could say that our quest for a maieutic debate at once is a quest for maieutic arguments, quality measures, forms of conclusions, as well as forms of writing.

* * *

Regarding the subject up for debate, the "*Homo academicus*" in the book's title, is, of course, an intertextual wink to Pierre Bourdieu's (1988) seminal text and other classics problematizing different versions of "*Homo*". By using this signifier, our intent is to convey the self-reflexive and critical, not to say emancipatory, reading effects that we are hoping for, problematizing assumptions about both scholarly positions and dispositions. However, the usage of "*Homo*" is not without controversy, and neither is our overarching generalized interest: to discuss ontological assumptions about academic "man" within the fields of management and organization, as both "*Homo*" and "man" have strong gendered connotations, not the least in Anglo-Saxon language communities. In this regard, we here face a delicate dilemma: *either* conveying the precise meaning we would like to attach to "Homo" and "man" ("a human being of either sex") and being accused of using gendering language, *or* using imprecise but non-gendered alternatives to "man" such as "humanity" or "mankind" (i.e. "human beings considered collectively" or "the human race" in the dictionary sense). "Human nature", as we occasionally used in our initial call for papers, narrows attention to general biological and/or psychological characteristics but might lead the reader in unwarranted directions. By comparison, "man" is significantly more open and inclusive of different aspects (and assumptions) of life.

We are of course not the first to face this dilemma, and sad to say there seems to be no complete escape out of the gendered intricacies of language. As we see it, however, there are strategies to mitigate the gap between *intentio auctoris* and the reading effects the use of language might trigger. On the one hand, we deem it fruitful to address the issue in an open and honest manner, revealing and discussing one's intentions and deliberations. On the other hand, we see it as necessary, as far as it is possible, to take responsibility, as both authors and editors, not only for the different texts in the book but also for the reading of it. The book you are holding in your hand is the outcome of these two strategies: we have omitted gendered expressions, such as "assumptions about man", in all but those cases where we openly scrutinize the assumption behind that assumption or are bound by explicit references that are not gender neutral (i.e., the Thomas theorem above); and we have actively rewritten text passages that could provoke gendering reading effects. However, we have kept "*Homo*" in the title, as well as in this introductory chapter and in most of the other chapters, since we reckon this to be one too well-established concept to abandon, given the positioning of the book and its contribution. Taken together, we sincerely hope that our dealings with our dilemma neither make the book into a gendered (or even worse, sexist) enterprise nor forfeit some of the book's core ideas and spirit.

* * *

Besides being fraught with background, the working title "Who do we think we are?" also entailed a troublesome reference to a "we". Although we (the editors) eventually came to abandon the working title, and although the "we" (in the working title) neither was intended to function as some sort of rhetorical device to create homogeneity or similarity between the contributors nor to create an intrusive or unwanted bond between the writers and the readers, this "we" triggered us (the editors) to reflect upon the position from which we (the editors and the contributors) speak—and what is spoken about. Some "empirical" specification was clearly needed in regard to both the contributors' collective and the content of the book.

After some deliberation, "management and organization" seemed to be the common denominator for both contributors and content. Despite our open call for contributions (in which the book title only was "Debating *Homo academicus*"), it turned out that almost all of the responders to the call, in one way or the other, explicitly positioned their texts in relation to "management and organization". It also seemed to be a matter of professional identity for them as they presented their professional areas of expertise and/or subject affiliations in terms of management and organization.

However, "management" and "organization" are two fuzzy and rather fluent concepts that could point in many different directions, and consequently could be used to draw up many different demarcation lines between people and subject areas—which in turn have different consequences for scholars in what they do and how they identify themselves. To acknowledge the plenitude of different research areas that are subsumed under the moniker "management and organization", we therefore find it important to specify that whenever we refer to "management and organization" we mean "scholars working in the fields of management and organization". Hopefully, this specification accommodates the contributors and their texts, as well as invites the reader, in an inclusive manner.

* * *

Last but not least, a short note on the book's subtitle, "Ontological assumptions and practical implications", in which "ontological assumptions" is intended to signify different basic assumptions about reality, i.e., "what is" vs. "what is not". In the context of "*Homo academicus* in management and organization", scholars in these fields could, for instance, assume that they are diligent and not lazy. However, this does not mean that they *are* diligent or that diligence is part of their identity or the role that they shoulder. It could very well be, not the least in light of self-fulfilling prophecies, that they become what they assume they are, but that is, in the end, an empirical question whose answer lies outside the scope of our book. Throughout the book we have therefore tried to steer away from essentialist thinking and identity or role categorizations, and to let "ontological assumptions" be nothing but just "ontological assumptions". In the pale cast of thought, this proved to be easier said than done, as ontological assumptions most often are tightly woven together with identity and role constructions. In this regard, one could say that issues of identity and roles are crucial parts of the "practical implications" indicated by the subtitle, but certainly not restricted to these issues.

On the Book's Narrative Structure and Content

By taking the above stands, we believe that we have positioned the book so that it is in line with the intention behind the publisher's book series, highlighting both the diversity of arguments and not a priori suppressing the arguments thematically or in any other way. As we see it, the book is not predicated upon any shared themes, and it was not construed in such a manner: we had an open call for contributions on the subject of the assumptions we make about ourselves as researchers, and the researchers that responded to the call got to develop their ideas freely in the abstracts. In different ways, each of the chapters discloses, problematizes, and criticizes different ontological assumptions about *Homo academicus* that underpins research in the fields of management and organization.

However, a posteriori (or rather: in the process of working with the book, editing and reviewing[1] the chapters) we came to develop an understanding of the ontological assumptions that seemed to be the basis for the assumptions discussed in the different chapters, sort of meta-assumptions. It seemed to us that our instigated debate revolved around two interrelated issues (or ideological tensions): (1) The extent to which scholars in the fields of management and organization are assumed to be—and should be—independent of social pressures, normative expectations, conventions, and institutional logics, and (2) The extent to which scholars in the fields of management and organization are assumed to speak—and should speak—from a position endowed with both obligations and privileges. And, through the different ways in which the book's contributors tackle these interrelated issues, we came to discern three more or less distinct argumentative ontological themes and positions:

Homo moralis: the assumption that scholars in the fields of management and organization on moral grounds should strive to be independent of social pressures, normative expectations, conventions, and institutional logics, and should be speaking from distinct privileged positions imbued with moral obligations.

Homo reflectivus: the assumption that scholars in the fields of management and organization are highly dependent on social pressures, normative expectations, conventions, and institutional logics, but should counteract such dependencies by speaking from positions based on self-reflexivity.

Homo mutatus: the assumption that scholars in the fields of management and organization are highly dependent on social pressures, normative expectations, conventions, and institutional logics, and therefore should strive to rethink the position from which to speak.

[1] All of the chapters have been subjected to double blind review, and we—the editors—would like to express our deepest gratitude to our colleagues who devoted their competence, time, and energy to act as reviewers: David Calås, Jeannie Holstein, Kai Inga Liehr Storm, Simon Parker, Suvi Satama, Ken Starkey, and Ruth Weatherall. We would also like to express our appreciation to the anonymous reviewers that commented upon our initial book proposal. It made us sharpen both our ideas and our arguments.

In the end, we decided to let these meta-assumptions form the narrative structure of the book and group the chapters in three different parts. On the one hand, the grouping made sense, for the sake of clarity of arguments, to highlight both similarities and dissimilarities between the chapters; and on the other hand, we deemed it fruitful to contribute with an overarching argumentative position, also in the introductory chapter, by means of the grouping per se. Arranging the chapters into three different parts was, however, not an unambiguous task. Some, not to say many or even all of the chapters, more or less fall in-between our imposed narrative structure. That is, *Homo moralis*, *Homo reflectivus*, and *Homo mutatus* are not mutually exclusive constructs. They are nothing but heuristic devices to even further stimulate a self-reflexive debate on *Homo academicus* within the fields of management and organization.

* * *

In Part One—*Homo moralis*—Daniel Ericsson and Pernilla Nilsson in "When management and organization came to the village of Jante" (Chapter 2) open up the debate by engaging with the question "who do we think we are?" through the moral lens of the Law of Jante—i.e. the moral imperative "you are not to think that you are anything special". Through their writing, the authors trace how the Law of Jante has been enacted within academia, business schools, and the fields of organization and management, and end up problematizing the (de)moralizing consequences for scholars in these fields in terms of, as they put it, "disbelief in oneself and one's ability and right to contribute to society".

Questioning oneself as an academic researcher is also the topic of Chapter 3, "Aren't we all human?: On the illusion of the extraordinary academic", in which Anders Örtenblad engages in the triggering reflection about the lack of self-reflection in conducting organization and management research. Örtenblad's starting point is the consideration that the *Homo academicus* tends to treat the people studied as human beings, as if they are biased, while considering their selves as being "extraordinary". In this chapter, the author delves into his own academic experiences in the area of management fashion, to discuss the extent to which scholars could be less gullible, irrational, and biased than those individuals they study.

First out in Part Two—*Homo reflectivus*—is Pär Vasko who in "Existential explorations of others and oneself as a researcher" (Chapter 4) engages in an exploration of others and oneself as a researcher through the illustration of three interwoven existential layers: (i) the existential paradoxes experienced by the author as a doctoral student in business administration; (ii) the theoretical key points of stewardship and agency theory; and (iii) the author's subjective exploration of taken-for-granted assumptions about human beings. Through these three existential layers, Vasko discusses how they contribute to the meaning of an "existential understanding" when theorizing about others while reflecting upon assumptions the researcher makes about oneself.

Martin Holgersson follows suit with "*Homo scribens*—Notes on writing management" (Chapter 5) in which he reflects on *Homo academicus* as a writing species. Whilst acknowledging the traditional assumption that sees management scholars as development consultants, who create knowledge in order to make organizations more efficient and well-functioning, Holgersson shifts the spotlight onto writing as the central and indispensable activity in developing management research. Far from being merely instrumental, writing is imbued with political aspects: something that places great responsibility on management scholars in the way they produce and disseminate scientific knowledge.

In "Living as an *academic-cum-something else*: How I learned to stop worrying and love academia" (Chapter 6), Carmelo Mazza earnestly reflects upon his personal struggle to be a *Homo academicus*, when another job (i.e. management consultancy) does not allow him to fully meet the requirements of being a *Homo academicus*. Interestingly, what the author refers to as "academic-cum-something else" allows him to keep loving academia without sharing the stress of the increasing managerialization of higher educational institutions, while relieving the burn-out of consultancy and management. In sharing his personal academic journey at the end of his Ph.D. in Organization Theory, Mazza seeks to answer the thought-provoking question of whether today's *Homo academicus* should, or should not, vanish into something else in order to make a new academia emerge.

Maira Babri titles Chapter 7 "*Homo academicus* as becoming nomadic: Reflections through a journey of pregnancy and motherhood". In it she outlines the shift she experienced in her academic identity from a static scholarly position toward a condition of "nomadism". Drawing from Braidotti's *Nomadic subject and nomadic ethics*, Babri initially delivers a somehow bitter and melancholic reflection on her positionality at the margins of the dominant and rational ideal academic, eventually acquiring strength through the conscious self-determination as "academic nomad"—one who is rooted and in becoming at the same time.

Kate Black, Gosia Ciesielska, and Dawn Whitton are the authors of Chapter 8, titled "'Dragged in the opposite direction': Identity tension facing women academics in business and management studies". The arguments develop between the three contributors, three female academics in the field of business and management, who take a reflexive-reflective approach to their academic experiences. Theoretically, the authors ground their conversation in the socio-cultural perspectives of identity, to question who they think they are, and to what extent they are who they want to be. Gender emerges as a central aspect of the chapter, with the authors examining an array of tensions they navigate as female academics in crafting their genuine sense of identity vis-à-vis the one expected by others—both inside and outside their institutions.

Gender is also at the core of the first chapter in Part Three—*Homo mutatus*. In "*Homo academicus* and gender: The cracking assumptions of rationality" (Chapter 9), Anna M. Górska delves into the ontological assumptions underlying academic identities in the fields of management and organization in the context of New Public Management (NPM). The author's study uncovers how NPM has reshaped the management scholars' ontological beliefs about their roles and capabilities, highlighting the gendered dimensions of these shifts. In particular, the focus is on how the tendency to prioritize research over teaching under NPM not only exacerbates gender inequalities but also leads to a reframing of academic identity. Hence, the quest for Higher Education institutions to reassess performance criteria to foster more equitable and supportive conditions.

In Chapter 10, "Beyond conventional leadership: On *Homo academicus (dux)* and ontological assumptions in academia", Mattias Jacobsson and Anders Söderholm explore what it means to be a *Homo academicus* in the fields of organization and management, and they do so in relation to the academic leader (*Homo academicus dux*). The authors reflect on three common yet (what they see as) incorrect assumptions held in the literature pertaining to *the distribution of power, the role of dependencies among units and practices*, and *how a sense of belonging is formed*. The authors envisage three alternative conditions that contour a new academic rationality and help move beyond conventional leadership. These are *reversed hierarchy, lateral independence*, and *community-based belonging*.

Mikael Lundgren and Martin Blom follow suit with "From *Homo academicus activistarum* to *Homo academicus imaginatus*" (Chapter 11). In focus is the assumption that forms the role and practice of the *Homo academic activistarum*: the scholar who ideologically turns to activism to balance the tension between a sense of urgency to solve pressing social problems, and a diminishing faith in traditional institutions such as universities. Problematizing this assumption, the authors turn to the fields of organization and management and envision the scholar as *Homo academicus imaginatus*. In both teaching and research, the imaginative scholar is one who engages in "imaginative performativity", promoting reflexivity and alternative thinking while avoiding the pitfalls and perils of academic activism.

Last but not least, Alf Westelius closes the *Homo mutatus* part of the book with "*Homo academicus* as guild, employment and attitude: The academy in transition" (Chapter 12). The chapter hosts Alf Westelius' consideration of three very different assumptions about who counts as *Homo academicus*: being part of a guild, holding employment at a university, or having internalized a specific attitude toward knowledge and learning in terms of passion, curiosity and the search for intellectual challenges. The author examines current transitions in the academy and provides an interesting read of how the three different conceptions interact, challenge and are challenged by each other and by trends in the societies of which they form parts.

A Maieutic Quest for Reflexivity

Having outlined the rationale behind our book project, positioned it in relation to three of the most prominent strands of research in the fields of management and organization that deal with ontological assumptions and practical consequences, and presented eleven (twelve with this introductory chapter) very different debate positions, we hope to have inspired a continued self-reflexive debate on *Homo academicus* within the fields of management and organization. In this regard, our project is a quest for reflexivity—as opposed to a search for it. Whereas "the search" is oriented toward a final end state—a pre-defined goal, "the quest" is oriented toward its very own intrinsic values. Whereas "the search" is about storytelling, "the quest" is epic in character: it is an adventure into the unknown, based on the recognition that the unknown never will (and cannot) be fully known. "The quest" is, as Kostera (2005) eloquently expresses it, "a textual travel in ideas".

And, as ours is an ongoing travel, we do not put a full stop to our quest. Instead, we end this introductory chapter with a colon. It is time for you, our reader, to read, reflect, and continue the debate:

References

Alvesson, M., & Sandberg, J. (2022). Pre-understanding: An interpretation-enhancer and horizon-expander in research. *Organization Studies, 43*(3), 395–412. https://doi.org/10.1177/0170840621994507

Alvesson, M., & Sköldberg, K. (2009). *Reflexive methodology: New vistas for qualitative research*. Sage.

Arendt, H. (1958/2018). *The human condition*. The University of Chicago Press.

Auerbach, E. (1953/1974). *Mimesis: The representation of reality in Western literature*. Princeton University Press.

Babad, E. Y., Inbar, J., & Rosenthal, R. (1982). Pygmalion, Galatea, and the Golem: Investigations of biased and unbiased teachers. *Journal of Educational Psychology, 74*(4), 459–474. https://doi.org/10.1037/0022-0663.74.4.459

Bass, B. M. (1985). *Leadership and performance beyond expectations*. Free Press.
Bell, E., Bryman, A., & Harley, B. (2022). *Business research methods*. Oxford University Press.
Berger, P. L., & Luckmann, T. (1966/1991). *The social construction of reality: A treatise in the sociology of knowledge*. Penguin.
Bourdieu, P. (1988). *Homo academicus*. Stanford University Press.
Brunsson, N. (1982). The irrationality of action and action rationality: Decisions, ideologies and organizational actions. *Journal of Management Studies, 19*(1), 29–44. https://doi.org/10.1111/j.1467-6486.1982.tb00058.x
Burrell, G., & Morgan, G. (1979). *Sociological paradigms and organisational analysis: Elements of the sociology of corporate life*. Heinemann.
Donaldson, L., & Davis, J. H. (1991). Stewardship theory or agency theory: CEO governance and shareholder returns. *Australian Journal of Management, 16*(1), 49–64. https://doi.org/10.1177/031289629101600103
Eden, D. (1986). OD and self-fulfilling prophecy: Boosting productivity by raising expectations. *The Journal of Applied Behavioral Science, 22*(1), 1–13. https://doi.org/10.1177/002188638602200104
Eden, D. (1992). Leadership and expectations: Pygmalion effects and other self-fulfilling prophecies in organizations. *The Leadership Quarterly, 3*(4), 271–305. https://doi.org/10.1016/1048-9843(92)90018-B
Ericsson, D., & Kostera, M. (2022). The university as the bringer of hope: A scaffolding for the future. *World Futures, 78*(5), 302–310. https://doi.org/10.1080/02604027.2021.2014750
Ericsson, D., & Nilsson, P. (2024). When management and organization came to the village of Jante. In S. Cinque & D. Ericsson (Eds.), *Debating Homo academicus in management and organization: Ontological assumptions and practical implications* (pp. 25–47). Palgrave.
Felin, T., & Foss, N. J. (2009). Social reality, the boundaries of self-fulfilling prophecy, and economics. *Organization Science, 20*(3), 654–668. https://doi.org/10.1287/orsc.1090.0431
Ferraro, F., Pfeffer, J., & Sutton, R. I. (2005). Economics language and assumptions: How theories can become self-fulfilling. *Academy of Management Review, 30*(1), 8–24. https://doi.org/doi.org/10.5465/amr.2005.15281412
Fleming, P. (2017). *The death of Homo economicus: Work, eebt and the myth of endless accumulation*. Pluto.
Gadamer, H. (1979). *Truth and method*. Sheed and Ward.
Giorgi, A. (1994). A phenomenological perspective on certain qualitative research methods. *Journal of Phenomenological Psychology, 25*, 190–220. https://doi.org/10.1163/156916294X00034

Haustein, H. D. (1981). Human resources, creativity, and innovation: The conflict between homo faber and homo ludens. *Behavioral Science, 26*(3), 243–255. https://doi.org/10.1002/bs.3830260307
Jacobsson, M., & Söderholm, A. (2021). An essay on 'Homo projecticus': Ontological assumptions in the projectified society. *International Journal of Project Management, 40*(4), 315–319. https://doi.org/10.1016/j.ijproman.2021.11.004
Jensen, M. C., & Meckling, W. H. (1976). Theory of the firm: Managerial behavior, agency costs and ownership structure. *Journal of Financial Economics, 3*(4), 305–360. https://doi.org/10.1016/0304-405X(76)90026-X
Jermier, J. M., & Forbes, L. C. (2011). Metaphor as the foundation of organizational studies: Images of organization and beyond. *Organization & Environment, 24*(4), 444–458. https://doi.org/10.1177/1086026611436328
Kakko, I., & Inkinen, S. (2009). Homo creativus: Creativity and serendipity management in third generation science and technology parks. *Science and Public Policy, 36*(7), 537–548. https://doi.org/10.3152/030234209X465570
Kent, M. L., & Taylor, M. (2016). From Homo economicus to Homo dialogicus: Rethinking social media use in CSR communication. *Public Relations Review, 42*(1), 60–67. https://doi.org/10.1016/j.pubrev.2015.11.003
Kierein, N. M., & Gold, M. A. (2000). Pygmalion in work organizations: A meta-analysis. *Journal of Organizational Behavior, 21*(8), 913–928. http://www.jstor.org/stable/3100361
Kluver, J., Frazier, R., & Haidt, J. (2014). Behavioral ethics for Homo economicus, Homo heuristicus, and Homo duplex. *Organizational Behavior and Human Decision Processes, 123*(2), 150–158. https://doi.org/10.1016/j.obhdp.2013.12.004
Kostera, M. (2005). *The quest for the self-actualizing organization.* Liber.
Lounsbury, M., Gehman, J., & Glynn, A. M. (2019). Beyond Homo entrepreneurus: Judgment and the theory of cultural entrepreneurship. *Journal of Management Studies, 56*(6), 1214–1236. https://doi.org/10.1111/joms.12429
McGregor, D. (1960). *The human side of enterprise.* McGraw-Hill.
Merton, R. K. (1948). The self-fulfilling prophecy. *Antioch Review, 8*, 193–210. https://doi.org/10.2307/4609267
Meyers, M. C., & Van Woerkom, M. (2014). The influence of underlying philosophies on talent management: Theory, implications for practice, and

research agenda. *Journal of World Business, 49*(2), 192–203. https://doi.org/10.1016/j.jwb.2013.11.003
Mill, J. S. (1863/1962). Utilitarianism. Reprinted in J. S. Mill (1962). *Utilitarianism, on liberty, essay on Bentham*. Meridian Books.
Mills, C. W. (1959). *The sociological imagination*. Evergreen Books.
Norén, L. (1995). *Tolkande företagsekonomisk forskning: en metodbok*. Studentlitteratur.
Nyborg, K. (2000). Homo economicus and homo politicus: Interpretation and aggregation of environmental values. *Journal of Economic Behavior & Organization, 42*(3), 305–322. https://doi.org/10.1016/S0167-2681(00)00091-3
Örtenblad, A. (Ed.). (2024). *The Oxford handbook of metaphor in organization studies*. Oxford University Press.
Potter, J. (1996). *Representing reality: Discourse, rhetoric and social construction*. Sage.
Rankin, H. D. (1983). *Sophists, Socratics and Cynics*. Barnes & Noble.
Redmalm, D., & Skoglund, A. (2020). Rethinking government and its economy with Giorgio Agamben: The homo sacer in alternative entrepreneurship. *The Sociological Review, 68*(5), 948–964. https://doi.org/10.1177/0038026120914538
Rosenthal, R., & Jacobson, L. (1968). Pygmalion in the classroom. *Urban Review, 3*, 16–20. https://doi.org/10.1007/BF02322211
Russ, M. (2014). *Homo Sustainabiliticus* and the "New Gold". In M. Russ (Ed.). *Value creation, reporting, and signaling for human capital and human assets*. Palgrave Macmillan. https://doi.org/10.1057/9781137472069_1
Simon, H. A. (1957). *Models of man: Social and rational. Mathematical essays on rational human behaviour in a social setting*. Wiley.
Smith, A. (1776/2012). *The wealth of nations*. Wordsworth Editions Limited.
Taylor, F. W. (1911/1913). *The principles of scientific management*. Harper & Brothers.
Vasquez, G. M. (1993). A homo narrans paradigm for public relations: Combining Bormann's symbolic convergence theory and Grunig's situational theory of publics. *Journal of Public Relations Research, 5*(3), 201–216. https://doi.org/10.1207/s1532754xjprr0503_03
Vroom, V. H. (1964). *Work and motivation*. Wiley.
Whiteley, P., Sy, T., & Johnson, S. K. (2012). Leaders' conceptions of followers: Implications for naturally occurring Pygmalion effects. *The Leadership Quarterly, 23*(5), 822–834. https://doi.org/10.1016/j.leaqua.2012.03.006

Part I

Homo Moralis

2

When Management and Organization Came to the Village of Jante

Daniel Ericsson and Pernilla Nilsson

Introduction

Once upon a time, not particularly long ago, it meant something very special to be an academic scholar. Not only were academic scholars given the power to act from an esteemed and consecrated position imbued with both symbolic and economic capital, they were also assumed to possess a distinctive disposition of resources and qualities of a scarce and delicate kind. The holders of the scholarly (dis)positions were, for instance, assumed to be highly educated, and as such experts in a specific knowledge domain; they were assumed to be well-trained in scientific methodology, and as such guarantors of valid and reliable knowledge claims; and they were assumed to stand free from both

D. Ericsson (✉)
School of Business and Economics, Linnaeus University, Växjö, Sweden
e-mail: daniel.ericsson@lnu.se

Department of Arts and Cultural Sciences, Lund University, Lund, Sweden

P. Nilsson
Alvesta, Sweden

S. Cinque and D. Ericsson (eds.), *Debating 'Homo Academicus' in Management and Organization*, Palgrave Debates in Business and Management,
https://doi.org/10.1007/978-3-031-58195-3_2

internal and external pressures, and as such be objective and non-opportunistic. Such (dis)positional powers and assumptions together formed the academic researcher's identity—and raison d'être: you are something special, offering qualifications provided by the very few.

However, that was then but this is now, and the (dis)position of the academic scholar is no longer what it used to be. On the one hand, the academic scholar's position has step by step been deconstructed, criticized, deconsecrated, and diluted, turning the once unique societal (dis)position of the scholar more or less into a staple. *Homo academicus* in this sense simply has become *Homo vulgaris*. On the other hand, the (dis)positional assumptions have been fundamentally challenged, questioned, and altered in favour of an alternative moral imperative, the Law of Jante: You shall not think that you are anything special.

In the following, we will present our arguments behind these seemingly bold statements of ours by sketching the contours of the many institutional changes that have radically transformed the academic landscape, such as the postmodern demise of science as a grand narrative, the expansion of higher education, the neoliberal university, and the Bologna reform. Each and every one of these changes, we argue, in different ways and to different extents, forms a fertile soil for the Law of Jante, and together contribute to the vulgarization of the academic scholar's (dis)position. Our focus is then directed toward business schools, which we believe occupy a precarious place in the academic landscape, particularly vulnerable to neoliberal reforms such as accreditation processes, marketization, and Thatcherian "There Is No Alternative" (TINA) management, and we outline how the Law of Jante has been enacted within the fields of management and organization. What are the moralizing consequences for scholars in these fields, to assume that you are not anything special? we ask. Does it lead to fear of exalting oneself, silence, or perhaps even exit?

Before we address these pressing questions, however, we need to present our overarching interpretative frame of reference, i.e., the Law of Jante.

The Law of Jante

As formulated by the Danish-Norwegian author Aksel Sandemose (1933/2010) in *En flykting korsar sitt spår* (*A Fugitive Crosses His Tracks*), the Law of Jante was once a satirical description of the social norms that Sandemose meant governed the behaviours and attitudes of working-class Norwegians and Danes into conformity and hostility towards individual success in the fictional village of Jante. Over the years, however, it has come to depict the egalitarian Scandinavian cultures as well as to acquire a kind of proverbial resonance both within and outside these cultures (see Cappelen & Dahlberg, 2018; Gopal, 2000).

Most often, the Law of Jante is distilled to the rule "You shall not think you are anything special". This is, however, only the first rule of a set of ten different rules or commandments, as Sandemose calls them (Sandemose, 1933/2010, p. 79):

1. You shall not think you *are* anything special.
2. You shall not think you are as (morally) good as *we* are.
3. You shall not think you are smarter than *we* are.
4. You shall not imagine yourself you are better than *we* are.
5. You shall not think you know more than *we* do.
6. You shall not think you are more important than *we* are.
7. You shall not think *you* are good for anything.
8. You shall not laugh at *us*.
9. You shall not think anyone cares about *you*.
10. You shall not think you can teach *us* anything.[1]

[1] The commandments are translated by us from the Norwegian original. We have, however, taken into consideration some of the established translations in Swedish and English, as we cannot but note that some of these translations deviate from the original in troublesome manners. For instance, the translation provided by Cappelen and Dahlberg (2018) consistently omits the modal verb "shall", uses italics to accentuate specific words not accentuated in the original, and uses "others" instead of "us": "You shall not think you are smarter than *we* are" becomes "Don't think you're smarter than others" (p. 420). Such a translation turns the commandment into more of a "good advice", and inscribes a generalized other instead of pinpointing a very concrete cultural collective. Neither of these is to be found in the original. The 2nd commandment is especially troublesome since both Swedish and English translations tend to use the word "good" ("god" in the Swedish language). To our mind, this misses the moralizing character of the goodness that Sandemose intended, and therefore we have added the word "morally" within brackets.

As Sandemose tells the story, these commandments have been mediated by oral tradition in Jante, and only recently been written down. Over the centuries, they have dictated life in Jante in a very muscular fashion similar to how Mosaic law has governed Judeo-Christian life. The Jante law is however not only law, Sandemose writes, it is "the heart of the language" (Sandemose, 1933/2010, p. 81, our translation) in the sense that everything said could be traced back to it. Sandemose therefore likens the law to the air that the inhabitants of Jante breathe, a poisonous fume that slowly suffocates everyone without mercy. With it, the inhabitants kill themselves, all their chances in life, all their dreams, hopes, and ambitions.

In Sandemose's hands, the Law of Jante is intended to portray a condescending culture in which individuality is severely suppressed, and in which there is a lack of tolerance—towards other people, their deviant ideas and behaviour, and success. The strong pressure on people to conform and to adapt to a "middle-of-the-road normality" (Cappelen & Dahlberg, 2018, p. 421) is considered to be destructive as it oppresses people, and prevents them from expressing themselves and living their lives to the fullest. There are, however, commentators that highlight the positive aspects of the Law of Jante: it is said to also foster social stability, harmony, and trust, even community (see Gentile, 2014; Uslaner, 2012), as well as desirable virtues such as equality and modesty (see Smith et al., 2003).

The Law of Jante resembles phenomena found outside the Scandinavian context. For instance, in many Anglosphere countries, especially in Australia and New Zealand, *the tall poppy syndrome* (Cappelen & Dahlberg, 2018; Peeters, 2004) refers to hostility towards successful people and most of all towards those who boast about their success. In the Netherlands, the concept *maaiveldcultuur* points to a culture in which everything above average is cut to the ground (Pierce et al., 2017). And in Japan, the tall poppy syndrome and the maaiveldcultuur is reflected in the proverb "the nail that sticks up gets hammered down" (Tokunaga, 2003). There is however an important difference between these concepts and the Law of Jante, as we see it. Whereas the tall poppy syndrome, maaiveldcultuur, and the Japanese proverb refer to reactions to people displaying their success, the Law of Jante is a social norm that prevents people from sticking out or exalting themselves. In this sense, the Law of Jante functions proactively not only stigmatizing those who experience success and/or boast about it but also inhibiting potentially successful people from wanting to stand out at all. In other words, the Law of Jante represents both a repressive and a suppressive culture.

A Changed Academic Landscape

Having outlined the Law of Jante as our overarching interpretative frame of reference, our first stop on our argumentative path is to reflect upon how some of the institutional changes that academia has undergone in the last couple of decades paved the way for the enactment of the Law of Jante. In this regard, we reckon that there are at least four different changes to consider.

The first institutional change to consider is the postmodern idea that truth always is contextual and relative. This idea represents a severe attack on the grand academic narrative as it has been told and retold throughout modernity (see Lyotard, 1984). Scholarly knowledge is now seen as nothing but a historically and socially situated language game, and as such on par with any other language game, such as politics or religion. At the same time, the scholar is now decentred as the protagonist of scientific knowledge and truth. As a consequence, faith in scientific knowledge is declining, and most so it seems when it comes to the humanities and the social sciences (Elías, 2019). The Sokal affair (1996), not the least, and other types of controversies (see Alvesson et al., 2017, p. 6 ff), have fuelled this loss of faith, and current scholarly debates on what to consider to be valid knowledge on pressing issues such as climate change, COVID-19, and international terrorism, is spreading disbelief in scholarly knowledge. Trust issues like these, of course, affect scholars and their identities—and the assumptions they make about themselves and the knowledge they contribute. Under the postmodern condition, it is close at hand to believe that scholars, especially within the social sciences and the humanities, are prone to question who they (think they) are, and to internalize the fifth and sixth commandments of the Law of Jante: I don't know more than anyone else, and I am—as a scholar—not more important than any other person.

A second institutional change to consider is the ongoing expansion of higher education. At no other time in history have there been as many universities, PhDs, and university professors as now. In Sweden, for example, the number of universities has increased from five to 16 in the last five decades, whereas the number of senior lecturers and professors has almost doubled between 2001 and 2022 (SCB, 2023). In regard to the Law of Jante, this expansion is however somewhat paradoxical. One could very well argue that the expansion of higher education in itself is a reflection of the both material and symbolical relevance of academic scholarship—which in turn signals the very antithesis to the Law of Jante. To become a scholar is indeed something special. However, one could at the same also argue that the expansion of higher education dilutes the significance of academic scholarship on the individual level in the sense that the thresholds have been lowered, making it easier to both enter academia and leave it with a degree. In this regard, the upscaled production of PhDs has been likened to the standardized and streamlined mass production found within Fordistic systems (Nilsson, 2003). Paraphrasing Henry Ford's dictum that the T-Ford of the 1920s comes in "any colour the customer wants, as long as it's black", one could thus argue that present-day PhDs appear equally uniform (Nilsson, 2003) and that the production system suppresses individuality. Seen through the lens of the Law of Jante, the expansion of higher education in this sense also suppresses scholarly notions of being something special, i.e., being smarter, better, more knowledgeable, or more important than others.

A third institutional change to dwell upon is the intrusion of New Public Management (NPM) into academia and its many adverse consequences such as a competitive publish-or-perish logic, increased managerial discretion, marketization of research results, and an increased focus on research output in quantitative performance indicators rather than in terms of quality, relevance, and excellence (see Amaral, 2008; Broucker & De Wit, 2015). Taken together, consequences such as these form an incredibly fertile soil for the enculturation of the Law of Jante in and through which not even the ones who completely surrender themselves to NPM are to think that they are anything special. They are only as special as their output in the last quarter permits them to believe. At the same time, scholarly work is devalued under the NPM regime, almost in a systematic manner. On the one hand, resources are increasingly transferred from the operating core (research and teaching) to management, technostructure, and support staff (see Baltaru & Soysal, 2018), thus escalating universities' overhead costs. On the other hand, administrative work is increasingly transferred from the technostructure and support staff to the operating core (see Schneijderberg & Merkator, 2013). As a result, both the symbolic and economic order in academia is being turned upside down, making the scholar not only less special but also less important.

The fourth and last institutional change to consider is the Bologna reform and its underlying mode of university governance. Intended to ensure the development of a qualified labour force in Europe, as well as to stimulate the free movement of students and teachers between European countries for the sake of the needs of their labour markets, the Bologna reform largely is a matter of standardization (or harmonization) of processes, programmes, curricula, courses, and—ultimately—students and scholars. The primary mode of governance therefore is benchmarking and quality assurance; however, this mode of governance has not resulted in some sort of organizational (structural) isomorphism (Brøgger, 2016). Instead, it is a mode of governance that has resulted in fierce competition through which universities mimic the performance of others without changing their structural nature. They (only) keep up their (presumably good) appearance. In this regard, Brøgger (2016) argues, the Bologna reform is a matter of *mimetic desire*, and with reference to Rene Girard (1966, p. 42) she explains this concept:

> Mimetic desire is an expansion of the structure of desire to encompass not only subject and object but also a third party: the mediator and initiator of the desire. The subject desires the object because it is desired by a third party who mediates the desire. As a mediator, the third party is both admired and despised as an ideal of and a barrier to the desired object: the closer the mediator comes, the more bitter the fruits of mimetic desire become. ... Desire turns into the mimesis of another's desire – which makes mimetic desire a 'borrowed' desire. (Brøgger, 2016, p. 85)

The consequence of this mimetic desire is, according to Brøgger, an affective peer pressure mediated by constant processes of comparison, monitoring, and self-evaluation; and under this pressure states, universities, and scholars are kept at bay, trying to navigate the Bologna politics—which in the end boils down to engaging in processes of naming, faming, and shaming.

In light of the Law of Jante, the Bologna reform both promotes and demotes scholarly ideas of being something special. It promotes such ideas by naming and faming, i.e., placing consecrated benchmarks in the centre of attention and fostering a normative imperative to strive towards becoming such a benchmark from the university level down to the individual scholar. Abiding by the Bologna reform is in this regard anti-Jante: to mimic the performance of esteemed peers is the guarantee of being seen as something special. The flip side of this mimetic desire, however, is the simultaneous shaming of those who do not live up to the expectations or who do not conform to the standards. In this regard, the Bologna reform is utterly pro-Jante: You shall not think you are as good as *we* are.

Business Schools—Between Mercury and Minerva

Our second stop on our argumentative path is to query the Business School phenomenon and its exposed position in between business and academia or, as Engwall (2009) has put it with reference to Roman mythology, in between Mercury and Minerva. The position is exposed not only because business schools need to strike a delicate balance between two different, not to say conflicting, institutional logics, being relevant and excellent in regard to both business and academic logics. It is also a position that is particularly exposed to the recent changes in the academic landscape in that NPM and the Bologna mode of governance in many ways are consistent with the Mercury logic, thus destabilizing, even unsettling, prior reached balances between Mercury and Minerva. To come to terms with how this exposedness of business schools is intertwined with the Law of Jante, we reckon that it is not enough to merely focus on the differences between the two logics. One also needs to account for the history behind the Business School phenomena. As we see it, it is a history of inferiority complex, legitimacy struggles, and shifting rights of interpretation.

The very first business school in the world—ESCP—was established in France in 1819, modeled after École Polytechnique, a militarized school set up to educate civilians and military men in engineering and science, founded in the late eighteenth century. As such, ESCP targeted the very same group of students as École Polytechnique, but with the explicit purpose of training business executives-to-be to solve problems related to management and organization, and to focus upon vocational subjects for the prosperity of running and developing firms (see Kaplan, 2014; Passant, 2022). ESCP was privately financed outside of the university system, and this soon became the role model for how to set up similar institutions across Europe (Kaplan, 2014).

The way business schools were initially institutionalized in Europe did not arouse any academic legitimacy issues to talk about. Mercury and Minerva lived their lives fully apart. In America, however, business schools were already from the beginning set up *within* the existing universities, and this aroused controversy. At the Wharton School of Finance and Economy, the very first business school in the US, established in 1881 at the University of Pennsylvania, the introduction of the subject "commerce" was met with resistance. As Üsdiken et al. (2021, p. 444) put it, it "…meant facing up to resistance from the dominant liberal arts education, which was based on the idea of learning for its own sake, and included subjects such as ancient classics, modern languages, history, philosophy, and science". "Commerce" was simply seen as redundant since, college faculty argued, the well-established liberal arts education already offered an adequate range of courses also contributing to business careers.

The controversy between Mercury and Minerva at the University of Pennsylvania, and at other universities that followed suit with establishing business schools in the US and eventually also in Europe, could very well be interpreted as a Jante issue. Minerva simply dismisses Mercury: You shall not think you are anything special. In this sense, educators at American business schools, already from the beginning, have had to deal with a sort of inferiority complex in relation to well-established educations such as law, medicine, and in some cases divinity (see Aaronson, 1990, p. 263), with a need to prove themselves as legitimate academic institutions.

The business schools' struggle for legitimacy in America was, however, not a unified project in which the business schools struggled together. Instead, they competed with different strategies for gaining legitimacy. After World War II, two different types of schools were chiselled out: the Graduate School of Business at Columbia (CBS) versus Harvard Business School (HBS). At the time, both schools were recognized by the Ford Foundation to be prime examples of MBA Educations for others to learn from, but the differences were fundamental. At Columbia, writes Aaronson (1990, p. 266), "students were prepared for business with academically respectable theories and models; they rarely studied real business problems. In addition, these students learned about business from faculty members who generally had little practical business experience". At Harvard, it was the other way around: students were prepared for business by analysing real-world problems—cases—instead of reading textbooks and following lectures. The intention behind this case study approach was not to prepare the students for operational decision-making, which was the intention behind the Columbia approach, but for entrepreneurial decision-making—and for leadership. At Harvard, the students therefore, Aaronson (1990, p. 267) concludes, "learned business from the vantage point of top management". Consequently, practical skills and experiences amongst Harvard faculty members were meritorious.

In retrospect, both Columbia's and Harvard's approaches to higher education have indeed been very successful. Both approaches are commonly used at business schools, on both sides of the Atlantic, regardless of whether the schools are backed by private or public funds (or a mix thereof), and regardless of whether they are part of a university or not. Both approaches are part of an institutionalized strategic repertoire for business schools to solve the legitimacy dilemma of being stuck in between Mercury and Minerva. Having said this, one must however acknowledge the power of Minerva, and the privileges and interpretative rights that historically have been attributed to academia and its scholars. The village of Jante is in this regard inhabited by *Homo academici* who, by default, are suppressing *Homo oeconomici*, a situation Fleming (2020, p. 1308) vividly testifies about: "Faculty in the humanities and sciences, for example, frequently assume that we're unscholarly corporate wannabes […] Mention T. W. Adorno and they look at you like a freak".

There seems, however, to be a glitch in this academic village as the hierarchy between Minerva and Mercury in many regards is shifting, at least a little bit. On the one hand, the neoliberal zeitgeist speaks in favour of the Mercury logic, at the same time consecrating business schools and transforming universities more and more into business schools. Not for nothing, E.P. Thomson (1970, p. 78) already more than fifty years ago likened business studies to a cuckoo in the university nest. On the other hand, the business schools have been very successful in speaking up for themselves, claiming their recognition, and influencing decision-makers both inside and outside academia. For example, from the 1950s onward, Harvard was a key actor not only in the expansion of MBAs in the US but also in successfully exporting the concept to Europe. This was, however, not accomplished in isolation; it was heavily fuelled by the school's long-time granted support from philanthropies such as the Ford Foundation and the Carnegie Corporation. The Marshall plan subsidies after World War II (Kaplan, 2014), which significantly helped to rebuild and develop higher education in Europe (with INSEAD in France as a noted example), also contributed to the spread of the Harvard approach (Bottom, 2009).

Yet another strategy employed by business schools to acquire legitimacy and build scholarly reputation, is to apply for, and partake in, different types of accreditation processes and rankings. There is a long history of assessments and accreditations of universities in the US, stretching all the way back to the late 1800s, to satisfy the need of different interest groups such as students and professional corps to be able to separate the chaff from the wheat (see Sandebring, 2004). In 1949, such services were so greatly in demand that the universities had to launch The National Commission on Accrediting (NCA) to assess the increasing number of accrediting organizations (Sandebring, 2004). As a result, NCA started to publish an annual list, covering all qualified accrediting firms, which still is updated by the commission's successor, The Council for Higher Education Accreditation (CHEA) (Sandebring, 2004). CHEA presents itself as "A primary national voice for accreditation and quality assurance to the U.S. Congress and U.S. Department of Education" and "A leading national voice for accreditation to the general public, opinion leaders, students, and families" (see CHEA.org). In Europe, accreditation was put on the agenda only in the 1970s as part of political interests in forming a European cohesive market for higher education. However, diversity in procedures amongst sovereign nation states, all having their own ministry and authorities for higher education, has inhibited the enactment of a joint accreditation system. For business schools, however, there are a number of internationally acclaimed accrediting organizations, amongst which AMBA, EQUIS, and AACSB are the most prominent. The latter is the oldest, established already in 1916 in North America, whereas the two former are European offsprings of more recent dates. Originally, these organizations were geographically restricted, but as AACSB started to expand its operations in the 1980s as a response to the world-wide proliferation of MBA programmes, EQUIS and AMBA followed suit in the 1990s (Hedmo et al., 2001).

From a Jante frame of reference, accreditation stands out as a contrarian artefact to the repressive and suppressive Jante culture. The very assumption behind accreditors such as AACSB, EQUIS, and AMBA is to stand out as something very special and to show it to the world. To get accreditation means to become part of, writes Engwall et al. (2022, p. 450), "an exclusive club of screened departments that deploy their accreditations as tools in reputation-building efforts". However, even if membership in this exclusive club is meant to be restricted by specific criteria, application fees, and peer reviews extended over long periods, the number of accredited schools tends to increase as time goes by. For example, AASCB reached 1000 accredited schools in 2023, "a milestone", as they marketed it (see www.aacsb.edu). However, in as much as this is something for AACSB to be proud of, it erodes the value of being accredited, and presents already accredited business schools with a dilemma with a Jante twist: You shall strive to be something special, but you shall not think you are anything special.

In this regard, the whole accreditation system thrives upon the Law of Jante, and the only way out of the dilemma seems to be to acquire even more exclusivity, i.e., to apply for accreditation from yet another accreditation organization. An aspirational goal for many business school managers is therefore to become "triple crowned", i.e. accredited by all three major accreditation organizations. The irony of it all, however, is that sooner or later the "triple crown" emblem will lose its appeal, as more and more schools get the mark. "This sets off an elusive and constantly ongoing search for exclusivity as business schools attempt to distinguish themselves from other business schools" (Engwall et al., 2022, p. 450).

It is at this point rankings become a central strategic tool for business schools to signify fame and fortune. Because, hand on heart, "accreditation does not distinguish the very best from the rest; instead ranking provides a means for this", as Hedmo et al. put it (2001, p. 18). Rankings also is an American invention, originating in the 1980s in trade journals such as Business Week, and spreading to leading papers in Europe in the 1990s. The most well-known ranking list is produced by the Financial Times who, since 1999, scrutinizes international MBAs (Engwall et al., 2022, p. 448; Sandebring, 2004, p. 25). Rankings obviously send an elitist message to the business school community, but they are at the same time an ambiguous Jante message. As with accreditations, rankings are meant to incite quality improvements and competition based on merit. But it is only the chosen few, those included in the rankings, that get to think that they are something special. The rest are left in awe: admiring the chosen few, and suppressing their own aspirations.

Management and Organization

The overarching institutional changes of the academic landscape, and the exposed situation of the business school in between Mercury and Minerva, undoubtedly form a fertile soil for the enculturation of the Law of Jante within business schools. Inside the business schools, however, we find a group of scholars that we believe to be more exposed to Jante than other groups. This group leans more to the Minerva side, extensively borrowing theories and methods from "soft" disciplines such as sociology, anthropology, and psychology, and as such finds itself in an inferior legitimacy position vis-a-vis those groups that are closer to the Mercury side, leaning on "hard" disciplines such as statistics and mathematics. Members of the former group most often also work in the hermeneutic traditions, not seldom embracing a critical theory position, which puts them in the shadow of mainstream positivist research. This group consists, we reckon, of scholars in the fields of management and organization.

To specify further the group we, above all, are referring to here, it seems a good idea to follow Jackson and Carter's (2007) distinction between the OB and the ob traditions in the fields of management and organization. The OB tradition, they argue, is the major and dominant one, whereas the ob tradition is the minor one (hence the former is uppercased, whereas the latter is lowercased). The OB tradition, Jackson and Carter go on to explain, is an American managerial tradition in which researchers seek to find the best organizational behaviour to increase business return on investment. Their ultimate goal is to formulate universal prescriptions for practitioners on how to behave and how to manipulate the world in a technical manner. In contrast, the ob tradition is European in character, based on social theory, and with the explicit aim to understand organizational behaviour through theoretically informed descriptions and explanations. As we see it, it is researchers within the ob tradition that are most prone to fall victim to the Law of Jante. Not only are they questioning the economic rationality of business practices and actors, thus creating a distance between themselves and Mercury. Epistemologically wise, they also turn away from objective and universal knowledge claims in favour of (inter)subjective and particular knowledge claims, thus contributing to the postmodern undermining of the grand academic narrative.

In our experience, scholars working in the ob tradition at business schools fall victim to the Law of Jante in many different situations. For the sake of argument, we find it beneficial to discriminate between four typical situations: teaching, collaborations with external partners, collegial conversations and interactions, and dealings with management.

In teaching situations, ob scholars meet students in courses that typically are based on a postmodern approach to the subject area. In introductory courses, the course literature (see, for instance, classics such as Bolman & Deal, 2017; Hatch, 2018; Morgan, 2006) typically acknowledges the incoherence of the theoretical field, and presents different perspectives through which aspects of management and organization are made intelligible instead of stating empirically deduced facts; and in courses at the advanced level, students get to discuss issues such as sense-making, institutional theory, discourse analysis, gender and power relations. All with the intent to prepare the students for a multi-faceted working life in which reflexivity and critical thinking are seen as key competencies.

The intention of ob scholars, however, is seldom in line with what the typical student expects. He or she expects to become a master of managing and organizing and expects to acquire leadership training and develop leadership skills. Management and organization theories are perceived as a set of tools, which the students not only want to gain access to but also want to learn to use to excel in "the real world" as managerial leaders. The teacher is consequently seen as a tool expert, and as someone who, in a strict normative manner, should have acquired the tool expertise through practical experience and mastery.

Normative expectations such as these are of course mediated through the grand academic narrative, but also by the business schools and their bias towards Mercury. The clash between the student and the ob teachers is therefore not a particularly equal one. Students have both *Homo academicus* and *Homo oeconomicus* at their side, whereas the ob teachers find support only amongst their colleagues working in the same tradition. It truly is a sort of David and Goliath encounter, and the result is the enactment of Jante's 10th commandment: "You shall not think you can teach *us* anything".

In situations of collaborations with external partners, the very same clash of expectations is at work as in the teaching situation. However, when ob researchers team up with practitioners in commissioned educational programmes, an additional typical expectation tends to flourish, namely the idea that researchers in the fields of management and organization should provide the practitioners some sort of theoretical absolution, i.e., to reassure them that their actions are consistent with the latest management and organization theories. For OB scholars, this does not in any way represent a problem, as it is part and parcel of the managerialist OB agenda to correct any deviances from theory. For ob scholars, however, such absolution is not consistent with the Minerva ethos. These researchers do not believe in the idea that theories are key answers to practical problems—or that theories represent a blueprint for reality. Theories are no more, no less, concepts and relations among concepts that could be used to describe and interpret the world, i.e., they represent a language or a grammar.

Confronted with the ob ethos, practitioners typically respond with resentment. The ob researchers' theoretical (dis)position is dismissed as being illegitimate, whereas their contributions are deemed useless in practice. Underneath such reactions, Jante lurks. On the one hand, the ob researcher's competence is brought into question and deemed subordinate to that of the practitioners. "You shall not think you know more than *we* do" is thus coupled with "You shall not think you can teach *us* anything" and "You shall not think *you* are good for anything". On the other hand, the ob researchers should not think that they are any more important than the practitioners are.

In situations of collegial conversations and interactions with researchers belonging to the OB tradition, the ob researchers tend to speak and act from a contested (dis)position. The close association with Mercury not only consecrates OB research but also gives the OB scholars the right of interpretation on research and educational matters, and on other important issues at the business schools, such as recruitment, tenure, and planning, i.e., who gets to do what, and with what resources. In our experience, the OB scholars' right of interpretation evokes the law of Jante in particular on two occasions: in processes of enculturation of neophytes into scholarly (dis)positions, and in processes of blind peer review, be it journals or applications for funds or positions.

In the first of these processes, new doctoral students tend to be approached by OB scholars wanting to provide some sort of "fatherly advice" (yes, we deem this type of advice-giving to be a gendered phenomenon) on how to navigate within the fields of management and organization. "Don't go there!", they warn about the ob tradition, and they continue with outlining the ob pitfalls: getting stuck in the "methodological morass" with the risk of never getting a Ph.D., not being able to get published in top-tier journals with the risk of discontinuing a career in academia, and not being able to contribute to real-life problems with the risk of being considered irrelevant or even strangely aloof. The OB arguments against ob are compelling, to say the least, so cursed be the doctoral student who does not follow the advice. "Who do you think you are?" "Do you think you are smarter than we are?" "Do you think you are more important than we are?" the OB scholars indignantly ask.

In the second of these processes in which we believe the Law of Jante particularly to be evoked, the OB scholars' right of interpretation functions as a gatekeeper to the fields and their resources. In the guise of blind review, OB research and researchers tend to pass the gate to journals, funding, and job positions more or less effortlessly, whereas ob research and researchers are efficiently kept outside. The effectuation of this is, however, not only mediated by the OB right of interpretation alone. Rather, it is mainly a result of the institutionalization of the OB tradition in the form of a great number of journals, editorships, professorships, and so on, fondly embracing the OB agenda. The probability that an ob scholar, testing his or her luck by submitting a paper to a journal or applying for external funds, will be peer reviewed by an OB scholar is therefore extremely high, regardless of the aim and scope of the journal or fund. If the paper or application is sent out for peer review, that is. Most often ob research is simply desk rejected by OB scholars acting as editors or managers of research funds. The message to ob scholars in such cases is loud and clear Jante: "You shall not think that anyone cares about *you*".

In situations of dealings with management, both OB and ob scholars tend to be looked upon with suspicion. As scholars, they not only are perceived to lack the practical experiences so highly valued by business school managers (and students). They also, as scholars in the fields of management and organization, seem to have some sort of deficiency in business morals that has led them to turn their backs on lucrative careers outside academia. As a consequence, OB and ob scholars find themselves to be less in demand at the business schools than their more Mercury-oriented colleagues belonging to subject areas such as accounting, marketing, and logistics—and this affects their dealings with managers accordingly. "You shall not think you *are* anything special" seems to be a common response from business schools' managers to both OB and ob scholars in negotiations concerning issues of management and organization. The Ob and ob scholars' expertise is simply not respected.

The expansion of the business school has furthermore led to an abundance of OB and ob graduates in the job market—or, if one likes, an army of unemployed OB and ob scholars competing for jobs. The fear of this army tends to keep already employed OB and ob scholars in order, making them refrain from voicing critiques, "clenching their fists in their pockets". It is also used by business school managers as an argument for keeping salaries for OB and ob scholars down. The combined effect of fear of being replaced by someone else and being underpaid further contributes to the enactment of the Law of Jante, making the OB and ob scholars internalize that they are not to think that they are anything special. They are nothing but replaceable cogs in the business schools' machinery.

Discussion

The totality of institutional changes academia has undergone in recent decades, the business schools' historic and ongoing strive for legitimacy, and the precarious situations that especially ob scholars are facing, we argue, pave the way for the spread of the Law of Jante. It is of course an empirical question, namely, to what extent individual scholars in the fields of management and organization internalize the different commandments that form the basis for the Law, and in turn, ground their research and teaching in the assumption that they are nothing special. There is always individual agency, and collective resistance to structural determination, to consider. However, as the sheer function of the Law of Jante is to deprive people of their agency, and to inhibit them from acting on the assumption that they are something special, we cannot rule out the possibility that Jante has gained a strong foothold, at least amongst ob scholars.

The consequences of the Law of Jante for academic scholars are in many regards devastating. Internalized fear of breaking the Law and disbelief in oneself and one's ability and right to contribute to society may not only lead to self-policing and avoidance of actions that are assumed to provoke the moralizing gaze of Jante, but may also lead to complete withdrawal from the public eye. The scholars that are fully enculturated into the Jante village do not partake in public debates, do not apply for funds, do not try to publish research in high-ranked journals, do not go to esteemed conferences, do not stand up for their merits and competencies, do not object to being wage discriminated, and so on. Instead, they abdicate from their academic duties—and their scholarly (dis)positions. To abdicate, however, is not a feasible option as it inexorably leads to a catch-22 situation. Either you are damned if you act against the Jante commandments or you are damned if you are not fulfilling your academic duties: Who do you think you are?

As we see it, there is a way out of this catch-22 situation for scholars within the fields of management and organization. It is not an easy trail to follow, especially not for ob scholars, burdened as they are by the weight of Mercury. The first step is, however, not to try to get rid of the yoke of capitalism; it is to embrace it, see right through it, and stick true to the ob traditions' intellectual legacy. The second step is to outright protest against the Law of Jante and its commandments—by articulating the law's adverse consequences, and by deliberately acting against its diminishing and inhibiting moral.

As we see it, the route to emancipation also goes via attempts to rewrite the Law of Jante—and the assumptions conveyed by it. In this regard, however, we do not propose some sort of inverted version of the Law of Jante, turning it upside down. The reason for this is that seven of the commandments rest upon a relation between you and a collective "we" that we find troublesome, not to say unsound, to reproduce. On the one hand, we want to abandon the Law's built-in bullying tendencies, ascribing unwarranted rights of interpretation to an invisible mob, to which scholars within the fields of management and organization are to subordinate themselves. On the other hand, we want to question the evaluative or judgemental character of the relation through which scholars within the fields of management and organization are supposed to benchmark themselves to others constantly. Instead, we would like to empower these scholars to see and appreciate themselves in their own right.

Our argumentation thus leads us to the formulation of a new set of commandments that we believe should form the basis for life in academia. Instead of ten commandments, we end up with seven, having omitted some overlaps and the one that focuses on laughing. (Laughing in academia these days is hard to do without being accused of using master suppression techniques.) Let us for the sake of clarity, call this list Anti-Jante:

1. You shall think you are something special.
2. You shall think you are good at what you do.
3. You shall think you are smart.
4. You shall think you are knowledgeable.
5. You shall think you are important.
6. You shall think many people care about you.
7. You shall think you can teach students a lot.

References

Aaronson, S. (1990). Without practice or practitioners: Graduate business education, 1945–1960. *Business and Economic History, 19*, 262–270. http://www.jstor.org/stable/23702953

Alvesson, M., Gabriel, Y., & Paulsen, R. (2017). *Return to meaning: A social science with something to say*. Oxford University Press.

Amaral, A. (2008). Transforming higher education. In A. Amaral, I. Bleiklie, & C. Musselin (Eds.), *From governance to identity: A festschrift for Mary Henkel* (pp. 81–94). Springer. https://doi.org/10.1007/978-1-4020-8994-7_7

Baltaru, R. D., & Soysal, Y. N. (2018). Administrators in higher education: Organizational expansion in a transforming institution. *Higher Education, 76*(2), 213–229. https://doi.org/10.1007/s10734-017-0204-3

Bolman, L. G., & Deal, T. E. (2017). *Reframing organizations: Artistry, choice, and leadership*. Jossey-Bass & Pfeiffer Imprints, Wiley.

Bottom, W. P. (2009). Organizing intelligence: Development of behavioral science and the research based model of business education. *Journal of the History of the Behavioral Sciences, 45*, 253–283. https://doi.org/10.1002/jhbs.20381

Broucker, B., & De Wit, K. (2015). New public management in higher education. In J. Huisman, H. Boer, D. D. Dill, & M. Souto-Otero (Eds.), *The Palgrave international handbook of higher education policy and governance* (pp. 57–75). Palgrave Macmillan UK. https://doi.org/10.1007/978-1-137-45617-5_4

Brøgger, K. (2016). The rule of mimetic desire in higher education: Governing through naming, shaming and faming. *British Journal of Sociology of Education, 37*(1), 72–91. https://doi.org/10.1080/01425692.2015.1096191

Cappelen, C., & Dahlberg, S. (2018). The Law of Jante and generalized trust. *Acta Sociologica, 61*(4), 419–440. https://www.jstor.org/stable/48595442

Elías, C. (2019). *Science on the ropes: Decline of scientific culture in the era of fake news*. Springer.

Engwall, L. (2009). *Mercury meets Minerva: Business studies and higher education: The Swedish case*. Economic Research Institute, Stockholm School of Economics.

Engwall, L., Edlund, P., & Wedlin, L. (2022). Who is to blame? Evaluations in academia spreading through relationships among multiple actor types. *Social Science Information, 61*(4), 439–456. https://doi.org/10.1177/05390184221146476

Fleming, P. (2020). Dark academia: Despair in the neoliberal business school. *Journal of Management Studies, 57*(6), 1305–1311. https://doi.org/10.1111/joms.12521

Gentile, I. (2014). A psychobiological approach to couple therapy and issues of reciprocity: The influence of Janteloven on Norwegian couples. *Psychotherapy in Australia, 21*(1), 42–47.

Girard, R. (1966). *Deceit, desire and the novel—Self and other in literary structure*. The John Hopkins University Press.

Gopal, K. (2000). Janteloven–modviljen mod forskellighed. Danske forestillinger om lighed som enshed. *Tidsskriftet Antropologi, 42*, 23–43.

Hatch, M. J. (2018). *Organization theory: Modern, symbolic, and postmodern perspectives*. Oxford University Press.

Hedmo, T., Sahlin Andersson, K., & Wedlin, L. (2001). *The emergence of a regulatory field of management education—Standardizing through accreditation, ranking and guidelines*. SCORE, Stockholm University.

Jackson, N., & Carter, P. (2007). *Rethinking organisational behavior: A post-structuralist framework*. Financial Times Prentice Hall.

Kaplan, A. (2014). European management and European business schools: Insights from the history of business schools. *European Management Journal, 32*(4), 529–534. https://doi.org/10.1016/j.emj.2014.03.006

Lyotard, J.-F. (1984). *The postmodern condition: A report on knowledge*. University of Minnesota Press.

Morgan, G. (2006). *Images of organization*. Sage.

Nilsson, P. (2003). Under huven på doktor Ford. In D. Ericsson (Ed.), *Det oavsedda ledarskapet* (pp. 44–57). Academia Adacta.

Passant, A. J. G. (2022). Making European managers in business schools: A longitudinal case study on evolution, processes, and actors from the late 1960s onward. *Enterprise & Society, 23*(2), 478–511. https://doi.org/10.1017/eso.2020.65

Peeters, B. (2004). Thou shalt not be a tall poppy: Describing an Australian communicative (and behavioral) norm. *Intercultural Pragmatics, 1*(1), 71–92. https://doi.org/10.1515/iprg.2004.008

Pierce, S., Hodge, K., Taylor, M., & Button, A. (2017). Tall poppy syndrome: Perceptions and experiences of elite New Zealand athletes. *International Journal of Sport and Exercise Psychology, 15*(4), 351–369. https://doi.org/10.1080/1612197X.2017.1280834

Sandebring, A. (2004). *Regler för högre utbildning. En historisk studie av regelsättande för högre utbildning i USA och Europa*. SCORE, rapportserie.

Sandemose, A. (1933/2010). *En flykting korsar sitt spår* (A fugitive crosses his tracks). Themis.

SCB. (2023). *Higher education: Employees in Higher education 2022*. https://www.scb.se/publication/49904

Schneijderberg, C., & Merkator, N. (2013). The new higher education professionals. In B. M. Kehm & U. Teichler (Eds.), *The academic profession in Europe: New tasks and new challenges* (pp. 53–92). Springer. https://doi.org/10.1007/978-94-007-4614-5_5

Smith, P. B., Andersen, J. A., Ekelund, B., Graversen, G., & Ropo, A. (2003). In search of Nordic management styles. *Scandinavian Journal of Management, 19*(4), 491–507. https://doi.org/10.1016/S0956-5221(03)00036-8

Sokal, A. D. (1996). Transgressing the boundaries: Toward a transformative hermeneutics of quantum gravity. *Social Text*, (46/47), 217–252. https://doi.org/10.2307/466856

Thompson, E. P. (1970). *Warwick University Ltd: Industry, management and the universities*. Penguin Education Specials.

Tokunaga, P. (2003). *Invitation to lead: Guidance for emerging Asian American leaders*. InterVarsity Press.

Uslaner, E. M. (2012). *Segregation and mistrust: Diversity, isolation and social cohesion*. Cambridge University Press.

Üsdiken, B., Kipping, M., & Engwall, L. (2021). Professional school obsession: An enduring yet shifting rhetoric by US business schools. *Academy of Management Learning & Education, 20*(3), 442–458. https://doi.org/10.5465/amle.2020.0109

3

Aren't We All Human?—On the Illusion of the Extraordinary Academic

Anders Örtenblad

Who Do We Think We Are?

I have my own, relatively clear image of who we, as academics, are. In this chapter, I use my more than 30 years of experience of being an academic to reflect upon the lack of self-reflection (!) that more often than not tends to characterize the typical academic. Many of us treat the people we study as if they are biased, due to being human and possessing a variety of weaknesses, while thinking of ourselves as being fairly extraordinary. This assumption about the people we study and ourselves is worth some further examination. I share my own experiences from academia and my reflections on to what extent we could be said to be any less gullible, irrational and biased than those whom we study. In the reasoning, I use examples from my own research area—organization studies—and especially the area of the spread of management knowledge

A. Örtenblad (✉)
Department of Working Life and Innovation, School of Business and Law, University of Agder, Grimstad, Norway
e-mail: anders.ortenblad@uia.no

S. Cinque and D. Ericsson (eds.), *Debating 'Homo Academicus' in Management and Organization*, Palgrave Debates in Business and Management,
https://doi.org/10.1007/978-3-031-58195-3_3

and ideas (see, e.g., Örtenblad, 2015), which I in this chapter will refer to by the term *management fashion.* Thus, the majority (but not everything) of what I deal with in this chapter has to do with the form of human weaknesses that are related to social acceptance and legitimacy, rather than those which are related to cognitive boundaries (e.g., Simon, 1991).

Organization studies is an area where we quite often make statements about organizational practitioners and whether they do the right things in the best way possible, such as making decisions, among others. The area of management fashion tries to understand how fashionable ideas are developed in the area of organization and management—such as *knowledge management, total quality management, business process engineering* and the *learning organization*—and, not least, how managers and other organization actors deal with these fashionable ideas. These questions are worth investigating since there is, according to researchers in this area, a continuous stream of new fashionable management ideas. The new ones, which are not always as new as they may seem (e.g., Örtenblad, 2007; Pruijt, 1998; Spell, 2001), make the existing ones irrelevant—that is, the life cycle of any such fashionable idea is short, and is getting increasingly shorter (e.g., Carson et al., 1999, 2000). These ideas are framed in a way so that they *appear* to be relevant for everyone, that is, for each and every organization (e.g., Rüling, 2015). On top of everything, these fashionable ideas are not always very easily grasped (Benders & van Veen, 2001; Benders & Verlaar, 2003; Benders et al., 1998; Kieser, 1997; Ryan & Hurley, 2004).

Unlike other scholars, I am not occupied with the relation between what researchers write themselves and the "management gurus" they criticize (e.g., Collins, 2001). Neither am I occupied here with the relation between consultants and managers, which others have written about:

> The tendency to see managers as "relatively powerless victims" goes hand in hand with the assumption that consultants are somehow immune to the insecurities of contemporary corporate life. (Fincham, 1999, p. 342)

I am instead, in this chapter, occupied with the relation between how we, academics, view the people we study, along with how we view ourselves and what/who we think we are. This chapter is, thus, aimed at discussing our own human weaknesses, as academics, and if it is reasonable to believe that we in fact are less gullible and show less herd-like behavior than those whom we study. The objective of the chapter is to increase awareness among the research community and to offer a basis for reflection on and debate about ourselves and who we are.

The chapter is structured as follows. First, I present some evidence of how researchers in the area of organization studies have considered practitioners as being human indeed. The next section offers arguments in favor of the fact that researchers themselves are human too. Thereafter, I suggest four possible assumptions, based on two distinctions—the degree to which practitioners can be assumed to be human, and the degree to which academics can be assumed to be human. The next section discusses some implications from two of these four assumptions. The chapter ends with a brief self-reflection.

Practitioners as Humans

The academic literature in the broad area of organization studies contains many statements of the type that claim that managers and other organization actors have, what I call, *human weaknesses*—that is, that they are biased in various ways and unable to act fully rationally—such as that they are gullible, fashion-followers or legitimacy seeking, rather than being able to focus on their work tasks and performing these in an unbiased way. As Stubbart (1989, p. 329) notes, "the field of organizational sciences itself was founded as an alternative to economists' assumptions about managerial rationality".

Let us take a look at only a few of the many examples, available in the literature, of statements indicating that practitioners are human. A few should be enough, since it is hardly any controversial thing to say that academics tend to treat organizational practitioners as humans, with their weaknesses. As early as the 1950s, managers were spoken of as "gullible". For instance, Dunnette suggested that

> businessmen are today behaving in a rather gullible fashion. Not a few industrial psychologists, both within firms and acting as consultants, are making heavy use of anecdotal validation in selling their wares to businessmen. In other words, they are widely prescribing methods which upon examination may be found to be similar to the medic's use of sugar pills. Surprisingly, these techniques are currently enjoying a good deal of acceptance. (Dunnette, 1957, p. 223)

Stagner (1958) talked about the "gullible personnel manager" who would "often purchase expensive 'employee selection' programs with no scientific evidence that the service offered has any value whatsoever" (p. 347) and suggested that "[t]he personnel manager should avoid being seduced by the flattening report on his [sic] own fine qualities into purchasing a test which is worthless when evaluated scientifically" (p. 352).

More lately, researchers—at least in the area of management fashion—have tended to leave the gullibility behind, stating that managers cannot be assumed to be as gullible as others have suggested, or as passively the victims of the producers of management knowledge. In a study of an organization that utilized a number of fashionable management ideas, Watson (1994, p. 903) found that "there was little evidence in the research of the existence of managers who were completely unreflective fad-mongers".

Nevertheless, the area of management fashion still uses concepts such as "herd behaviour" (Sorge & van Witteloostuijn, 2004) and "bandwagoning" (e.g., Rosenkopf & Abrahamson, 1999), which hardly indicate that practitioners have come to be regarded as anything but human. Neither does the following quote represent an image of organizational practitioners as being other than human:

> The shelves of bookshops are piled with the next generation of management guru bestsellers for tired, bored, or frustrated managers hungry for vision and cookbook recipes. (Sorge & van Witteloostuijn, 2004, p. 1207)

In a paper where the perspective taken is that of memetics, Williams (2004) suggests that some management concepts, techniques and ideas prosper because of their interpersonal reproductive capacity, rather than because they are economically reproductive. One explanation for such imitation, offered by the management fashion literature, is that the organization actors need to legitimize themselves in relation to various stakeholders, by referring to the ideas that currently are fashionable (DiMaggio & Powell, 1983; Meyer & Rowan, 1977).

Organization actors experience various problems stemming from the need to relate to the same ideas, not least the fact that the same, currently fashionable idea does not fit all organizations, with their different situations, conditions and problems. There are various ways to deal with this, described in the literature. One is that organization actors decouple practice from talk about practice,[1] something that Westphal and Zajac (2001) call "symbolic decoupling". For instance, they gain legitimacy through using fashionable terms such as "artificial intelligence" (to take a current example) on their websites, while they in practice have done little or nothing to implement it. Nystrom and Starbuck (1984, p. 182) argue that to appear legitimate in the eyes of the people who control resources, managers construct a "false front" or "organizational facade", to "deceive diverse people and institutions", which "mislead external stakeholders, organizational members, researchers, other managers, and even themselves". Brunsson (1993, p. 502) suggests the term "hypocracy", by which he refers to:

> what can and should be said is said, not only by ordinary people but also by important people such as executives and actors, but without the talk leading to the corresponding action.

This form of decoupling tends to go hand in hand with some of my own experiences of, especially, discussing various fashionable management ideas with organization actors. During the 1990s, when the *learning organization* was quite fashionable in Sweden, I talked with several practitioners who argued for the exceptionality of the guru of and bible in the area—Peter Senge's *The Fifth Discipline* (Senge, 1990). Later on, during the conversation, it became clear to me that they had not read

---

[1] Whether such behavior is more intentional or rather unintentional could be discussed (see, e.g., Örtenblad, 2005).

that book. In a few cases they had not even purchased the book, but claimed that they were about to do so. Another, similar experience of mine is from the beginning of the 2000s, when I visited one of the biggest companies in one of the Nordic countries. The person I talked to claimed, when I asked if they were interested in any of the contemporary management ideas, that they were doing knowledge management. When I showed interest in what they said and asked them to elaborate, it became clear that they were interested in knowledge management but had not yet begun their efforts to try to understand what was meant by the management label considered.

Another way to deal with the mismatch between what organizations actually need in practice—which may also be "no need to change anything"—and the current thinking is that organization actors change the ideas—something that often comes under the notion of *translation*—to fit the actual needs of the individual organization (see, e.g., Czarniawska & Sevón, 1996; Stensaker, 2007).

While such approaches for dealing with the experience of an imperative to relate to management ideas that are not (fully) usable in an instrumental sense (for a definition—see, e.g., Pelz, 1978), may appear as rational, they could still be considered originating in human weakness. Neither decoupling talk from practice nor translation seem to contradict how researchers in the area of organization studies tend to view practitioners as humans that possess various forms of weaknesses. It could be assumed that disconnecting talk from practice and presenting such decoupled talk would take more energy than merely acting in a way that corresponds with one's talk. It could also be considered as less rational that many organizations make changes to one and the same idea instead of each organization deciding to implement an idea that fits their particular situation and problems.

The research area of management fashion is far from the only one where researchers make assumptions about the people they study as possessing human weaknesses. An example from another, neighboring research area, organizational learning, is from Levitt and March, who used the term "superstitious" and claimed that

> [s]uperstitious learning occurs when the subjective experience of learning is compelling, but the connections between actions and outcomes are misspecified. Numerous opportunities exist for such misunderstandings in learning from experience in organizations. (Levitt & March, 1988, p. 325)

Levitt and March exemplify by suggesting that

> the promotion of managers on the basis of performance produces self-confidence among top executives that is partly superstitious, leading them to overestimate the extent to which they can control the risks their organizations face... (Levitt & March, 1988, pp. 325–326)

They continue with another example, namely that in "an organization that is invariantly successful, routines that are followed are associated with success and are reinforced" (Levitt & March, 1988, p. 326). An example of this is the heroification/scapegoating that leaders are frequently subjected to when an organization succeeds or when it fails. An alternative explanation would instead be to claim that to be successful as a leader one needs to have some luck, such as entering an organization when everything is settled for success (see, e.g., Svensson & Wood, 2005; see also Andersen, 2006).

To me this all makes sense. As Good writes in an article entitled "How rational should a manager be?":

> Our decisions are necessarily determined in part by unconscious mental events, by physiological events and by external forces; and it is impossible to make conscious use of the theory of rationality for all our decisions, before the decisions are made. (Good, 1962, p. 385)

Often, practitioners are definitely not completely unbiased, even if it also is true to say that some organization actors are more reflective, show more skepticism toward fashionable management ideas and, perhaps, are more unbiased than others. In this sense I generally tend to agree with the management fashion literature, as well as academics in other areas of organization studies.

Let us now take a look at academics—are we any less gullible, fashion-following or legitimacy-seeking than practitioners are? Are we any less biased, less subjective, or less myopic than organization actors?

Academics as Humans

It is not that difficult to find signs, even evidence, that we, as academics, are human, just like those we do research on and write about.

For instance, a fairly large number of us—not least the more successful ones—tend to be more occupied with our own success than with the importance of conducting and publishing research that helps to make the world a better place:

> Academic journal articles are generally read by very few people, and most academic books (apart from textbooks) suffer a similar fate. They are really not written to be read, but published (and the distinction is important) in order to signify a particular form of status game. (Parker, 2023, p. 408)

Harney (2008) has commented on similar matters in the British academy, which "values individual success at the expense of the common good of society" and where "[m]oney, respect and promotion flow from the way the RAE [Research Assessment Exercise] rates departments and, indirectly, individual scholars on their research" (see also De Rond et al., 2005; Elangovan & Hoffman, 2021). At one university where I worked, I was responsible for the research seminars. We had invited a scholar who was fairly well recognized within her/his field, to present a paper that was almost ready to be submitted to the selected journal. After the presentation, when the paper was discussed and commented on, I asked the author-presenter what the relevance of the paper was, since I did not understand much from the four lines that were written about it in the paper. My intention was to initiate a discussion with the author about the relevance, which for me is a significant topic in any research paper, as well as at any research seminar. The scholar answered that for the journal to which s/he intended to submit the paper, four lines about the relevance would be enough, that "the journal that the paper will be submitted to demands no more than four lines on relevance". Implicitly, I guess, s/he was saying that there thus was no reason to discuss it any further. I was completely flabbergasted by the response, to such an extent, in fact, that I remained silent and did not even try to follow the question up.

One could even go so far as to say that quite a number of us, in academia, view and value ourselves in terms of number of citations, number of publications, and so forth (e.g., Elangovan & Hoffman, 2021). In the academy, we often compare ourselves with our peers, and have a fairly clear picture of who is better—in terms of getting cited more often; having more publications in top-tier journals, and so forth—than us (hopefully nobody) and who is worse than us (hopefully many). We are, to say the least, keen on getting published in top-ranked journals, something that our employers motivate us to do but that we are pretty good at motivating ourselves to do as well (see, e.g., Quijada, 2021). We willingly take part in the publishing game, as if doing research (especially the publishing part) was some kind of sport or game (e.g., Butler & Spoelstra, 2020). For this, we could blame our employers, we could blame ourselves, or one could blame the zeitgeist:

> The whole Zeitgeist seems to encourage research efforts that earn big grants, crank out publications frequently and regularly, self-perpetuate themselves.... (J. P. Campbell, quoted in Dunnette, 1966, p. 348)

Not that many years ago, I attended a conference where most attendees had some kind of critical approach to management and organization studies, a conference where one theme, in fact, was "resistance". During the discussion after a plenary presentation, I raised my hand and asked why so few of us show resistance ourselves, for instance, resistance to the publishing hysteria that has come to be so dominating, not least at business schools, but that also has come to characterize the academy in general. A well-recognized scholar replied that her/his way of resisting was to do research on (others') resistance, and another, equally well-recognized scholar raised her/his hand and said that "I resist against the publishing system by sticking to the system". I have to say that I never understood what any of them meant...

The academy is indeed hierarchic, much more than the existence of a limited number of academic titles (e.g., assistant professor, associate professor, professor) suggests. Talking about *gurus*, it happens also within the academy—in fact, fairly often—that it is so very much more important who the person is who says something, than what is being said (see, e.g., Bort & Kieser, 2011). For instance, it sometimes seems to be more important whom we cite and that the papers we cite were published in high-ranked journals than that we cite relevant works (see, e.g., Bort & Kieser, 2011). For what and for whom is this a good thing? A reasonable interpretation is that we do it to gain legitimacy. As academics, we, just like the practitioners we write about, are dependent on appearing legitimate (e.g., De Rond et al., 2005). We legitimize ourselves by referring to the "right" journals, authors and works, not necessarily the ones that best explain what we refer to or support what we want to claim. The academy, in contrast to arts, is so very focused on citations, it is citation-heavy, not least in comparison with art, as the late artist and art historian Lars Vilks once expressed it at a presentation he gave in Sweden in autumn 2008, if I remember correctly. Sunstein argues that "[t]here is also a market for academic ideas, and this market will have significant effects on what academics do" (Sunstein, 2001, p. 1253).

Moreover, we are just as keen to follow fashion as we claim those are whom we write about. At an EGOS conference in the 1990s, I presented a paper named "'Fashion as fashion' or 'researchers have their fashions too'" (Örtenblad, 1999). At that time I had begun to take interest in the management fashion literature, and found it bit awkward that the researchers them-/ourselves so rarely were regarded as anything but completely rational and unbiased actors. In my paper, "fashion" and the interest in it among management scholars was used as the main case in point, when arguing that scholars, too, are fashion-followers. A young scholar protested right after my presentation, and claimed that "while managers of course have their fashions, researchers do not". An established scholar in the area stepped in, though, and defended my position, which made the young scholar cease. (Again, it is important in the academy who the person is that says something.) The paper I presented was never published, although the idea that the huge interest among scholars in fashionable management ideas in itself may be a fashion, was published by another scholar (Clark, 2004). Similarly, scholars such as Carson et al. (2000, p. 1143) have suggested that "fashion bashing itself is becoming fashionable". In any case, I have since then brought with me the ideas of the paper. I should not, though, take credit for having been the first person on Earth to think along these lines (see, e.g., McKinley, 1996).

The other idea that was stated in that conference paper (Örtenblad, 1999)—that researchers, too, have fashions—has also been dealt with by others. Bort and Kieser (2011, p. 660) suggest that "the diffusion of articles using concepts will also follow the typical bell-shaped fashion lifecycle". Similarly, Sunstein claims, mainly about the academic field of law, that "academic life has its own fads and fashions" (Sunstein, 2001, p. 1263) and that "[a]cademics, like everyone else, are subject to *cascade effects*. They start, join, and accelerate bandwagons" (Sunstein, 2001, p. 1251, emphasis in original). Bort and Kieser present a similar argument:

> The more peers choose certain topics, theories, concepts or methods, the more attractive these appear. In this way, fashion could find its way into science. (Bort & Kieser, 2011, p. 658)

It is easy to find examples of fashions within the academic community of organization studies. Researchers, claim Bort and Kieser (2011), may do things such as suggesting new paradigms just to impress their peers. Paradigms have become a matter of fashion, insofar as it is possible to choose paradigm—well, at least it is possible for any particular person to profess to and even preach a particular paradigm, whether or not one actually also practices it. Among some research communities, critical realism is the right paradigm to have, while other communities within the organization studies area favor, for instance, interpretivism, radical humanism or postmodernism. This can be seen as fashion-following, just like *social constructionism* can be regarded as a fashion among quite a number of doctoral students (see also Andersson, 2008). Anyone who, as a doctoral student in organization studies, takes any other position may find it difficult to appear legitimate. This is at least how it is at some universities, according to my own experiences.

Andersson (2008) argues that researchers, too, are victims of fashions and that researchers and practitioners, within the area of management, surf on the same fashion waves—not only do the researchers study the practitioners' fashions, they are also part, Andersson claims, of the same "time collective". Examples of "fashions of researchers" are the enormous current interest in "sustainability", "innovation" and "entrepreneurship". But, as in the case with practitioner fashions, there is an end to any researcher fashion, too. As Starbuck (2009, p. 115) suggests, "[a]lthough each successive fad – contingency theory, population ecology, institutional theory – has left a small residual of devotees, the great majority of researchers have moved on".

During the last few decades, it has become fashionable among a not-that-small group of researchers within the area of organization studies to refer to philosophical texts. Many of these researchers specifically refer to Habermas and/or Foucault. One could perhaps take it as far as claiming that some academics even seem to refer to those philosophers in somewhat of a herd-like way (see also Sunstein, 2001, pp. 1262–1263). Thus, "heroification" or "guruification" is apparent also among researchers. Nothing wrong with that, of course, but there is clearly a tendency that a researcher can no longer say anything critical—or, at the least, few would listen—without referring to any of these two philosophers, or to any other philosopher that it is legitimate within the research area in question to refer to. As Parker (2002) has argued, for one or another reason researchers in organization studies are not allowed to put forward much critique without these kind of references to philosophers, even if there are others—such as Naomi Klein—who are entitled to be critical without leaning on references to academic theory.

Thus, according to the above reasoning, academics also seem to possess at least some degree of human weakness. But not everyone would agree. In the next section, I sketch four assumptions about the relation between how unbiased practitioners can be considered to be, in relation to how unbiased academics may be.

Assumptions About the Degree of Human Weakness Among Academics Versus Practitioners

How human, then, are academics in relation to practitioners?[2] There are those who tend to assume that practitioners are more biased, gullible, and so on, than they are themselves. I call this assumption the *extraordinary academic assumption.* This is an assumption, as it seems, that those who criticize debunkers of management fashions claim that the debunkers usually have:

> management's gurus live in a false or deluded world, while critical scholars of management enjoy unique access to a world which provides true and objective information regarding the nature and performance of organizations. In seeking to debunk guru ideas as fads therefore, critical scholars seem to substitute the totalising world-view of the gurus, for their preferred totalising world-view. (Collins, 2001, p. 28)

An example is the younger scholar I wrote about above, who, at an EGOS conference, seemed to be convinced that practitioners are fashion-followers but denied that academics could be regarded as such. Without having any evidence to show in support of my claim, I dare to say that this is still a common assumption among academics—at least in the area of organization studies. Perhaps it is even the most common assumption among scholars in this research area.

Those who suggest that managers are not to be regarded as passive victims of management fashions (Collins, 2001, 2003), or as gullible (Cox et al., 2005) as others have suggested, while at the same time avoid questioning (or at least bringing it up for reflection) their own extraordinariness, could be said to have an assumption where both practitioners and academics are regarded as being fairly extraordinary. I call this position the *Übermensch assumption.* Without knowing how reflexive those who criticize others for wanting to debunk management fashions

[2] It is perfectly correct to say that the four assumptions to some extent can be characterized as caricatures. It is also correct to claim that neither "human" nor "extraordinary" are given the exact same meanings in all four assumptions.

in order to assist seduced managers are, a qualified guess would be that at least many of them have this assumption.

Others may view organization actors, in fact, as less biased and gullible than academics, an assumption that I suggest is called the *ivory tower assumption.* On the top of such towers is where academics are assumed to sit, by those who criticize the usefulness of academic work (especially research). As Parker has argued,

> [a]cademics continue to overproduce words that most people never read, and "critical" academics spend time imagining that writing a "critical" piece and tweeting about it is the same as engaging in politics. (Parker, 2023, p. 414)

Anyone suggesting that what academics do is far too distanced from practice and reality and has little—if any—value, while arguing that people outside of the academy in fact do know what they are talking about, would have this assumption. Perhaps those who question the relevance of academic management studies for managerial practice (e.g., Bennis & O'Toole, 2005; Nicolai & Röbken, 2005; Pfeffer & Fong, 2002), implying that the outcome of such studies never actually gets utilized, could be placed here. Academics, thus, exist within a bubble, writing things for one another merely to gain legitimacy among peers. In contrast, practitioners, according to this assumption, are—thanks to their ability to thrive without being dependent on gaining legitimacy—able to contribute instrumentally.

The fourth assumption comes under the notion, so I suggest, of the *ordinary citizen assumption* (see Fig. 3.1). It is here assumed that academics are as biased and as human, with weaknesses such as gullibility, as any practitioner they may study. McKinley (1996, p. 614) argues that "[a]s is true in the creation of popular management rhetoric, the production of management scholarship is subject to the influence of fashion". Bort and Kieser (2011, p. 655) claim that there is no reason why science should be an exception to the fact that "all areas of human culture are subjected to the whims of fashion". Similarly, Sunstein argues that "people care about what others think of them, and most academics are, on this count, like most other people" (Sunstein, 2001, p. 1257), and explains:

> Academics, like everyone else, are also susceptible to the *reputational pressures* imposed by the (perceived) beliefs of others. They respond to these pressures, and by so doing, they help to amplify them. It is for these reasons that fads, fashions, and bandwagon effects can be found in academia, including the academic study of law. (Sunstein, 2001, p. 1251, emphasis in original)

"Fashion" is here regarded "not as an evil but as a social phenomenon that permeates science just as it permeates other areas of social life" (Bort & Kieser, 2011, p. 656). A similar argument is put forward by Stubbart (1989, p. 338), who suggested that "[e]ven scientists prove vulnerable to cognitive simplification and errors".

The ordinary citizen assumption is the one that I identify the most with myself. At the least, it is the assumption I appreciate the most, the one that I would want to be associated with as an academic. In the remainder of the chapter, I discuss some implications and problems stemming from two of the above assumptions—the extraordinary academic assumption, which I think is a common one in academia, and the ordinary citizen assumption, which is the assumption I want to believe is the one that is closest to my own heart (and brain).

ACADEMICS

PRACTITIONERS	Human	Extraordinary
Extraordinary	The ivory tower assumption	The Übermensch assumption
Human	The ordinary citizen assumption	The extraordinary academic assumption

Fig. 3.1 Four assumptions about the extent to which practitioners versus academics possess human weakness

Comments and Implications

If I am correct when claiming that quite a few academics in the area of organization studies tend to view themselves as possessing less human weakness than the people they study, then this has some problematic implications. These researchers tend to believe that it is possible to stand externally of what they are studying. I tend to disagree.

Such elitism, as I want to call it, is not anything I have any problem with per se, even if it is perhaps not really my cup of tea. Neither do I mind that academics do not practice what they preach in the sense of, obviously, defining the humans they are themselves differently from how they define the humans they study. But the elitism nevertheless gives rise to problems. It makes researchers and their research appear far less credible. It may even make it more difficult for those researchers to reach out to their audiences, at least as long as the audience consists of the same type of practitioners as those who participated in the researcher's study. These people may not feel comfortable being told by "elitist researchers" that they are human and possess human weaknesses. It is important that researchers show respect for those whom they study and show humbleness in relation to them:

> A first step in the direction of better research is to make researchers aware of the biases that infuse their work and how these biases undermine their efforts…as this article tries to do. Researchers themselves can take a second step by enlisting people other than academics in the evaluation of research. (Starbuck, 2009, p. 115; see also Arnold, 2024)

Without such humbleness and respect, there is a clear risk that practitioners—completely understandably—no longer want us to do research on or about them, which may lead to access problems (see also Arnold, 2024).

Self-reflexivity is certainly a part of such humbleness. Too rarely does it happen that academics apply the same theories in studies of themselves (introspective studies), as they do when studying organization actors (and claiming that these are "human" in various forms). A notable exception is Engstrom (2012), who offers a very introspective, self-reflexive, autoethnographic analysis of his own experiences from entrepreneurship. The experiences he shares and his interpretations of these are far from only positive, which is refreshing. I would like to see more introspection within the academy, in terms of researchers who examine themselves by the use of the same theories they use to examine others. Thus, as some have argued (e.g., Alvesson et al., 2024; Driver, 2017; Letiche & De Loo, 2024), it would be better if academics would turn more self-reflexive. Or we could, at the least, insert the same kind of reflection in our studies as Watson does:

> ...I am anxious to point out that my examination of their discourse, as an "academic analyst", is no less an exercise of rhetoric skills than their "lay" talk. The sociological writer is constructing realities just as much as the managers are. (Watson, 1995, p. 807)

Even more problematic does it get if I am right in my other observation too. If we assume that academics in fact are as human as those are whom they study, then what researchers are saying about organization actors can be questioned for the same reasons as the academics question organization actors (that is, not making rational decisions, being gullible, etc.). It is not only that we can put as little trust in researchers as we can in practitioners, but their choices of paradigms, theories, perspectives, methods, among others, that they use may also be flawed.

A Few Final Reflections

On the basis of what I have written in this chapter, readers may think "as if he is any less human than those academics he writes about" or "as if he thinks he could gain credence by pointing out how human academics are". In fact, there is no reason to believe that I am any more rational or unbiased than those academics I have been criticizing. As a matter of fact, I have never meant to exclude myself from those whom I criticize.

To claim that one is reflective is hardly enough. We must remember that even the claim that researchers have fashions too could be considered as a fashionable claim to make—that is, the fashion to claim that fashion is a fashion—when it gets popular to do so, which could be said to have been the case during the first decade of the 2000s. Not least, my claim that I hold the ordinary citizen assumption, while simultaneously claiming that the potentially most common position within the area of organization studies is that of the extraordinary academic assumption, is per se evidence enough for the fact that I am human. For believing that one is a bit better than the rest is, indeed, human.

References

Alvesson, M., Gabriel, Y., & Sandberg, J. (2024). Using metaphors critically and reflexively in empirical organizational research. In A. Örtenblad (Ed.), *The Oxford handbook of metaphor in organization studies* (pp. 251–264). Oxford University Press.

Andersen, J. A. (2006). Leadership, personality and effectiveness. *The Journal of Socio-Economics, 35*(6), 1078–1091. https://doi.org/10.1016/j.socec.2005.11.066

Andersson, T. (2008). Personal growth and sensitivity training as fashions in management and management research. *International Studies of Management & Organization, 38*(2), 71–96. https://doi.org/10.2753/IMO0020-8825380204

Arnold, L. B. (2024). Just like a freefall: The freedoms and pitfalls of critical metaphor analysis. In A. Örtenblad (Ed.), *The Oxford handbook of metaphor in organization studies* (pp. 314–327). Oxford University Press.

Benders, J., van den Berg, R., & van Bijsterveld, M. (1998). Hitch-hiking on a hype: Dutch consultants engineering re-engineering. *Journal of Organizational Change Management, 11*(3), 201–215. https://doi.org/10.1108/09534819810216247

Benders, J., & van Veen, K. (2001). What's in a fashion? Interpretative viability and management fashions. *Organization, 8*(1), 33–53. https://doi.org/10.1177/135050840181003

Benders, J., & Verlaar, S. (2003). Lifting parts: Putting conceptual insights into practice. *International Journal of Operations & Production Management, 23*(7), 757–774. https://doi.org/10.1108/01443570310481540

Bennis, W. G., & O'Toole, J. (2005). How business schools lost their way. *Harvard Business Review, 83*(5), 96–104. https://hbr.org/2005/05/how-business-schools-lost-their-way

Bort, S., & Kieser, A. (2011). Fashion in organization theory: An empirical analysis of the diffusion of theoretical concepts. *Organization Studies, 32*(5), 655–681. https://doi.org/10.1177/0170840611405427

Brunsson, N. (1993). Ideas and actions: Justification and hypocrisy as alternatives to control. *Accounting, Organizations and Society, 18*(6), 489–506. https://doi.org/10.1016/0361-3682(93)90001-M

Butler, N., & Spoelstra, S. (2020). Academics at play: Why the "publication game" is more than a metaphor. *Management Learning, 51*(4), 414–430. https://doi.org/10.1177/1350507620917257

Carson, P. P., Lanier, P. A., Carson, K. D., & Birkenmeier, B. J. (1999). A historical perspective on fad adoption and abandonment. *Journal of Management History, 5*(6), 320–333. https://doi.org/10.1108/13552529910288109

Carson, P. P., Lanier, P. A., Carson, K. D., & Guidry, B. N. (2000). Clearing a path through the management fashion jungle: Some preliminary trailblazing. *Academy of Management Journal, 43*(6), 1143–1158. https://doi.org/10.2307/1556342

Clark, T. (2004). The fashion of management fashion: A surge too far? *Organization, 11*(2), 297–306. https://doi.org/10.1177/1350508404030659

Collins, D. (2001). The fad motif in management scholarship. *Employee Relations, 23*(1), 26–37. https://doi.org/10.1108/01425450110366255

Collins, D. (2003). The branding of management knowledge: Rethinking management "fads." *Journal of Organizational Change Management, 16*(2), 186–204. https://doi.org/10.1108/09534810310468152

Cox, A., Lonsdale, C., Sanderson, J., & Watson, G. (2005). *The right tools for the job: On the use and performance of management tools and techniques.* Palgrave Macmillan. https://doi.org/10.1057/9780230509207

Czarniawska, B., & Sevón, G. (Eds.). (1996). *Translating organizational change.* Walter de Gruyter. https://doi.org/10.1515/9783110879735

De Rond, M., & Miller, A. N. (2005). Publish or perish: Bane or boon of academic life? *Journal of Management Inquiry, 14*(4), 321–329. https://doi.org/10.1177/1056492605276850

DiMaggio, P. J., & Powell, W. W. (1983). The iron cage revisited: Institutional isomorphism and collective rationality in organizational fields. *American Sociological Review, 48*(2), 147–160. https://doi.org/10.2307/2095101

Driver, M. (2017). Toward more reflexive, empowering, and ethical metaphorical organizational research. *Management Learning, 48*(5), 552–565. https://doi.org/10.1177/1350507617712430
Dunnette, M. D. (1957). Use of the sugar pill by industrial psychologists. *American Psychologist, 12*(4), 223–225. https://doi.org/10.1037/h0048809
Dunnette, M. D. (1966). Fads, fashions, and folderol in psychology. *American Psychologist, 21*(4), 343–352. https://doi.org/10.1037/h0023535
Elangovan, A. R., & Hoffman, A. J. (2021). The pursuit of success in academia: Plato's ghost asks "what then?" *Journal of Management Inquiry, 30*(1), 68–73. https://doi.org/10.1177/1056492619836729
Engstrom, C. (2012). An autoethnographic account of prosaic entrepreneurship. *Tamara: Journal of Critical Organization Inquiry, 10*(1), 41–54. https://journals.kozminski.edu.pl/system/files/146-539-1-PB.pdf
Fincham, R. (1999). The consultant–client relationship: Critical perspectives on the management of organizational change. *Journal of Management Studies, 36*(3), 336–351. https://doi.org/10.1111/1467-6486.00139
Good, I. J. (1962). How rational should a manager be? *Management Science, 8*(4), 383–393. https://doi.org/10.1287/mnsc.8.4.383
Harney, S. (2008, November 20). Business schools must spurn rewards culture that shamed the city. *Times Higher Education.* https://www.researchgate.net/publication/328216214_Business_schools_must_spurn_rewards_culhe_City_Times_Higher_Education_THE
Kieser, A. (1997). Rhetoric and myth in management fashion. *Organization, 4*(1), 49–74. https://doi.org/10.1177/135050849741004
Letiche, H., & De Loo, I. (2024). Research: Invitation to metaphor. In A. Örtenblad (Ed.), *The Oxford handbook of metaphor in organization studies* (pp. 434–447). Oxford University Press.
Levitt, B., & March, J. G. (1988). Organizational learning. *Annual Review of Sociology, 14*, 319–338. https://doi.org/10.1146/annurev.so.14.080188.001535
McKinley, W. (1996). What's hot and what's not. *Academy of Management Review, 21*(3), 614–616. http://www.jstor.org/stable/258995
Meyer, J. W., & Rowan, B. (1977). Institutionalized organizations: Formal structure as myth and ceremony. *American Journal of Sociology, 83*(2), 340–363. https://doi.org/10.1086/226550
Nicolai, A. T., & Röbken, H. (2005). Scientification, immune responses, and reflection: The changing relationship between management studies and consulting. *Journal of Organizational Change Management, 18*(5), 416–434. https://doi.org/10.1108/09534810510614922

Nystrom, P. C., & Starbuck, W. H. (1984). Organizational facades. *Academy of Management Annual Meeting Proceedings, 1*, 182–185. https://doi.org/10.5465/ambpp.1984.4978761

Örtenblad, A. (1999, July 4–6). *"The fashionable fashion concept" or "researchers have their fashions too"* [Conference presentation]. European Group for Organizational Studies 15th colloquium, Warwick University, UK.

Örtenblad, A. (2005). Vague and attractive: Five explanations of the use of ambiguous management ideas. *Philosophy of Management, 5*(1), 45–54. https://doi.org/10.5840/pom20055130

Örtenblad, A. (2007). The evolution of popular management ideas: An exploration and extension of the old wine in new bottles metaphor. *International Journal of Management Concepts and Philosophy, 2*(4), 365–388. https://doi.org/10.1504/IJMCP.2007.015131

Örtenblad, A. (2015). *Handbook of research on management ideas and panaceas: Adaptation and context*. Edward Elgar. https://doi.org/10.4337/9781783475605

Parker, M. (2002). *Against management*. Polity.

Parker, M. (2023). Against management: Auto-critique. *Organization, 30*(2), 407–415. https://doi.org/10.1177/13505084211020922

Pelz, D. C. (1978). Some expanded perspectives on use of social science in public policy. In J. M. Yinger & S. J. Cutler (Eds.), *Major social issues: A multidisciplinary view* (pp. 346–357). The Free Press.

Pfeffer, J., & Fong, C. T. (2002). The end of business schools? Less that meets the eye. *Academy of Management Learning & Education, 1*(1), 78–95. https://doi.org/10.5465/amle.2002.7373679

Pruijt, H. (1998). Multiple personalities: The case of business process reengineering. *Journal of Organizational Change Management, 11*(3), 260–268. https://doi.org/10.1108/09534819810216283

Quijada, M. A. (2021). My mental health struggle in academia: What I wish all business school faculty, students, and administration knew. *Journal of Management Education, 45*(1), 19–42. https://doi.org/10.1177/1052562920958433

Rosenkopf, L., & Abrahamson, E. (1999). Modeling reputational and informational influences in threshold models of bandwagon innovation diffusion. *Computational & Mathematical Organization Theory, 5*(4), 361–384. https://doi.org/10.1023/A:1009620618662

Rüling, C-C. (2015). Managerial panaceas, sensemaking and identity construction in contemporary organizations. In A. Örtenblad (Ed.), *Handbook of research on management ideas and panaceas: Adaptation and context* (pp. 427–441). Edward Elgar. https://doi.org/10.4337/9781783475605.00041

Ryan, S., & Hurley, J. (2004). Have total quality management, business process re-engineering and the learning organisation been replaced by knowledge management? *Irish Journal of Management, 25*(1), 41–55. https://www.proquest.com/openview/4c1a1dce5769ec7bcafd84bccab135d2/1?pq-origsite=gscholar&cbl=10069

Senge, P. M. (1990). *The fifth discipline: The art and practice of the learning organization.* Doubleday.

Simon, H. A. (1991). Bounded rationality and organizational learning. *Organization Science, 2*(1), 125–134. https://doi.org/10.1287/orsc.2.1.125

Sorge, A., & van Witteloostuijn, A. (2004). The (non)sense of organizational change: An essai about universal management hypes, sick consultancy metaphors, and healthy organization theories. *Organization Studies, 25*(7), 1205–1231. https://doi.org/10.1177/0170840604046360

Spell, C. S. (2001). Management fashions: Where do they come from, and are they old wine in new bottles? *Journal of Management Inquiry, 10*(4), 358–373. https://doi.org/10.1177/1056492601104009

Stagner, R. (1958). The gullibility of personnel managers. *Personnel Psychology, 11*(3), 347–352. https://doi.org/10.1111/j.1744-6570.1958.tb00022.x

Starbuck, W. H. (2009). The constant causes of never-ending faddishness in the behavioral and social sciences. *Scandinavian Journal of Management, 25*(1), 108–116. https://doi.org/10.1016/j.scaman.2008.11.005

Stensaker, B. (2007). Quality as fashion: Exploring the translation of a management idea into higher education. In D. F. Westerheijden, B. Stensaker, & M. J. Rosa (Eds.), *Quality assurance in higher education: Trends in regulation, translation and transmission* (pp. 99–118). Springer. https://doi.org/10.1007/978-1-4020-6012-0_4

Stubbart, C. I. (1989). Managerial cognition: A missing link in strategic management research. *Journal of Management Studies, 26*(4), 325–347. https://doi.org/10.1111/j.1467-6486.1989.tb00732.x

Sunstein, C. R. (2001). Foreword: On academic fads and fashions. *Michigan Law Review, 99*(6), 1251–1264. https://dash.harvard.edu/bitstream/handle/1/13614522/Sunstein_OnAcademicFads.pdf?sequence=3&isAllowed=y

Svensson, G., & Wood, G. (2005). The serendipity of leadership effectiveness in management and business practices. *Management Decision, 43*(7–8), 1001–1009. https://doi.org/10.1108/00251740510609992

Watson, T. J. (1994). Management "flavours of the month": Their role in managers' lives. *The International Journal of Human Resource Management, 5*(4), 893–909. https://doi.org/10.1080/09585199400000071
Watson, T. J. (1995). Rhetoric, discourse and argument in organizational sense making: A reflexive tale. *Organization Studies, 16*(5), 805–821. https://doi.org/10.1177/017084069501600503
Westphal, J. D., & Zajac, E. J. (2001). Decoupling policy from practice: The case of stock repurchase programs. *Administrative Science Quarterly, 46*(2), 202–228. https://www.proquest.com/scholarly-journals/decoupling-policy-practice-case-stock-repurchase/docview/203978821/se-2?accountid=45259
Williams, R. (2004). Management fashions and fads: Understanding the role of consultants and managers in the evolution of ideas. *Management Decision, 42*(6), 769–780. https://doi.org/10.1108/00251740410542339

Part II

Homo Reflectivus

4

Existential Explorations of Others and Oneself as a Researcher

Pär Vasko

Researchers in the interpretative fields of management and organization often find themselves theorizing about others, curious to understand the doings and decisions of managers, leaders, employees, board members and investors. Taking an existential stance, in this chapter I would like to reflexively turn the gaze upon myself and my existential adventure into the depths of research, thereby engaging in a wider wondering about existence. Reasoning at length about faith and truth in the light of objectivity and subjectivity, Kierkegaard argued that life is paradoxical and that those paradoxes of life become thrown into sharp relief when one seeks to create an understanding of existence as a human being (Kierkegaard, 1844/1977).

To help accomplish this reflexive undertaking, I intend to illustrate three existential layers interwoven into the text of this chapter. The first concerns (some of) the existential paradoxes I experienced as a doctoral student in business administration and how these paradoxes influenced

P. Vasko (✉)
School of Business and Economics, Linnaeus University, Växjö, Sweden
e-mail: par.vasko@lnu.se

S. Cinque and D. Ericsson (eds.), *Debating 'Homo Academicus' in Management and Organization*, Palgrave Debates in Business and Management,
https://doi.org/10.1007/978-3-031-58195-3_4

the course of the dissertation and my writing process. The second layer regards my use of stewardship theory and agency theory for the dissertation, highlighting some of the key points that came to function as my theoretical focus. In the third layer I explore the theoretical discourse as a subjective way of wondering about researchers' taken-for-granted assumptions about themselves—a way of wondering that in turn underpins both the stewardship and the agency positions. Finally, I hope with these three layers to contribute to what an existential understanding means—and could mean—as I, a researcher in management and organization, theorize about others while reflecting on assumptions I make about myself as that researcher.

The Start of a Non-Linear Journey

I applied and was one of six accepted to the doctoral program in business administration at the School of Business and Economics at Linnaeus University in the midst of summer 2017. The number of applicants for those six positions had been historically high, but we, the six singled out to join the adventure of becoming researchers, were eager to get going.

The first course, an ambitious intellectual odyssey into the classics and research frontiers of business administration, set the tone for the road ahead, a route that promised waypoints in entrepreneurship, corporate governance, management accounting, finance, international business, marketing as well as management and leadership theory. Thousands of pages compiled in articles and books lay waiting to be read, reflected upon and analyzed in written papers. These were the expected initial challenges to be met by a person embarking on a quest to understand the variegated field of business administration. The trade-off for the quest was inevitable: family time lounging by the sea in exchange for long hours fettered to books and texts.

In an opening speech, the dean explained to the six of us that we were all specializing in different sub-fields, but nonetheless enrolled in the broader field of business administration. I was enrolled in international business. Given my previous studies, international business was, all in all, uncharted intellectual territory, which is why the speech felt like a breath of fresh air. Maybe because I already knew that my dissertation would never fall within the confines of international business and that my decisions along the way would have consequences leading me in another direction. At the outset I assumed that my preconceived research process would play out linearly: My text would gradually evolve, be critiqued and therefore automatically improved and certainly be challenged over and over again. Although the process perhaps unfolded in precisely that manner, when I look in the rearview mirror, I notice how back there at the beginning I had demarcated myself and the text as two separate entities. As the adventure continued, however, I came to realize that the text I was writing was not separate from myself but rather something I had written myself into. This symbiosis between myself and my writing meant the journey was to evolve as anything but linear.

What I had failed to realize was how changing direction would metamorphize from an existential crisis into a leap of faith in existential philosophy as a way to understand stewardship theory and agency theory. In retrospect, I see my naivety as a budding researcher who understood the process as involving an object—the dissertation—which was supposed to undergo a series of rather instrumental, mechanical, almost linear changes, while I, my being, would be left untouched by the whole debacle of theorizing. Needless to say, I was wrong—or as Nilsén (2000) eloquently put it, and I paraphrase: Few decisions in life are taken on so uninformed basis as the decision to start writing a dissertation. Learning this truth did not scare me off but rather left me wondering what I had gotten myself into. Naivety is not necessarily negative; indeed, not actually knowing or even guessing the consequences of our decisions is what it means to exist as a human being (Beauvoir, 1944/2020, 1947/2018; Sartre, 1943/2003, 1945/2007). We might anticipate, sometimes with certainty, the consequences of our decisions and where they will lead us, but never absolutely. That said, my naivety, my inability to fully grasp the ramifications of my undertaking for my own existence, gave me the actual courage to throw myself into the world of doctoral studies.

Certainly, my own numerous attempts to bring the being of a dissertation into existence were hardly unique. The anthology *The Dissertation* [my translation] (Strannegård, 2000) offers an abundance of perspectives on what it means to write a dissertation. The dark passages in the writing process can bring up a wellspring of emotions—anxiety, doubt, self-criticism, fear and trembling, but also moments of joy, excitement and the thrill of discovery. Reflecting on these emotional modes of being, experienced researchers can grasp and relate to them as lived experiences. For the novice, however, feeling these emotions for the first time is something else. Considering the reflections of both the master and myself as the novice, I have come to see how writing a dissertation is—or can at least also—be understood as an existential endeavor. The aim of creating an object (a physical product in the form of a book) is equally a creation of the subject (the person writing the book). Framed existentially, an ongoing dialectic runs between the writing and the writer, and this dialectic can be understood as an engagement in existence itself: The text changes the being of the writer, just as the writer changes the being of the text.

One finds oneself lurching between emotional extremes—a confidence in one's capacity to write that instantaneously falls into a bottomless pit of self-doubt, of utter ignorance. In my experience this thin, frail line between the two requires a delicate tread as one gropes in the dark—all sense of direction lost as some clarion questions cross one's path: What are you writing about? When will you finish? What is your contribution to extant literature? I was taken off guard every time these fully reasonable questions were asked. What *was* I really writing about? My inner editor had already doomed my writing, burying it in a cemetery of broken thoughts and malformed texts. In hindsight, I can see that I overcame my fear of that question by staying open to changing my line of thought as well as the text I was writing—a trial that was an existential conquest of being in movement. There is no shame in not knowing the answer; the answer moves in parallel with the writer's changes just as much as the constant revisions of the text.

The second matter of finishing had, though, a more linear answer, as the finish line for the doctoral studies was absolute, fixed in time. A period measured in money had been allotted to me and my intellectual development. Running out of money equaled running out of time. Formally, I was to complete the dissertation in 2022. That was the short answer, but a slightly longer, existential answer would have been more honest: When will I finish, you ask? I seriously doubt I'll ever finish what

I have started, and I make no guarantees of ever bringing this project home. In fact, a dissertation is never done until actually done, a harsh truth that left me trembling with the sensation that I would be stuck forever with an uncompleted work. Especially in view of where I now found myself: lost. I mean really lost, with only the slightest chance of finding my way.

At about the halfway mark, about two and a half years in temporal terms, I found myself caught in limbo. Every day played out in exactly the same loop: writing from morning to late afternoon and the inevitable deletion of all text by nightfall. A creeping sensation began to take hold of me. I had an argument I wanted to explore, an argument worth striving for, yet I lacked the capacity to bend the words to my will. The rich contrasts in my idea are more apparent now, but at the time my only inkling was that, although the stewardship vs. agency discourse lies, rightly, in corporate governance, it *also* concerns something else: These two vastly different ways of understanding managers and board members ultimately represent two different ways of making assumptions about human beings. The point, therefore, was not so much about stewardship theory and agency theory per se, but rather the stewards and the agents themselves—or more precisely the theoretical ideals on which they were constructed. There was the benevolent steward, on the one hand, and the self-interested economic man on the other. To me, the researcher engaging in one theory was also choosing how to study and understand others. As such, not only was the theoretical engagement to be chosen at stake, but also a view and understanding of managers as either benevolent stewards or self-interested agents. Understanding human beings as either one or the other was theoretically neat, but in practice? Where does a one-sided view of the people being studied go?

My inquiry was empirically grounded, as I had for some time engaged with Interior Cluster Sweden, a membership-driven, non-profit organization active in the interior design and furniture industry. I had obtained access to the CEO and the board members, participated in workshops and board meetings and also attended a few events hosted for other companies in the industry. The longer I spent in their business context, the more human the managers I encountered became. There was more to them than their job titles implied, which I found surprisingly puzzling.

Paradoxically, they bridged the theoretical ideals and dichotomous categories of stewardship and agency simply by being who they were. For example, I sought to untangle why they at once engaged in an organization that stood only to benefit the overall industry without any obvious direct economic gain for them while simultaneously underscoring their expectation of financial payoff from the engagement. Either side of that statement would fall neatly into one theoretical ideal or the other; stewards would act with a collective responsibility in the best interest of the group, whereas agents would strive for direct economic gain and a positive bottom line. An alternative understanding, I thought, could bridge the dichotomous discourse and the ambiguous practice but would have to operate on a different premise able to capacitate this ambiguity. In other words, both collective responsibility and direct economic gain could be understood to illustrate what it means to act as a manager in practice. More importantly, to reach beyond the theoretical ideals, I had to escape the same essential frame of mind in which the ideals had been constructed. I had become a paradox to myself. I now knew I had to transcend the dichotomies, but without yet understanding how, or even whether, it could be done. I needed to dig myself out of my own thinking and find a philosophical fundament from which to work. What this foundation might be was still nebulous.

At the time I was reading Sartre's Nausea (1938/2021), strongly identifying with the main character, Antonine Roquentin, and his struggles to finish a book project. The sluggishness and nausea permeated every page I turned, and by the end I realized that I was not alone, someone else, albeit a fictional character, was also experiencing the dread of being lost. In my mind, the argument seemed coherent and solid enough to underpin my ideas, but whenever I tried to commit the argument to paper, it somehow evaporated. Around then I also came across the Swedish poet Tomas Tranströmer and his famous poem *The Meadow* [my translation]. The first line resonated with me in a pitch-perfect tone: "In the middle of the woods, there is an unexpected meadow that only one who is lost is able to find" (Tranströmer, 2001, p. 193, my translation). In spite of my bleak outlook on my dissertation, I found comfort in at least knowing that I was lost, but also felt an emergent realization that I might be at a crossroads.

Through experience I had finally lifted the shroud of my naivety and could hope for a new dawn to break. Could I look to existential philosophy as a means of revisiting the theoretical positions of stewardship theory and agency theory from an alternative angle? Perhaps I might write not with the eloquence of Tranströmer or the winding reasonings of Sartre and Beauvoir, but in a voice that felt personal and explorative. I decided to call a professor I had met during two courses in qualitative methods, both of which had felt filled with invigorating possibilities. For example, I handed in an assignment in the form of a journal note my then therapist might have written about me. I even embellished the note with a client number, upcoming bookings and a reminder that I rarely answer the phone—all to complete the illusion that this was an actual journal entry concerning an actual client. I remember finding putting myself in my therapist's place an intriguing exercise of the imagination.

I had decided not to cry when I called the professor responsible for the doctoral program to explain my plans of taking the dissertation in another direction—a decision I had to abandon about two sentences after saying hello. The new direction was, of course, existential philosophy as a way of exploring fundamental assumptions about managers and leaders in the discourse on stewardship theory and agency theory. After reading my latest draft, the professor gave me both encouraging comments and a friendly warning. I could write differently, he assured me; I could finish on time and could even contribute to the field of corporate governance, but choosing this direction was also likely to entail conflict borne of office politics and criticism from more traditional research streams—but, he added, my choice also carried a touch of courage.

A New Direction

The professor agreed to step in as my new supervisor, and a reasonably dignified solution was found to manage the office politics. I had officially changed course but would continue to theoretically explore the discourse on stewardship theory and agency theory, two central positions in the corporate governance field (Eriksson-Zetterqvist et al., 2020). Soon after, a number of supporting arguments began to emerge in the guise of three articles I had come across in the *Journal of Management Studies*. The articles resembled a conversation between a stewardship theorist and an agency theorist, each representing a vastly different view of managers. The conversation between these scholars sparked my interest. On the one hand, Donaldson (1990a, 1990b) proposed stewardship and the conception of the steward as an alternative to the dominating conception of the agent. A steward, he clarified, is a manager intrinsically motivated to act in the group's best interest even when individual self-interest and the interests of the collective conflict. To support his argument, he pointed out that not all managers are rational, wealth-maximizers motivated by self-interest, as would be the case in the theoretical conception of the agent. Barney (1990) retorted that extensive empirical observation had supported the theory of the agent more strongly than that of the steward. What grabbed me about this polemic was less the debate itself than the way it seemed to present me, as an aspiring researcher, with a choice: *either* stewardship theory *or* agency theory, with all that the respective theories entail. Why not recognize, I wondered, that managers and board members, and by extension human beings, are more complex and paradoxical than to be understood as fitting neatly into one theoretical ideal or the other?

This question led me to challenge the assumptions about how I as a researcher in becoming should think. Dichotomies, categories and extremes were three academically appealing concepts gathered under this normative assumption. To think differently, or alternatively, I first had to challenge extant norms as well as myself—to find solid intellectual ground and work from there. At stake were two seemingly opposite conceptions of managers based on two opposite theoretical ideals that, to my mind, scholars had polemically constructed as an either/or dichotomy. Although academically appealing, dichotomizing managers and leaders into stewards or agents forestalls a more complex and paradoxical exploration aligned with Kierkegaard's (1844/1977) notion of the paradoxes of existence. When one has already decided how to view others, the absence of self-reflection becomes clear. Indeed, the fundamental assumptions of a theory hold an uncharted potentiality that, if taken, enables one to explore one's own preconceived notions and taken-for-granted assumptions in broad terms.

The literature following the initial discussion between Donaldson (1990a, 1990b) and Barney (1990) appears to continue constructing the discourse on stewardship and agency as a dichotomy between two theoretical ideals taken for granted as they are (Albrecht et al., 2004; Chrisman, 2019; Davis et al., 1997; Hernandez, 2012; Madison, 2014), and thus to close any avenue moving somewhere other than either/or.

In that initial feverish debate, scholars fought from their respective corners, hurling accusations that the others were mushy headed liberals or economic fascists (see Barney, 1990). That rhetoric has since been toned down, but the dichotomous shape of the discourse itself seemed to go unnoticed and the question of which theoretical ideal to choose unanswered. To my mind, there was more at stake than discriminating between theoretical ideals, as the discourse at large struck me as a way of choosing how to theoretically conceive human beings. From this understanding sprang these questions: Could my understanding of the discourse as a dichotomy be a springboard to an alternative understanding of managers and leaders? Could this alternative allow me to explore managers and leaders as existential beings? My wanderer's spirit came alive, raising me out of the depths of anxiety into a world of adventure glimpsed through my inquisitive thoughts. If not constantly, at least occasionally. As I had come to understand the discourse, read literally, it seemed that few researchers were scrutinizing the fundamental assumptions underpinning the theories, ideals and categories, but to me this was the whole point. An interesting trail I thought I might follow: What could be gleaned from trying to see what lay beneath the fundamental assumptions rather than taking them for granted?

Three works by social psychologist Johan Asplund opened my eyes to the possibility of finding an alternative route on which to theorize. In his book, *In wonder about society* [my translation], the reader is encouraged to explore their own understanding by wondering. This wondering entails not accepting established theoretical ideals in their absolute terms, but critically delving into the fundamental assumption beneath a given text (Asplund, 1970). The notion of wondering resonated with me and my newfound excitement over the research project. By approaching the theoretical positions from another angle and considering what lies beneath the text, I felt the entire project getting back into motion. As I embarked on my critical foray into this territory beneath the discourse on stewardship theory and agency theory, I was able to see three layers of the discourse. The first concerned two opposite theoretical positions, the second outlined how these positions are fundamentally anchored in two different theoretical ideals (e.g., stewards and agents), and the third involved the notion that the two ideals are constructed on two opposite sets of fundamental assumptions about human beings (e.g., hedonistic wealth-maximizers or altruistic collectivists). The intricate fabric of these three interwoven layers offered a means of meaningfully arguing how the construction of the discourse as dichotomous could be understood. Still, merely concluding that the dichotomous shape could be seen as layered was not enough, the mightier challenge was to move beyond the dichotomy itself—a movement with its own value (Asplund, 1987, 1991).

Asplund's encouragement to go beneath the surface guided me to a fourth, philosophical layer embodied in a simple question: What philosophical foundation engenders dichotomies? In my view essentialism was key, so I looked further into Blackburn (1996), learning that an essence consists of elements it cannot be without. Remove any one element and the given essence would cease to exist.

I was now walking a trail I was eager to travel and curious to see where it would take me in my dissertation. About the same time, I realized that I needed to invite the ultimate reader, critics and supporters to follow along and hopefully experience my way of writing as an adventure of sorts. The adventure unfolded in three main passageways. First, I strove to create an understanding for Asplund's way of reasoning. Second, I provided an overview of the discourse in question, but with the aim of attempting to move beyond dichotomies, an endeavor that could offer an alternative way of understanding managers and leaders—with existential philosophy to light the way. Lastly, I wanted to write in a tone and voice congenial with the existential tradition and that also said something about myself, the writer.

Who did I think I was in my capacity as an aspiring researcher in business administration, as someone about to interweave corporate governance, existentialism and social psychology into one and the same dissertation?

The question may sound arrogant, which is not my intention, although I do believe that it says something about myself as a writer and as a person. Rather, the question is primarily meant to connote the main points I have sought to convey in my dissertation *Moving beyond stewards versus agents*. That said, in this next and final part of the chapter, I reflect on these main points in an attempt to make a reflexive turn upon myself.

To Wonder About Dichotomies

"You live your life forwards, but understands it backwards." This famous quote by Kierkegaard is also the title of an overview of Kierkegaardian existentialism (Thielst, 1994). I can certainly relate to these words as I now engage in reflecting on my own experiences of what it existentially means to write a dissertation. More precisely, what it has meant to me.

Existentially, my own fear of conflict and oft-employed social strategy of mending or compensating for any disharmony in a group underlie my understanding of uneasiness. Notably, although strong criticism is a valuable aspect of life in academia, its sharpening arguments and clarifying intellectual thinking, in my view a dichotomous conversation tends to digress into a zero-sum game and therefore to shape a discourse into a matter of one winner, one loser—either/or. With my predisposition to harmony, I prefer to partake in discussions providing an opportunity to openly wonder in terms of both/and.

My own conflict aversion thus brought another aspect of the extant dichotomous conversation into sight, which is where Asplund's (1970, 1979, 1991) reasoning became fruitful. He argues that a theory, or conversation about a theory, is not exclusively about determining which party is right or wrong, but rather what the theory or conversation enables one to see and, more importantly, wonder about what the point is—and could be. As such, thinking beyond the dichotomy does not absolutely determine what-is, but instead enables what-could-be. I became grounded in this two-pronged assumption, which one might astutely note resembles a … dichotomy. However, what-is and what-could-be are not mutually exclusive as the rules of a zero-sum game would dictate. Rather, they complement each other and require the reader to keep two thoughts in play at once.

To Question Theoretical Ideals

In my dissertation I present the criticism aimed at the economic man, *Homo oeconomicus*. This criticism proved to be a starting point for an exploration into alternative ways of seeing and thinking beyond dichotomies. I am, however, hardly alone in criticizing the economic man as a theoretical ideal (Asplund, 1970; Chrisman, 2019; Davis et al., 1997; Friedberg, 2000). Theoretical ideals are based on a set of fundamental assumptions that allow some assumptions to be made to the exclusion of others—a limitation that certainly sets a direction for arguments. So, I instead inquired into the consequences of utilizing theoretical ideals as fixed, asking what this fixation leads to in terms of understanding managers and leaders.

Instead of accepting the two theoretical ideals (the economic man/agent and the empathetic man/steward) as they are constructed, I leaned into existential philosophy's understanding of human beings as not an essence but an existence. In other words, I framed humans in an understanding lurking somewhere beyond those two ideals, of them as existences, as beings in becoming. Theorizing about human beings (e.g., managers and leaders) from an existential viewpoint enables one to employ seemingly contradictory assumptions about them. For example, one can claim that showing empathy is motivated by self-interest and vice versa. Expanding outwards from contradictions aligns perfectly well with existential philosophy. Beauvoir (1947/2018), for example, maintains that human beings can be understood as ambiguous simply because the condition of existing is ambiguous.

My continuing adventure now rested on the existential assumption that existence is in constant movement and that existing as a human being is ambiguous. Ambiguity, broadly speaking, could partly explain my anxiety during the dissertation process. For a long stretch of the journey I could not wrap my head around what I was doing or even where I was headed. Although claiming to be out on an existential endeavor, I was locked in an essential mindset of striving for absolute insights into what-was. I thought I might define my essence and thereby reach a place of serenity. The existential argument of being in movement seemed to elude me. I guess this illustrated how I, too, am a paradoxical, ambiguous human being.

The empirical insights I gained from experiencing the motivations for engagement, actions and thoughts of managers and board members active in the interior design and furniture industry led me to rethink my own thinking. In practice these motivations appeared quite paradoxical, at least when understood through a theoretical discourse that provided a dichotomous way of understanding them. I wanted to bridge the theoretical abstractions and the empirical concreteness, but to do so required me to break with my own essential thinking. I wanted to understand the paradoxical managers and board members, not just explain them. This compelled me to delve into what it would mean to profoundly think existentially when working empirically. At that point it dawned on me that I was equally trying to understand myself as an aspiring researcher—and ultimately as a human being. Without my experiences from the managers and board members, I myself would probably not have changed.

To Theorize About Managers as Existential Beings

I realized that managers, as paradoxical beings in movement, cannot be defined according to one set of assumptions (or more), a realization that created the potential to bridge contradictory assumptions adherent to a fixed model or ideal. Bridging assumptions meant that they were constantly moving ambiguously, at times contradictorily. An empirical example of this bridging occurred during a workshop in which the Swedish furniture industry managers evaluated a business event, held in New York, they had collectively created and participated in. Their aim with the event was to exhibit furniture collections and hopefully close a deal or two. At the workshop back in Sweden, the managers expressed skepticism about their business trip: The venue had been "ugly," the organization "messy" and the visits to potential clients difficult to get to. In short, New York was definitely not an option for the future. They made these comments in the morning session. After lunch, the managers were asked to brainstorm some possible venues for future events. Following a few stumbling suggestions, someone piped up, "New York—again?" The morning's criticism had done an about face. Discussions took off and by the end of the day the managers had decided to return to New York and execute the same event one more time. Their collective notion now expressed a belief that this time it would be different. The managers returned to New York in spring 2020.

A key takeaway from this empirical illustration of existential ambiguity lies in the shifting way the managers discussed the event, initially with criticism but later with a desire to try an encore performance. Illustrating such empirical ambiguity is one way of attempting to write about managers as existential beings. As I see it, when seeking to understand the bridge between theory and practice, a researcher can move beyond dichotomies by allowing for paradoxes and contradictions.

Closing Comments

The dissertation's submission date had finally arrived. I still faced a grueling 40 straight hours finalizing the entire text, but that was all that stood between me and the send-off to Linnaeus University Press. An intense adventure was about to come to an end, one that has probably changed me more than I realize, definitely more than this chapter expresses. My experiences are surely not unique; many researchers and scholars can bear witness to the chain of existential crises they have lived through. Writing a dissertation is unquestionably a life-changing experience, perhaps not for all, but for some. Definitely for me.

I see now how much I took for granted during my doctoral journey. I criticized scholars in the extant literature for being overly dichotomous, yet had myself been stuck in the same frame of mind for some time. In my eagerness to determine and explain, I neglected to explore and understand. Only when an interest in understanding what it means to be human caught my attention could I see the discourse on stewardship theory and agent theory as something other than a mere debate about two theoretical positions. This insight took me from a unidirectional way of thinking, where I tried to categorize managers and board members as consistent with one or the other ideal, to a more reciprocal way of understanding myself in relation to others. Still, I would never have reached this understanding without the people engaged in my dissertation project. They pointed out that a taken-for-granted assumption in a discourse is not a wall but a hatchway through which to explore what is beneath the text—and that's where the adventure begins.

With the story related in this chapter, I hope to have created a bridge between the writer (the subject, e.g., me) and the content of the text (the object, e.g., the dissertation). However, this endeavor has left me with two questions: Who is writing whom—was I writing the dissertation, or was it writing me? Perhaps the oscillation between the two could be understood as a movement that illustrates how the being of the subject changes over time. This movement could provide some perspective on the existential anxiety so many experience during a dissertation project. The movement's direction is in constant flux as both the text and the subject change over time. Experiencing this movement for the first time, certainly in an academic context, can be quite daunting. A second question is: Why does the writer write the way he or she does? I sincerely believe that the different parts of my dissertation reflect many of my lifelong struggles. I have been a dichotomous thinker, yet driven to change my thinking. I have set unattainable standards for myself, yet realized that ideals are unreachable in practice but fully possible to move between. Fearing conflict, I have tried to change the tone of conversations and pointed out that results can also be reached through cordial discussion. I have tried to compose a text in the spirit of jazz, labelling my chapters "refrain," "bridge," "coda" and so on, simply because I think a winding jazz song says something about movement and existence. So much of me lies in—and beneath—the text. This writing adventure manifested itself into quite an unusual bird, but I finally came to enjoy the blue notes she sings.

References

Albrecht, W., Albrech, C. C., & Albrecht, C. O. (2004). Fraud and corporate executives: Agency, stewardship and broken trust. *Journal of Forensic Accounting, 5*, 109–130.

Asplund, J. (1970). *Om undran inför samhället*. Argos.

Asplund, J. (1979). *Teorier om framtiden*. Liber Förlag.

Asplund, J. (1987). *Det sociala livets elementära former*. Bokförlaget Korpen.

Asplund, J. (1991). *Essä om Gemeinschaft och Gesellschaft*. Bokförlaget Korpen.

Barney, J. B. (1990). The debate between traditional management theory and organizational economics: Substantive differences or intergroup conflict? *Academy of Management Review, 15*(3), 382–393. https://doi.org/10.5465/amr.1990.4308815

Beauvoir, S. (1944/2020). *What is existentialism?* Penguin Classics.

Beauvoir, S. (1947/2018). *The ambiguity of ethics*. Open Road Integrated Media.

Blackburn, S. (1996). *The Oxford dictionary of philosophy*. Oxford University Press.

Chrisman, J. J. (2019). Stewardship theory: Realism, relevance, and family firm governance. *Entrepreneurship Theory and Practice, 43*(6), 1051–1066. https://doi.org/10.1177/1042258719838472

Davis, J. H., Schoorman, F. D., & Donaldson, L. (1997). Toward a stewardship theory of management. *Academy of Management Review, 22*(1), 20–47. https://doi.org/10.5465/amr.1997.9707180258

Donaldson, L. (1990a). The ethereal hand: Organizational economics and management theory. *Academy of Management Review, 15*(3), 369–381. https://doi.org/10.5465/amr.1990.4308806

Donaldson, L. (1990b). A rational basis for criticisms of organizational economics: A reply to Barney. *Academy of Management Review, 15*(3), 394–401. https://doi.org/10.5465/amr.1990.4308821

Eriksson-Zetterquist, U., Hansson, M., & Nilsson, F. (2020). *Theories and perspectives in business administration*. Studentlitteratur.

Friedberg, E. (2000). Going beyond the either/or. *Journal of Management & Governance, 4*(1–2), 35–52. https://doi.org/10.1023/a:1009977815841

Hernandez, M. (2012). Toward an understanding of the psychology of stewardship. *Academy of Management Review, 37*(2), 172–193. https://doi.org/10.5465/amr.2010.0363

Kierkegaard, S. (1844/1977). *Sören Kierkegaard – skrifter i urval.* Wahlström & Widstrand.

Madison, K. J. (2014). *Agency theory and stewardship theory integrated, expanded, and bounded by context: An empirical investigation of structure, behavior, and performance within family firms* [Doctoral dissertation]. University of Tennessee Press.

Nilsén, Å. (2000). *En empirisk vetenskap om duet – Om Alfred Schutz bidrag till sociologin.* Lund University Press.

Sartre, J-P. (1943/2003). *Being and nothingness.* Routledge.

Sartre, J-P. (1945/2007). *Existentialism is a humanism.* Yale University Press.

Sartre, J. P. (1938/2021). *Nausea.* Penguin Books.

Strannegård, L. (Ed.). (2003). *Avhandlingen – Om att formas till forskare.* Studentlitteratur.

Thielst, P. (1994). *Man förstår livet baklänges – men måste leva det framlänges: historien om Søren Kirkegaard.* Rabén och Sjögren.

Tranströmer, T. (2001). *Samlade dikter 1954–1996.* Albert Bonniers Förlag.

5

Homo Scribens—Notes on Writing Management

Martin Holgersson

Introduction

The cover of *Writing Culture*, a classic anthropology publication edited by Clifford and Marcus in 1986, features a striking image that evokes various associations and prompts reflections on the representation of other cultures and societies. The photograph depicts a white man hunched over a wicker bed, intently writing on a piece of paper. In the background, a hut looms and what appears to be the hut's owner is visible. The sandy ground and bright sun add to the scene's atmosphere. To protect himself from the sun, and to be able to write, the man has draped a handkerchief over one side of his face, held in place by his glasses. While the photograph invites diverse thoughts about representation, at its most basic level, the editors seem to be emphasizing that research is an act of writing and that this fact, although self-evident, is easily overlooked.

M. Holgersson (✉)
School of Business and Economics, Linnaeus University, Växjö, Sweden
e-mail: martin.holgersson@lnu.se

S. Cinque and D. Ericsson (eds.), *Debating 'Homo Academicus' in Management and Organization*, Palgrave Debates in Business and Management,
https://doi.org/10.1007/978-3-031-58195-3_5

There are multiple ways to frame the craft of scientific work, and the perspective presented in this text is one of many. From my perspective, it is a valuable approach and one that is often forgotten or underdeveloped. The main idea is quite straightforward: researchers write. Other formulations that point in the same direction could be "science is written text" and "researchers produce books and articles". Regardless of how we phrase it, the crux of the matter is that science depends on, and is a consequence of, writing. Writing is an essential part of scientific work, without which it would not exist. Every scientist is in that sense a writer, and we could refer to them as *Homo scribens*—people who write.

Broadly speaking, similar claims have been suggested in various forms for quite some time in management and organization studies (see Czarniawska, 1999; Cloutier, 2016; Rhodes, 2001). Currently, there is even a growing research program based on the fundamental assumption of *Homo scribens*, called "writing differently" (Boncori, 2022; Gilmore et al., 2019; Kostera, 2022). However, even though we start from the same assumption about the connectedness between research and writing, we end up in slightly different places, and suggestions. The "writing differently" program makes a case for breaking away from traditional norms (restrictions) to explore alternative ways of writing (Gilmore et al., 2019). The sources of inspiration for new directions concerning both form and content can, for example, come from poetry, emotions, and novels. The core feature of the program seems to be to explore what is possible if you leave conventional scientific norms behind. My ambition is more modest and slightly different. Using the principal words from the tradition above, one could say that my point is that *we all write, and we do it differently*, but that this is not recognized and elaborated enough. By making this assumption visible and looking at several different aspects of writing and management, I hope to make room for a more explicit relationship between management research and writing. Before I elaborate further on this, I would like to discuss a more conventional assumption and idea, of who researchers are, and what they do.

Taylor as a Consultant, and a Writer

There are many ways to approach the scientific enterprise, and one way is to examine the field's predecessors and classics. In contrast to anthropology, business administration—or more specifically, management—has its roots in the nineteenth-century factory. The industrial shift from agriculture to industry marked a starting point for the emergence of the entire field. The challenges associated with accounting, control, and management that arose during this time prompted the need for new knowledge. Companies became a new object of study that had not been previously examined extensively in the existing social sciences, which focused on nations, people, and societies. In line with the modern zeitgeist, knowledge about companies successively became the subject of a new scientific field, as it represented a pressing and timely area of inquiry.

Perhaps the most notable and pioneering figure in management research is Frederick Winslow Taylor, an engineer who published *The Principles of Scientific Management* in 1911 (Taylor, 1911/1998). Taylor's work is worth exploring because it can shed light on this new "science" as well as its "scientists". In the preface, Taylor emphasizes the economic aspect of his work, quoting President Theodore Roosevelt on the importance of national efficiency and optimal resource utilization for the nation's success. Roosevelt's focus is on conserving natural resources such as forests and water, but Taylor's interests lie in improving labor in manufacturing. He is interested in social resources, not natural.

Taylor argues that human labor is a valuable resource that should not be squandered any more than natural resources should. As a result, he takes on the task of developing principles for "scientific management" to optimize labor. His book outlines strategies and techniques for improving efficiency in the workplace; more specifically, he suggests making use of time-based studies, standardization of work processes, and division of labor. Through his work, Taylor aims to make the best use of labor in the pursuit of increased efficiency, effectiveness, and profitability.

According to Taylor, the central problem in organizations is the inefficient execution of work, and he believes that, with the right approach, it can be improved. To support his argument, he provides examples of workers who follow traditional rules of thumb and therefore fail to maximize their work potential. Taylor advocates for the study of work processes, emphasizing that every activity involved should be mapped, to identify ways of optimizing the labor process. Even something as simple as loading a truck can be broken down into sub-activities that can be allocated to appropriate workers who have mastered the optimal work method. Through systematic and scientific analysis and experimentation, Taylor believes that work processes and division of labor can be optimized to achieve higher output for lower input. According to Taylor, the philosophy is a win–win situation, with both employees and owners benefiting from scientific management. Taylor summarizes his principles in the following four points:

> First. The development of true science.
> Second. The scientific selection of the workman.
> Third. His scientific education and development.
> Fourth. The intimate friendly cooperation between the management and the men. (p. 68)

First, it is essential to establish a scientific understanding of the work process, followed by the scientific selection—the right person for the right job—of workers who are then scientifically trained, according to Taylor's philosophy. Finally, Taylor emphasizes the importance of cooperation between supervisors and workers. The key concept that underpins this approach is *science*. Although the word is used in slightly different ways, the core is consistent. Science is systematic, rational, and based on empirical observations, experiments, and evidence. Science seeks to identify the underlying laws that govern the efficiency of the work process and the associated division of labor. In practical terms, time studies and the standardization of work tasks are the foundation of this philosophy. Given Taylor's perspective on what "science" is about, a follow-up question is then: Who is the scientist?

Following the examples presented in the book, where Taylor himself is often the protagonist and shares his experiences with "scientific management", the role of the researcher is to measure, clock, and analyze work processes to optimize the distribution of tasks. The researcher is a *consultant* who is tasked with developing and optimizing the work processes in a business, using scientific methods.

Even though the methods might have changed over time, the perspective remains. Management scholars are expected to generate knowledge that promotes improved organizational performance and greater efficiency based on a win–win rationale. Not least, practitioners typically view management from this perspective, which positions the researcher as a person who studies organizations to help make them work better.

The perspective is difficult to oppose. Simply opening a basic book on the subject reveals how research-based knowledge can facilitate the development and enhancement of organizations and management (Bolman & Deal, 2017). However, in addition to this perspective on the researcher as a consultant, I wish to propose an alternative approach, built on other assumptions. Just as Taylor (1911/1998) acted as an improvement consultant who advocated for principles and methods to aid in organizational development, he was also a *writer*, writing texts on management and organization. To introduce this perspective, let us once again examine a few lines from Taylor's introduction:

> This paper has been written:
>
> First. To point out, through a series of simple illustrations, the great loss that the whole country is suffering through inefficiency in almost all of our daily acts.
> Second. To try to convince the reader that the remedy for this inefficiency lies in systematic management, rather than in searching for some unusual or extraordinary man.
> Third. To prove that the best management is a true science, resting upon clearly defined laws, rules, and principles, as a foundation. And further to show that the fundamental principles of scientific management are applicable to all kinds of human activities, from our simplest individual acts to the work of our great corporations, which call for the most elaborate cooperation. And, briefly, through a series of illustrations, to convince the reader that whenever these principles are correctly applied, results must follow which are truly astounding. (p. iv)

The first sentence of the passage underscores its focus. The phrase "This paper has been written" suggests that the text was produced—written—by an individual for a specific purpose. Furthermore, the text is argumentative, employing illustrations to demonstrate inefficiency and support a thesis. The writing aims to persuade the reader that the inefficiency is attributable to deficiencies in systematic management and that a more scientific division of labor and work process is the solution. Later studies of Taylor and his work even go so far as to say he *manipulated* his anecdotes and empirical findings to better fit his argument and authoritative way of making his case in writing (Wrege & Hodgett, 2000).

Moreover, Taylor has dedicated himself to composing a text that advocates for his views and ideas regarding what ought to be done in organizations and why. It is also possible to approach the writing from other perspectives. The methodology itself, for those who practice "scientific management", can be viewed as a form of writing. Time studies and associated analyses are expected to rely on detailed documentation of work processes and the workforce, which requires diligent note taking. This documentation is not self-created but rather requires large amounts of time spent writing notes. Consider Taylor, the factory, and his post-clocking routine of sitting in an office, taking notes, and writing.

Another way to approach Taylor's work as a writer is to consider the language dimension. Prior to Taylor, there was no language that systematized what he referred to as "scientific management" in the way he did, through examples, principles, and a distinct view of science and leadership. By introducing new words, combinations of words, and language, he created a way for others to engage with the subject matter. He effectively established a new management language or, alternatively, contributed to an emerging one.

Taken together, the act of writing, documentation, and language development all highlight different aspects of the researcher as a writer. However, in research contexts, this perspective is seldom acknowledged, and there is little recognition given to the idea that researchers are also writers. This lack of recognition has implications, leading to missed opportunities associated with writing. In the following discussion, I will focus on three specific aspects: methodology, empirical material, and theory formulation, before turning to some of the political implications of management writing.

Writing as Methodology

One of the few chapters that have endured in all the new editions of the methodological landmark, *The Sage Handbook of Qualitative Research*, is authored by Laurel Richardson and Elizabeth Adams St. Pierre (2018). This chapter focuses on writing in relation to research methodology and science. Every time I read this chapter, I am struck by a passage in the introduction where Richardson expresses that many texts in the social sciences are boring. According to her, this is problematic because qualitative research needs to be read to be meaningful. Therefore, it can be said that the purpose of the chapter is to encourage better writing and to increase readership and engagement. In the following discussion, I will mainly refer to the second part of the chapter, which is written by St. Pierre. To begin, I would like to cite a quote that encapsulates the spirit of the section:

> I have called my work in academia "nomadic inquiry", and a great part of that inquiry is accomplished in the writing because, for me, writing *is* thinking, writing *is* analysis, and writing *is* indeed a seductive and tangled *method* of discovery. (2018, p. 827; italics original)

The key message conveyed in the quote is that writing assumes a critical and intricate role in the research process. According to the authors, it is not preferable, or sufficient, to perceive writing as a mundane activity separate from the broader research endeavor (see also Cloutier, 2016). On the contrary, writing gives life to thoughts, facilitates analysis, and serves as a means of making new discoveries. One aspect of this is the recognition that certain empirical data do not truly exist until they are transcribed onto paper. The act of writing has the power to manifest data that may otherwise remain elusive or take different forms. Most empirical data only assume shape and potential scientific significance when they are documented in writing, on paper or electronically. Ideas that exist solely within an individual's mind or among multiple individuals cannot be effectively studied or examined.

Another crucial aspect to consider is that writing plays a pivotal role in the testing of ideas. Assessing the value of an idea or exploring its potential intersections with other ideas becomes challenging if it remains confined within one's thoughts. To determine the worth of an idea, it must be transcribed onto paper and subjected to potential modifications and refinements over successive stages until it reaches its final form. Additionally, writing can lead researchers toward previously unseen avenues. It unveils new pathways that can be either pursued or discarded. Once again, writing assumes the form of a methodological tool that exerts influence on research, ultimately facilitating the discovery of new insights. This perspective is also evident in Taylor's work and the development of his principles of "scientific management", as he devoted himself to his desk, diligently typing, employing writing as a method to shape and refine his ideas.

The ideas of Richardson and St. Pierre can easily be associated with a well-established, yet often neglected, scholarly form: the essay. The essay enjoys a rich history and is often linked to esteemed figures such as Michel de Montaigne and Virginia Woolf. Nowadays, it has also found its place in the management literature (Brewis & Bell, 2020; Gabriel, 2016). Essays can be regarded as critical and reflective attempts to explore phenomena or ideas, by allowing the writing itself to guide the inquiry. Within the scientific context, this approach can be seen as somewhat rebellious. Neither the personal tone nor the tentative nature of essays aligns with the conventional self-perception of science. Perhaps this discrepancy arises from the notion that writing occupies a significant role, and that the act of writing itself can be considered the essay's methodology. Unlike deductive empirical studies, which verify or falsify their findings, essays do not seek to prove, but rather to demonstrate through their words and sentences. Often, they lack definitive conclusions or explicit messages for the reader. Here is an extract from an essay about (why we need) essays by Yiannis Gabriel (2016), to illustrate the personal tone and thought-provoking way of reasoning.

> Each essay represents not only an intellectual exploration into some aspect of the world, but also an exploration into the mind of its author, indeed not only the conscious mind, but the unconscious mind too. The connections, the illustrations, the metaphors and analogies, the wit, the discontinuities, the very words deployed by an essayist, the idiosyncrasies of style and expression, are not incidental but core features of the text. In this regard, an essay is as much a work of art, as a scientific text. At its best, the essay is an object of beauty, affording readers a degree of aesthetic pleasure in the text itself, while provoking them to look at the world with fresh eyes.
>
> Given its experimental nature, the essay offers no guaranteed road to success—if anything, failure may be its more common destination, though failure itself can be the mother of subsequent experiments and essays. Nor do successful essays necessarily deliver what is now comfortably described as a 'contribution'. Indeed some of the most successful essays, including some of those listed above, do not reach any firm conclusions. What successful essays always do, however, is enable us to consider possibilities of thought and of action that seemed inconceivable before. (p. 246)

A slightly different approach to writing and methodology is found in an article by Ericsson and Kostera (2020) where they introduce something called *alterethnography*. The fusion of the word "alterity" (otherness) with ethnography highlights that the representation of empirical material (dealing with the other, "Others", otherness) is fundamentally a matter of methodology. In their words "[w]riting is not a consequence or a follow-up, but is part of ethnographic work" (p. 1405). In other words, *how* you write and relate to empirical material, for example, ethically, is from their point of view very much an issue of methodology. Rephrased as a straightforward question, their primary idea can be condensed as follows: How do you aim to represent the persons and situations that constitute your empirical material in an ethically just way? If questions of writing and relating to "others" are not considered, management research risks reinforcing the ideological elements of business and management. Consequently, writing is also a methodological concern.

Overall, this section assigns writing a place within the domain commonly referred to as "method". Typically, writing is not accorded such a place. In methodological contexts, writing is frequently overlooked, despite being an indispensable and foundational component of all scientific endeavors—from data collection or construction to idea generation and testing. Regardless of how we approach writing, it is undeniable that it constitutes a vital part of scientific knowledge creation.

Writing Empirical Material

Most research relies on empirical studies and empirical material. This places the presentation of empirical material in an important light. Despite this requirement, researchers rarely engage in serious discussions about the form and style in which empirical material should be reported. One scholar who has delved into this topic is John van Maanen (2011) in his book *Tales of the Field*. Although his focus is on ethnographies and ethnographers, I believe his ideas are valid beyond that domain. The premise of the book is that the description of empirical material can—and perhaps should—incorporate a stance regarding how it should be presented. Van Maanen proposes three distinct styles from which researchers can choose and draw inspiration: realist, confessional, or impressionistic.

The most prevalent style is the realistic one, characterized by the absence of the author's presence, thereby creating an impression of "neutrality" in the text. The emphasis lies on the material itself rather than the writer, resulting in descriptions that are perceived as objective and documentary in tone. The presentation often has a sense of systematicity, with details and nuances following a coherent logic. It should, however, be noted that the researcher holds the responsibility for what is presented and how it is interpreted in a realistic description.

The second style is confessional. Here the researcher's personal experiences and reflections are given more prominence. It provides space for the exploration of how and why certain outcomes were obtained. In this sense, the confessional style can complement the realistic style as an addition. The distinctive feature of this style is that it acknowledges that science does not speak independently but through the researcher and author. Things are not simply what they are, and this recognition is affirmed within the confessional style.

The third style draws inspiration from impressionist painters such as Monet, Renoir, and van Gogh. They aimed to capture the appearance of objects under specific lighting conditions and unique circumstances. Similarly, in this style, the researcher takes center stage, and the essence lies in conveying the researcher's viewpoint from their distinct vantage point. The goal is to write in a way that enables the reader to see what the researcher saw. Tools employed can include metaphors, poetic expressions, and figurative language. Self-awareness and innovation are key aspects of this style.

In what follows, I provide three (very) shortened examples from the book by van Maanen to illustrate the different approaches to styles of writing and presenting empirical material. The purpose is to provide a quick look into the traditions with an emphasis on the different styles. For more extensive, in-depth examples, together with descriptions and arguments, I urge the reader to go to the source. It is well worth reading.

Realist:

> Among first-level supervisors in American police agencies are patrol sergeants. These men (and they are overwhelmingly men) differentiate their position from those of patrolmen on the assumptive grounds that they are "responsible for the activities of patrolmen" whereas patrolmen are responsible for the activities taking place on their beats". This seemingly clear-cut contrast is pregnant with operational difficulty, for it is apparent to anyone spending more than a trivial amount of time within large police departments that "being responsible for the men" can be demonstrated in a variety of ways, under a bewildering set of circumstances. (p. 58)

Confessional:

> In my study, I entered the police academy as a self-acknowledged researcher who, I wanted made known, would stay with the class through graduation and spend some time working with the recruits after they had left the academy. During training, I consciously avoided establishing obvious links with the academy staff. When asked, I turned down offers to sit with staff members at lunch, visit their offices

> on breaks, or go drinking with them after work. I felt this appropriate since a very strict formality normally obtains between recruits and staff members. (pp. 86-87)

Impressionistic:

> The chase is real police work. The chase is action. It's the symbolic enactment of your basic war-on-crime mythology involving search, pursuit, capture; the holy trinity for cops. In contrast to the mundane reality of aimless patrol duties and endless public order work, the chase is excitement extraordinaire and something of an acid test of one's courage and commitment.
> David motions for me to buckle up and heads the cruiser toward Interstate 13, where he thinks our culprit will head trying to get out of town. We make the interstate and are soon hitting speeds close to a hundred with lights flashing and siren ringing. (p. 110)

To do justice to van Maanen's proposal, it should be acknowledged that the three main styles are not the sole possibilities. He emphasizes that there are various other ways (or styles) of writing distinguished by different characteristics. For our purposes, however, the fundamental point itself is of interest. Empirical work can be written in different ways and from different perspectives, depending on the author, audience, and context (see Ericsson, 2020). Regardless of whether the researcher takes a deliberate stance on style or not, the activity is inevitably entwined with various authorial challenges and perspectives. Writing empirical work "scientifically" in a definitive manner is impossible; there is no single scientific way. Furthermore, there is no reason to restrict the application of styles solely to empirical narratives and discussions. Entire research papers and reports can be formulated in different styles with distinct underlying features, emphasizing different aspects.

In contrast to Richardson and St. Pierre (2018), whose texts could arguably be classified as a mix of confessional and impressionistic, Taylor's texts lean toward the realistic style, occasionally incorporating confessional elements. It can also be argued that Taylor could be classified within van Maanen's framework of "advocacy tales" (van Maanen, 2011, p. 170), as his text is strongly normative. Nevertheless, in my opinion, what they have in common is that they accurately adapt their writing style to the content and intended recipients. If Taylor had written more poetically, or if he had presented his case descriptions as unique, his writing would not have expressed the universality he aimed for. The text would also not have signaled the kind of "scientism" that his readers anticipated at the time. If Taylor had employed a different style, it would, in some senses, not have been the same scientific work.

Turning to the writing of the present text, I have had some inspiration from the impressionistic style, together with some explicit confessional remarks (like this one), as well as some normative elements. But above all, I have tried to write in a clear, albeit somewhat essayistic, style employing an informative structure, a conventional introduction, and well-defined headings. While certain academic writers inspired by the essay form tend to write dense and ambiguous prose (see Weick, 1995), the overarching principle guiding this text has been clarity. I want the perspective presented—*Homo scribens*—to be clear, easily understood, and free from tendentious jargon (cf. Grey & Sinclair, 2006). So, in that sense, I follow the classic scientific norms of logic and rationality, but through a more personalized tone.

Writing Theory

While the overarching goal of science, arguably, is the development of theories, the exact definition of what constitutes a theory is not straightforward. Furthermore, researchers often have diverse understandings of the nature of theory (Corvellec, 2013). I perceive theory, in simplified terms, as a collection of interrelated statements and (defined) concepts that seek to comprehend or explain a specific phenomenon. A theory typically serves as both the foundation and the outcome of a study. Therefore, the term "theoretical contribution" signifies what is added or refined within the original collection. Because of the principal role of theory in science, one might assume that it would be presented in clear and standardized ways. However, this is not the case. For instance, consider agency theory, one of the prominent theories in business administration and economics, which is presented in various articles by different researchers, each with slightly different structures and ways of reasoning (see Jensen & Meckling, 1976; Fama & Jensen, 1983, and how the use of arguments, as well as mathematics, varies).

One way to approach theory is through Barbara Czarniawska's (1999, 2014) notion of theories as *narratives* that unfold through various actions and eventually come together to create a meaningful and coherent narrative for the reader. While it is challenging to provide a concise summary of Czarniawska's position or theory, her starting point and essential elements are effectively captured in a quote where she draws upon Marie-Laure Ryan's categorization and "guide" to those seeking to write a scientific and theoretical story.

- Constructing *characters* (which, in social science texts, often begin as nonhuman actants: a newspaper article, new unemployment statistics, a new computer technology);
- Attributing *functions* to single events and actions (a crisis in the newspaper industry led to a search for spectacular scoops, which resulted in dramatizing the mistakes of the city council, and so on); and
- Finding an *interpretative theme* (global financial crisis? loss of trust in elective democracy?). (Ryan in Czarniawska, 2014, p. 127)

Put more concisely, it is a question of creating characters, places, and events as well as themes that are suitable for, or are the outcome of, a scientific study. The next step is to—with the help of the overall plot—weave the parts together into a meaningful story that works, and that the reader can follow along with and understand the meaning of. Science and scientific theories then take the form of classic storytelling which, of course, must be written to come into being. A similar view, although portrayed in a more minimalistic form, is presented by Richard L. Daft (1983):

> Research is storytelling. The scientific method is more like guess work, the making up and revising of stories. Storytelling means explaining what the data mean, using data to describe how organizations work. Stories are theories. Theory need not be formal or complex. Theories simply explain why. (p. 541)

Another way of understanding theory is through van Maanen (1995) and his idea that style and theory are connected. Perhaps one could summarize his idea as meaning that the way scientists write, reason, and argue—their style—constitutes the theory itself. From this angle, the theory is impossible to detach from the act of writing and the way the researcher expresses himself. As an example, van Maanen (1995) highlights the renowned organizational theorist Karl Weick and his distinctive essay style, characterized by its peculiarity, dialectical nature, and occasional cryptic elements. Regarding Weick's writing style, van Maanen (1995) asserts the following:

> The work reads as something of a personal reflection, a meditation on a theme, and is put forth in terse, highly qualified and personal prose. Moreover, the matters that occupy Weick's interest in the paper are not presented as things to which one must agree or disagree but as ideas tossed out to complicate our thinking about current problems in organizational theory (and elsewhere). (p. 136)

Weick's theorizing exhibits a distinct and unconventional character, deviating from conventional norms. Through the introduction of the concept of style in theoretical contexts, van Maanen ascribes a sense of uniqueness and inimitability to theories and the process of theorizing itself. This perspective emphasizes the significant role of researchers and their writing abilities in the research process. Both Czarniawska and van Maanen emphasize the inherently rhetorical nature of theories and theory development, challenging the common perception that they are distinct from writing. By recognizing the rhetorical aspect of theory, these scholars shed light on the interplay between writing and scientific knowledge.

Returning to Taylor and his presentation of "scientific management", his style is authoritative, persuasive, and relies on one-sided—even erroneous (Wrege & Hodgett, 2000)—empirical examples that support his fundamental thesis. It lacks self-criticism, self-reflection, dialectical elements, and exploratory aspects. The theory is formulated in line with the confidently argumentative style in which Taylor writes.

Politics of Writing

The norms and constraints of conventional academic writing should not be seen as neutral and apolitical. Martin Parker (2014) has reflected upon this:

> As any sociologist of knowledge will tell you, we can't collectively step outside the power of institutions to some place in which we are free to write whatever the fuck we want, whenever the fuck we want, and publish it on dried leaves which we will throw to the wind. However, understanding the spider's web of gentle constraints might help us think harder about writing itself, and make it visible in ways that it very often isn't. (p. 222)

The "power" under scrutiny by Parker is the current academic system of journals and rankings. To be an academic, the tacit rules of the system need to be obeyed. Research cannot be published on "dried leaves" and be distributed by the wind; there is an entire institutional machinery that provides science with its present setup. The papers and writing promoted by journals, their editors, and reviewers set the standard to which researchers must conform. According to Parker, the academic institutional world is dominated by white male professors from North America and northern Europe, with English as their first language.

> By definition, these are people who have done rather well from the publishing and ranking system and are unlikely to feel highly motivated to deny its effectiveness at encouraging the best to rise the top. Those who occupy high-status positions are also often those who claim to believe in the meritocratic nature of existing hierarchies. We could describe these people as those who define the centre of the discipline, in the sense that they work in the most prestigious universities, sit on the boards of journals, occupy positions in professional associations, examine PhDs, sit on promotions committees and so on. (2014, pp. 214–215)

The subordination to the system results in our "normal science" with its distinctively neutral—"author-free"—scientific style and form, in English (see also Boussebaa & Tienari, 2021, and the Englishization of academia). Paradoxically enough, Parker notes that this style is often difficult to read, with its over-use of "sophisticated" and theoretically informed words and concepts, long sentences, and long lists of references. Parker efficiently points to all of this, and its exclusionary effects on people outside—and often even inside—the academic community and makes a case for a more responsible and passionate academic writing. However, as indicated above, writing is not just a matter of esthetics but of *politics*. Writing good, clever, original papers does not guarantee getting published. To be accepted, a text must adhere to strict writing and style expectations.

An additional aspect of the political dimension is what the writing that is allowed and considered right is expressing. A strong case has been made for this point in and through the feminist tradition, where taken-for-granted scientific ideals such as rigor, rationality, and objectivity have been discussed through socio-political aspects highlighting the relationship between what we perceive as good, true science and masculinity (Phillips et al., 2014; Rhodes & Pullen, 2009). Traditional "scientific" texts often assert themselves with a confident, authoritative voice, prescribing what is, and what is true. They typically exclude elements of doubt, nuances, emotions, and other indications of ambivalence. From this standpoint, a considerable portion of management research can be viewed as contributing to a masculine and patriarchal discourse, embodied and reinforced by the conventional scientific format.

In the feminist tradition, there is a great deal of management research that has tried to encapsulate the critique and move beyond it by encouraging other forms of writing, not least in the "writing differently" direction (Gilmore et al., 2019). A challenge is how to work without running the risk of reproducing the binaries and dichotomic thinking present in gender categories. Muhr and Rehn (2015) suggest an interesting way to think about this. Drawing inspiration from Donna Haraway, they introduce the concept of *cyborg writing*, delving into the politics of the technologies employed in the writing process. The key notion is that writing is never accomplished "purely" by an individual researcher but is always mediated through the use of various technologies. Unlike the historical image of dipping pens in ink and making finely calibrated motions on paper, contemporary scientific writing involves the use of machines. Muhr and Rehn term this phenomenon cyborg writing, emphasizing the inseparability of technology from the practice and process of scientific writing. While the term "cyborg" may initially evoke a sci-fi connotation, it becomes more comprehensible when likened to a person coexisting with a pacemaker.

Muhr and Rehn (2015) initiate their discussion by examining the impact of the typewriter, highlighting its revolutionary role in transforming the production of texts (here, I look away from the gender dimension of the technologies, and focus exclusively on cyborg writing). The typewriter facilitated widespread and rapid writing and rewriting. Fast-forwarding through a century of technological evolution and examining contemporary management writing, it becomes crucial to acknowledge the role of technologies such as the computer (equipped with highly efficient word processing programs), web browsers and search engines (like Safari and Google), helpful websites (such as Wikipedia), digital publishing systems, and artificial intelligence (AI). Reflecting on the process of crafting this text, essential technologies include my computer, with Microsoft Word for editing, email for file exchange and communication with editors, Google Scholar for academic literature searches, and ChatGPT for assistance with English grammar. Without these tools, the nature of this text would be fundamentally different, even though "I" would have been "the same". In this sense, *Homo scribens* is (always) engaged in "cyborg writing", as texts emerge as products of individuals "merged" with machines.

Additionally, one can explore the connection between technology and material spaces, considering how the advent of laptops has revolutionized the locations *where* scientific writing occurs and what effects that has had on writing. The academic shift toward open office spaces and the diminishing prevalence of physical texts in favor of digital formats present other material factors. Campus and university ownership is another consideration, influencing office designs, the overall university environment, maintenance, and more. Technology and physical spaces are undeniably intertwined, forming the foundational material conditions for writing management.

In summary, this section has brought to light various political implications and underpinnings of writing in management. These can be categorized into three subtopics: (1) the institutional setting of writing and publishing, (2) the discourse of scientific writing, and (3) the technologies of writing. Collectively, this emphasizes the socio-political aspects of what is written and distributed, illustrating how all written text is part of discourses and products of the prevailing technologies of the time. This observation is true for classic works like Taylor's *Principles of Scientific Management* as well as for the current text.

Homo Scribens

In this chapter, I have aimed to discuss and challenge a conventional assumption behind how we understand the management researcher and the research process. Instead of framing the scholar as a development consultant who comes up with ideas for improving organizations, I have emphasized the role of writing and established a perspective of the researcher as a writer. I did this by pointing out that science is text, and that writing, therefore, is an indispensable part of the research process. Furthermore, I highlighted that various forms of documentation are integral to almost all research endeavors. Additionally, writing can also be seen as part of the process and effort to develop concepts and language that enable us to perceive and understand new and differently.

I deepened the perspective by discussing three different aspects of the research process: methodology, empirical material, and theory. Regarding the method, I emphasized that writing can be seen as part of testing ideas: before ideas are set down in writing, it is difficult to know whether they will hold, or even what they will look like. A second point is that the act of writing itself—the time spent with paper and pen, the typing on the typewriter or keyboard—gives birth to ideas that otherwise would not have existed. Again, writing acquires a kind of methodological status.

The second aspect made the case that empirical material can (must) be written in a particular style. The conventional scientific style is just one style among many—and one that meets certain expectations and suits some recipients. However, there are also other more reflective, personal, and poetic styles through which science can be expressed. The main point was that the writing style should be adapted to ambition, tradition, and audience.

The next aspect focused on theory. Scholars seem to understand theory in slightly different ways, and I introduced two different approaches that merit writing in different manners. The first approach was that writing can be seen as a form of storytelling, where characters, places, and themes are woven together in a plot. The second approach claimed that theory is part of the style, and that, for instance, essay writing offers an alternative to the conventional, more monotonous, and assertive scientific style when presenting "theory". Following this, I also reflected upon some of the political implications of writing management by discussing the current institutional settings for publishing, as well as the discourse of conventional scientific forms together with how technology is always present and part of writing.

Whether we approach writing from the perspective as a whole—the researcher as a writer—or from some of the aspects (method, empirics, theory, politics), writing emerges as the perhaps most fundamental research activity. Without writing, there is no research, and we can see the researcher as a writing person—a *Homo scribens*. Despite this, other perspectives and understandings of science tend to overshadow the multiple aspects and implications of "writing". For example, conventional science often appears devoid of style. Another deeply rooted idea would be to consider "writing" as a detachable part of the research process that is performed after a study has taken place, the so-called "writing up". I hope that this chapter can help challenge these and other understandings and thereby allow writing to occupy a larger space in discussions about science and knowledge. I find this especially important, since the social sciences are experiencing something of a supply crisis, with influential researchers even speaking of much research as meaningless (Alvesson et al., 2017).

One way to make science more meaningful and widely read may be to acknowledge that there are different styles and approaches suited for different studies and purposes. Which style or approach is appropriate is very much a situational and individual issue. Taylor would probably not be comfortable writing an impressionistic ethnography on worker experiences in factories. Given that management research and studies can be written in a myriad of ways, the point made is that the writer needs to get to know oneself, to get a sense of what kind of texts to produce (write). Based on the assumption of *Homo scribens*, researchers could ask themselves the following two questions: "What kind of writer am I?" and "What kind of writer do I aim to be?".

By placing writing at the heart of the research activity, I believe that potential readers also are given a greater place and influence in research endeavors. Today some texts seem to be written just to be written. It is unfortunate if we forget that science is ultimately written to be read. From a practice (as in a working manager) point of view, the conventional form (prose and style) is not very welcoming, and sometimes even inappropriate. It does not invite the non-academic reader in a friendly and engaging way. Taking seriously the assumption of *Homo scribens* opens the door to other, new possibilities, more tailored to the reader. One potential outcome could be to try other forms of writing or to try writing for other forums and audiences.

A complementary—but a bit more extreme—voice on the topic is found in Badley (2019) and his idea of *post-academic* writing. In its broadest sense, it is a case for realizing who we as academics are, and why we have social science in the first place, namely, to create and share knowledge (see also Badley, 2020). In the current academic world, with its dense, abstract, and sometimes even unreadable prose, that is often lost. Badley therefore urges us to write post-academically: "[s]imply put, post-academic writing is human writing for human readers. And that means human writing for the enhancement of human life" (2019, p. 180). However pretentious that may sound, sometimes it's good to remind oneself of the big picture; otherwise, it's easy to get trapped in the routines of everyday academic thinking and writing.

The two main perspectives elaborated in this chapter—the researcher as a consultant and as a writer, respectively—are built on fundamentally different assumptions about who the researcher is and what the researcher does. Additionally, the consultant- and development-oriented perspective tends to be how we conventionally picture the management scholar. To conclude, I believe that a shift in perspective, where writing is given a greater place and recognized with higher status, can contribute to a more challenging, stimulating, and sophisticated social science well worth reading. I also think that would be a place where *Homo scribens* would feel more at home.

References

Alvesson, M., Gabriel, Y., & Paulsen, R. (2017). *Return to meaning: A social science with something to say*. Oxford University Press. https://doi.org/10.1093/oso/9780198787099.001.0001

Bolman, L. G., & Deal, T. E. (2017). *Reframing organizations: Artistry, choice, and leadership*. John Wiley & Sons. https://doi.org/10.1002/9781119281856

Boncori, I. (2022). *Researching and writing differently*. Bristol University Press.

Boussebaa, M., & Tienari, J. (2021). Englishization and the politics of knowledge production in management studies. *Journal of Management Inquiry, 30*(1), 59–67. https://doi.org/10.1177/1056492619835314

Badley, G. F. (2019). Post-academic writing: Human writing for human readers. *Qualitative Inquiry, 25*(2), 180–191. https://doi.org/10.1177/1077800417736334

Badley, G. F. (2020). Why and how academics write. *Qualitative Inquiry, 26*(3–4), 247–256. https://doi.org/10.1177/1077800418810722

Brewis, D. N., & Bell, E. (2020). Provocation essays editorial: On the importance of moving and being moved. *Management Learning, 51*(5), 533–536. https://doi.org/10.1177/1350507620957111

Clifford, J., & Marcus, G. E. (Eds.). (1986). *Writing culture: The poetics and politics of ethnography*. University of California Press.

Cloutier, C. (2016). How I write: An inquiry into the writing practices of academics. *Journal of Management Inquiry, 25*(1), 69–84. https://doi.org/10.1177/1056492615585875

Corvellec, H. (2013) *What is theory? Answers from the social and cultural sciences*. Liber.

Czarniawska, B. (1999). *Writing management: Organization theory as a literary genre*. Oxford University Press on Demand.

Czarniawska, B. (2014). *Social science research: From field to desk*. Sage. https://doi.org/10.4135/9781529799613

Daft, R. L. (1983). Learning the craft of organizational research. *Academy of Management Review, 8*(4), 539–546. https://doi.org/10.2307/258255

Ericsson, D. (2020). Exercises in sensemaking: 3,628,800 ways of writing organization and management. In M. Kostera & C. Wozniak (Eds.), *Aesthetics, organization, and humanistic management* (pp. 190–202). Palgrave Macmillan. https://doi.org/10.4324/9781003091530-13

Ericsson, D., & Kostera, M. (2020). Alterethnography: Reading and writing otherness in organizations. *Gender, Work & Organization, 27*(6), 1402–1417. https://doi.org/10.1111/gwao.12503

Fama, E. F., & Jensen, M. C. (1983). Agency problems and residual claims. *The Journal of Law and Economics, 26*(2), 327–349.

Gabriel, Y. (2016). The essay as an endangered species: Should we care. *Journal of Management Studies, 53*(2), 244–249. https://doi.org/10.1111/joms.12176

Gilmore, S., Harding, N., Helin, J., & Pullen, A. (2019). Writing differently. *Management Learning, 50*(1), 3–10. https://doi.org/10.1177/1350507618811027

Grey, C., & Sinclair, A. (2006). Writing differently. *Organization, 13*(3), 443–453. https://doi.org/10.1177/1350508406063492

Jensen, M. C., & Meckling, W. H. (1976). Theory of the firm: Managerial behavior, agency costs and ownership structure. *Journal of Financial Economics, 3*(4), 305–360.

Kostera, M. (Ed.). (2022). *How to write differently: A quest for meaningful academic writing*. Edward Elgar.

Muhr, S. L., & Rehn, A. (2015). On gendered technologies and cyborg writing. *Gender, Work & Organization, 22*(2), 129–138. https://doi.org/10.1111/gwao.12057

Parker, M. (2014). Writing: What can be said, by who, and where? In E. Jeanes & T. Huzzard (Eds.), *Critical management research: Reflections from the field* (pp. 211–226). Sage. https://doi.org/10.4135/9781446288610

Phillips, M., Pullen, A., & Rhodes, C. (2014). Writing organization as gendered practice: Interrupting the libidinal economy. *Organization Studies, 35*(3), 313–333. https://doi.org/10.1177/0170840613483656

Rhodes, C. (2001). *Writing organization: (Re)presentation and control in narratives at work.* John Benjamins.

Rhodes, C., & Pullen, A. (2009). Narrative and stories in organizational research: An exploration of gendered politics in research methodology. In D. A. Bryman & D. Buchanan (Eds.), *The Sage handbook of Organizational research methods* (pp. 583–601). Sage.

Richardson, L., & St Pierre, E. (2018). A method of inquiry. In N. K. Denzin & Y. S. Lincoln (Eds.), *Sage handbook of qualitative research* (pp. 818–838). Sage.
Taylor, F. W. (1911/1998). *The principles of scientific management*. Routledge.
Van Maanen, J. (1995). Crossroads style as theory. *Organization Science, 6*(1), 133–143.
Van Maanen, J. (2011). *Tales of the field: On writing ethnography*. University of Chicago Press.
Weick, K. E. (1995). *Sensemaking in organizations*. Sage.
Wrege, C. D., & Hodgetts, R. M. (2000). Frederick W. Taylor's 1899 pig iron observations: Examining fact, fiction, and lessons for the new millennium. *Academy of Management Journal*, *43*(6), 1283–1291. https://doi.org/10.5465/1556350

6

Living as an *Academic-Cum-Something-Else*: How I Learned to Stop Worrying and Love Academia

Carmelo Mazza

O homem que diz "sou" não é porque quem é mesmo é "não sou"
(The one who says "I am" Is not because who really is Says "I am not").
(Vinicius de Moraes *Canto de Ossanha* 1966)

Introduction

I have read several research works unfolding almost each nuance the word *Homo* may contain. I started from the rational and efficient *Homo oeconomicus* described in the works of classical economic theory at the end of the eighteenth century. Then I learned of, among others: *Homo faber* (Arendt, 1958), *Homo typographicus* (McLuhan, 1962), *Homo sacer* (Agamben, 2018), *Homo consumens* (Bauman, 2021), *Homo*

C. Mazza (✉)
INSEAD—Corporate Governance Center, Fontainebleau, France
e-mail: mazza.carmelo@gmail.com

S. Cinque and D. Ericsson (eds.), *Debating 'Homo Academicus' in Management and Organization*, Palgrave Debates in Business and Management,
https://doi.org/10.1007/978-3-031-58195-3_6

entrepreneurus (Lounsbury et al., 2019), *Homo creativus* (Kakko & Inkinen, 2009). I distinguish two different approaches in these research works. First, the attempt to philosophically qualify and describe what *Homo* is. It is the case of *Homo faber*, *Homo sacer, and Homo typographicus.* In the other cases listed above, the researchers tried to identify ideal types of behaviors and attitudes characterizing what each kind of *Homo* ought to think, value, and act. Within this last large array of sociological and philosophical research, Bourdieu's (1984) *Homo academicus* raised my interested attention.

I say "interested attention" because when I read Bourdieu's book, I was wondering which was my place within academia. I had a lively international experience in business education after my PhD and, at the same time, a stimulating contamination with consulting and managerial engagements. Therefore, was I trying to become another stressed full-time academic struggling with an increasingly oppressive competitive environment where my ideals about academia were sacrificed on the altar of managerialization, individual advancement, and university ranking? Or was I looking for a way-out where my position across different fields could reveal a multiplicity of belongings behind the multiple positions I held? I saw the stress of my colleagues coping with new challenges that had nothing to do with the authentic academic behaviors and attitudes. On the other side, I wonder whether a multiplicity of belongings crossing academia, consulting and management, was a viable solution for this stress or just a *limbo* excluding me from each of the belongings.

In this chapter, I will try to deal with these questions building on my peculiar experiential perspective: that of the one who spent most of his professional career as an "academic-cum-something else". From "academic-cum-consultant" described in Czarniawska and Mazza (2003), to "academic-cum-manager" due to the position I have been holding from the last eight years, until the current "early scholar again" status I had the privilege to acquire by approaching again conferences and workshops, like during my PhD time, with early drafts looking for constructive feedbacks from well-recognized professors, many of them almost twenty-five years younger than me.

So, in this paper, I chose to write about my personal experience. The roots of this choice laid back to the work of Barbara Czarniawska

(1999) on organization theory as a literary genre. The reflections and theorizations of experience as *Homo academicus* followed a wide range of literary genres so far, from pamphlet (Parker, 2018) to fairy tale (Mazza & Quattrone, 2017). In this case, I adopted a more autobiographic style, reporting self-reflexive, *post-hoc* rationalizations of events. The autobiographic genre allowed me to report my observations about *Homo academicus* at the same time as an insider, sharing the "ought to", and as an outsider, critically assess constraints and habits. Therefore, the experience I described in this chapter is ambivalent. On one side, it includes the reflections on the academic life by somebody who was on the edge of being what a full-time *Homo academicus* ought to be. On the other side, it includes the critical observations on *Homo academicus* by somebody who has been living for thirty years in the limbo of *academic-cum-something else*. The ambivalence may help shedding light on controversial aspects of what the life of a *Homo academicus* meant to be over the last three decades and on the extent to which roles and trajectories in different fields could coincide in a single life. In other words, this ambivalence leads to a paradox: by staying in the *limbo,* I can feel the enchantment of the *illusio* of different fields but, reflexively, I could doubt of the real value of the stakes of their memberships (Bourdieu, 2000), thus experiencing disenchantment.

This chapter is divided into three parts. First, I outline what the *Homo academicus* ought to be from the perspective of my personal experience. Then, I described the *limbo* where I found myself by sharing my academic status with consultancy and management. Finally, I discuss how the *Homo academicus* may benefit from staying in the *limbo* and if and how a new academia may emerge from the liminality of the academic profession nowadays.

The *Homo Academicus* I Dreamt About

Today, managerialization strongly affects the academic field. I see at least three factors supporting this assumption: bureaucracy, quantitative measurement, and precarity. Already in 2010 in an article on The Guardian, Tahir (2010) reported the academic concern on the sharp rise in bureaucracy in university education and a 33% growth in the number of academic managers in UK from 2005 to 2010. Then, the research assessment frameworks in most EU countries juxtapose the academic activity—just by naming it "production" this reveals a very clear semantic choice about roles and tasks within academia—with measurable impacts of economic return, even more after COVID-19 (Fleming, 2023). Finally, an army of precarious teachers populates university, and criteria for selection and access have become highly hierarchical and bureaucratized (De Boer et al., 2007).

This trend of managerialization has been shaping academia for the last twenty years now. At the same time, an increasing number of scholars begins to feel the urge of having a public say on current big challenges and tragic events (Delmestri, 2023; Gümüşay, 2023). If Richard Winter (2009) described a schism between academic managers and managed academia, the very same year New York Times published an article claiming the end of university as we know it (Taylor, 2009). Within academia, many questions its future and no recipes seem to gain a wide consensus among academics and stakeholders (Izak et al., 2017).

However, this was not the academic field that drove my aspiration in 1992, when I decided to start a PhD program aiming at an academic career. I was eager to know the rules and excited to "be taken in and by the game" (Bourdieu & Wacquant, 1992, p. 116) of academia. I was ready to enthusiastically have in common with the other young colleagues the *illusio* (Bourdieu, 1984) of academia, the "fundamental belief in the interest of the game and the value of the stakes which is inherent in … membership" (Bourdieu, 2000, p. 11), convinced that the benefits of participating in the academic field were well worth all the needed efforts. I knew that, in Bourdieu's (2000, p. 51) words, *illusio* was an illusion for those outside the field. Therefore, I did not expect to have this *illusio* in common with other people outside the academic field; for those outside there was no *illusio* in dealing with the rules of academia and being part of academic games like, for instance, *publishing or perishing*.

The academic field was not homogeneous throughout the world and not even throughout Europe. At the time of my PhD, I perceived that while I share the *illusio* with those participating in the academic field, my individual *investment* was oriented toward the process of internationalization of business education taking place across Europe following to significant funding efforts by EU to promote the so-called *Bologna process*. The internationalized academic context was deeply different from the local academic contexts and, to a certain extent, even in competition with them. Following to Bourdieu's interpretation of Loic Wacquant (Bourdieu & Wacquant, 1992), I can hold that my *investment* referred to the *Homo academicus internationalus*, who differed from the *Homo academicus gallicus* described for the French academic context by Bourdieu (1984). *Homo academicus internationalus* I experienced was the *avant-garde* of the development of a European research area on management, identified in an EU-funded project—Creation of a European Management Practice (CEMP)—involving academic institutions from several EU countries such as Spain, UK, Sweden, France, Norway, Denmark, Italy, Germany and the Netherlands (D.G. Innovation and Research and European Commission, 2005).

However, as it is widespread for *Homo academicus italicus* (Giannini, 2013), my participation in the academic games did not prevent me from exploring consulting and management, always by keeping my academic reputation. This gave me two opportunities: first, to play the academic game without being a full-time *Homo academicus* and, second, to *invest* in the stake of membership of different fields with distinct people. The possibility to participate in different fields personally investing in each of them with those inhabiting each field proved very effective in professional terms and my overall reputation benefited of this duality. In terms of role, I was the "professor" among managers and consultants, and the "manager" among teachers, researchers, and even students. This condition was well described in Czarniawska and Mazza (2003) outlining the key issues of being an *academic-cum-consultant*. To move across the academic and the consulting fields allowed obtaining a kind of special status especially for Public Administration clients where my exposure as *Homo academicus* received a high recognition.

Despite the success, in brackets, in the consulting field, it was increasingly difficult for me to keep the needed investment to be *academic-cum-consultant*. My personal investment in academia decreased and my enthusiasm about academia decreased as well. The same happened when I experienced an *academic-cum-manager* position.[1] In this case, the duality was even more complicated. The workaholic managerial rhetoric does not allow investing in other fields. Managerial positions are to absorb 100% of personal time and effort and even more. It looks against the management game to show that time can be also devoted to preparing classes, read articles and book, and write papers for conference presentations. I felt management is not compatible with investment in the academia, it does not accept to share resources with any other personal ambition. Therefore, the *academic-cum-manager* remained on the paper, and I was not able to practice actively the *Homo academicus* life until I found a way to narrow down managerial responsibility. Membership in academia could coexist with membership of the consulting field but not with membership of the managerial field.

In all the years of *academic-cum-something else*, I have been able to write and publish as well as giving classes from time to time. This shows that on one side it was possible to be part of multiple positions and *illusio* in academic life. On the other side, nevertheless, I felt my *investment* in academia was not enough because of missing the full dedication to the field: with the words of the leading music composer John Zorn (2014), I have not fully "paid my dues" with academia. Paraphrasing his argument for artists, I cannot just get up and say I am a *Homo academicus*: I have to earn the right to say "I am a *Homo academicus*", not only in terms of curriculum vitae or a number of publications. Well, I have not done that. In Bourdieu's terms, the unpaid dues correspond to the missing adoption of the full *habitus* in academia, defined as a "set of socially constituted desires, drives, and abilities at once cognitive, emotive, aesthetic and ethical" (Wacquant, 2002, p. 183). To be able to share *illusio* across fields may be professionally rewarding to the extent that belonging is not a requisite to fully enjoy fields' benefits. Once belonging, and not simply membership, starts being required by showing full adherence to a given *habitus*, for instance under the form of the usual remark I received in many academic conferences "where are you affiliated now? Any time I see

[1] In 2015, I was appointed CEO of a company with above 50 employees in a highly regulated industry.

you, you show a different affiliation...", the lack of personal *investment* in the field becomes evident.

Moreover, multiple belongings dilute the capacity to catch weak signals or assess the impact of changes. In my case, being physically out of the academic institution, I almost completely missed the actual impact on academic lives of the trend of managerialization of university (Izak et al., 2017; Slaughter & Leslie, 1997). Too I missed the chance of meeting and confronting with the new professions gaining power within the university institutions such as the academic manager (Winter, 2009). Finally, I missed the technological transition of university institutions, whose speed skyrocketed during the COVID-19 pandemic. Classes I have been prepared are now outdated and need deep revision not only content-wise, which was the funny part, but also completely re-thought for a different audience and a different communication medium. The ability to give classes, part of the core investment to belong to the academic field, was at stake in just a couple of years.

In March 2023, Times Higher Education published a short article (Akefe et al., 2023) where the authors highlighted the drivers for a vision of the university in 2035. Three over the four identified drivers concerned with new technology and the fourth with the need to align university education to wider societal changes, of course mainly driven by technology. As an *academic-cum-something else,* I have been able to move across different domains, but I was not able to inhabit the changes that the academic field was experiencing. I had been surfing on the academic institutions. I claimed of belonging to the academic field and had in common the *illusio* of the field with academics but my position of *academic-cum-something else* made me loose the new tracks academia seems to be about to undertake as well as the emerging feeling of disappointment of colleagues on these new tracks. When a colleague and close friend of mine told me during a coffee-break of a conference "what are you doing here? Here everything has changed. *Nothing is like we dreamt about thirty years ago*", I suddenly understood that the rules had changed and perhaps it was not worth playing the academic game. The value of the stake inherent in the academic membership, and so the *illusio,* was vanishing and I felt disappointed.

Rationalizing the Disappointment: The Life in the Limbo of Multiple Belongings

If *Homo academicus* is somebody who holds a full-time professorship for more than two years in an academic institution, then I failed. I was not able, perhaps not even available, to stay in a full-time position for more than two academic years. My fault, indeed: I did not pay my dues. Nevertheless, along my own career, I cannot ignore that I largely benefited from being an *academic-cum-something else* and inhabit a *limbo* of multiple positions and multiple belongings. In this section, I will describe how and where I benefited from the *limbo* that I have been inhabiting for almost three decades.

To stay in a liminal space, here I use the word *limbo* whose Latin etymology refers to the word *border*, provides special qualities (Van Gennep, 1909/1960). Those who live in a limbo can stay within a transition time/space where people may assume temporary prerogatives (Turner, 1969) and special events may occur (Rottenburg, 2000). My experience in the academic limbo allowed me to receive additional reputation from my academic role when I was a consultant, even though I was not a full-time *Homo academicus* (Czarniawska & Mazza, 2012). On the contrary, the academic limbo forced me into the professional cage of abstract strategy thinker once I was an *academic-cum-manager*. In this case, I was never able to receive acknowledgment for practical organizational solutions or for substantial accomplishments. My contribution remained within the theoretical domain, while micro-management—like daily HR processes and procedures, product innovation, and daily relation with suppliers—very soon remained outside my duties. A sentence by another top manager I spent most of my managerial experience with, represents an effective synthesis.

> Oh professor, my dear professor! You are invaluable as a sounding board when decisions need to be made, and when we need a deep understanding of the different implications inside and outside the company. Nevertheless, once you understand what is going on, it seems like you do not care of getting things done. It is like you are very brilliant in class, but you don't put any effort into the homework. (October 2018)

The use of the label professor by other managers in the company was the landmark of my *academic-cum-manager* status. I have not managed to be simply a manager; the *Homo academicus* emerges to describe my role within the professional domain. I was neither located in the management space nor in the academic space. I was bounded in a space of my own where I did not have full accreditation for the managerial prerogatives, as I could not access the full academic prerogatives in the academic world. In other words, the managerial context, as for the consulting context analyzed in Czarniawska and Mazza (2003), constrained me into a liminal space in the same vein it happened when I was in the academic domain because I was not a full-time *Homo academicus*. I was not in an academic limbo; my whole professional life was in a *limbo*!

To summarize my condition, I was not perceived as simply a manager, but I was not a *Homo academicus*. Therefore, to fully display my belonging, I decided to move out of academia, and I focused on the activity requiring the most time and effort: to be a manager. I accepted a new status to try to exit the limbo and enter the apparently magnificent world of management. However, after a few years of being a dedicated manager, the situation had not changed significantly. Still the "oh professor, my dear professor" mantra was widespread in the organization and among the most important stakeholders. Although I had almost stopped my academic efforts, I had not been able to remove the *aura* of *Homo academicus* around me. I was still inhabiting a *limbo* where I was an outsider as a manager although I set progressively apart from academia, losing touch with conferences, new publications, and old academic friends, and emerging new scholars. Interestingly, I felt that my managerial experience was giving me a much better awareness and understanding of the strengths and weaknesses of different organizational theories. This would have been highly valuable in the academic context of management education. However, by withdrawing the *investment* as *Homo economicus*, my experience as a manager did not serve any academic performance both teaching-wise and research-wise. This reveals a paradox of my liminal condition: on one side the condition allowed me to be enchanted by the *illusio* of belonging to the academic field and the managerial field, on the other side, it allowed to experience disenchantment of both fields by doubting of the seriousness of both academic and management games.

For instance, from the perspective of a manager who had been sharing the *illusio* of academia with colleagues since PhD time, academia reveals many weaknesses. The very same weaknesses were under scrutiny by many scholars. The criticism on MBA education and management education in general, rooted in the work of two highly distinguished gurus like Rakesh Khurana (2002, 2007) and Henry Mintzberg (2004), diffused very quickly and questioned the value of management education for today's managerial job. Despite its lasting reputation, the contributions academia provides to the corporate world is less and less clear. *Homo academicus* seems highly self-referential. Academic reflections do not usually provide valuable solutions to concrete corporate problems, according to the opinion of a growing number of managers and higher education experts and consultants (Friday, 2022). At the same time, the practitioner-oriented literature, highly successful in the eighties and nineties, ended up reducing the complexity of corporate world and seems to aim at highlighting just a few normative clues. Managers' trust upon simplistic recipes today gets lower and lower as they do not match the big challenges top managers need to face after the financial crisis of 2008. More importantly, after the financial crisis, managers started thinking that academic books and research were not able to anticipate challenges. In other words, self-referential *Homo academicus* was arriving late to deal with the new challenges set by technology and by a volatile context. Therefore, managers believe it is better to listen to peers.

Another weakness was the bureaucratization of university reducing the relevance of faculty members against administrative managers (Ginsberg, 2011; Tahir, 2010). This weakness led to a wide array of research dealing with the depression hitting precarious faculty members (Fleming, 2020). The ongoing complaints I heard from former colleagues were: (i) the research assessment exercise and the managerialization of university had changed the academic role, (ii) publishing rules were tighter and tighter and constraining the creativity of researchers and the selection of topics,

(iii) journals acquired an unreasonable power, (iv) the excess of administrative works was killing the time for research and reflections, and (v) the increasingly negative relation with the academic managers.

Despite these weaknesses, when I got tired of the managerial condition, I started to look again at the academic field. This surely happened because of the sweet memories of my early career Since belonging to the academic field still represented to me a source of benefits worth the personal investment, I gave the *Homo academicus* in me another try. However, the required *investment* is high to get out of the limbo I was in: I had to start again from scratch, learning the new academic field. I was an *early scholar again*, writing early drafts far from publication standards, joining conferences and workshops, meeting again old academic friends very curious to see me active in the academic community after so many years, asking feedback to valuable scholars on average twenty years younger than me. Unfortunately, to be an *early scholar again* in my fifties put a great distance between my younger colleagues and my memories of the old times. In the words of an old colleague of mine:

> They are different today. They know the rules of the game and they follow them very tightly. They do not invest time in what has no competitive value for them. We spent our early time in academia to reflect upon the meaning of life. Today, they do not care less until it becomes strategic to increase reputation, publish in a top journal and achieve a tenured position.

They are simply the new *Homo academicus* and I still wonder whether the benefits of the academic field are worth the high investment required.

Where Do I Go from Here?

The *illusio* I have in common with the academic field members was shaped by the old-style academic life and the old reputation of university professorship. What current colleagues share in the academic field is very different today. Universities can be *of the past* (Friday, 2022). For others (KPMG, 2020), *the Golden age of university is passing*. When I studied the transition of university after the Bologna process (Mazza et al., 2008), I would have never imagined writing (or even reading) what after only 10 years I read from a report by one of the leading consulting firm, *EY*.

> Universities must reinvent themselves. But reinvention is challenging when organizations are trapped by today's assumptions. To help university leaders form a credible vision of their institution's role in the new future of higher education, EY has developed a thought experiment, exploring how converging technologies, shifting demographics and new business models might change the sector's structure. (Friday, 2022)

Universities must reinvent themselves. Therefore, those living, working, dreaming, and playing within universities should reinvent too. Even students need to reinvent themselves as clients/customers. However, what is reinvention about? The following sentence included in the 2020 report on Higher Education by another leading consulting firm KPMG may help shedding light on what is the expected reinvention.

> Fewer students will wish to undertake full-service degrees. However, more students will be interested in micro-credentialing, competence-based education, nanodegrees and curated degrees. (KPMG, 2020, p. 15)

Homo academicus needs to cope with these needs, as a supplier needs to cope with customer needs. Customers like *micro-credentialing* and *nanodegrees*. The future is tough time for an old-style *Homo academicus* and seems it arrived abruptly.

It is beyond the scope of this chapter to dig into the roots of academia transformation. However, I understood I keep loving academia and I still feel to belong to this field; perhaps because I am not directly involved into this process of transformation. I was not sharing the current stress of living within academic institutions with many colleagues of mine. This helped me saving the original dream of my early PhD times. Therefore, as staying in the liminal stage of *academic-cum-something else* prevented me to become a full-time *Homo academicus*, at the same time, the *limbo* I was in protected my academic dream from the stress and disillusionment of the current time in academia.

Of course, there is a paradox emerging from my personal experience. Being full-time academic allows to benefit from the *illusio* and the commitment shared with colleagues within the academic field and academic institutions. Benefits are in terms of displaying the belonging to the academic field without coexisting belongings to other fields. Therefore, not being a full-time academic brings a feeling of inadequacy, of not being not up to date with theories and within the field; in simple terms of not being able to redeem the *Homo academicus* reputation. However, not being a full-time academic is not only a limitation. Not being a full-time academic allows deeper reflections on the changing rules of the academic game and its consequences on the academic institutions and on the lives of those working there. In a similar vein, not being a full-time manager may open rooms for deeper reflection on the implications of managerialism and its impact on institutional life. Enjoying multiple positioning, and multiple *illusio,* can be therefore a resource for deeper understanding of fields in the same way a liminal state can offer opportunities to understand what is beyond liminality (Czarniawska & Mazza, 2003).

The paradox above highlights a way to potentially deal with the stress and challenges of academic life that many would like to reinvent, as I mentioned above. If being an *academic-cum-something else* prevented me to be a full-time *Homo academicus,* it does not stop me loving the academic work, research, publishing, and meeting colleagues in conferences and workshops. Rather, to mix academia with a different professional interest works as a relief from the pain of today's academic life. In my personal experience, I tried to combine different professional engagements, i.e., being academic and storyteller for company gatherings. This brought me to conclude that it might be better if the other interests are more personal and disconnected to academia. I know of colleagues interested, for instance, in playing music and in poetry. By distancing from academia, those academics have developed a critical stance toward current academic practices and have relieved from the stress of struggling, for instance, with managerialization. It is beyond the scope of the present chapter but worth mentioning that it is today questionable whether academic institutions are ready to allow full-time *Homo academicus* such a distancing from the daily academic nuts and bolts. In this sense, I add that the individual tension between full-time *Homo academicus* and *academic-cum-something else* practices would deeply affect the way academic institutions work and, likely, reframe some of the above-mentioned visions of the future of university.

Concluding Remarks

In this chapter, I used my personal experience to illustrate three apparently contrasting dynamics. First, not being a full-time *Homo academicus*, rather an *academic-cum-something else*, I benefited from the reputation of academia in different fields without suffering from the increasing stress provoked by the recent transformation of the academic field and institutions. Second, being an *academic-cum-something else* I inhabited a liminal space that prevented me to enjoy the benefits of exclusive belongings, which in the academic field is of great relevance. Third, I showed how the liminal condition of *academic-cum-something else* by protecting me from the disillusionment of the current academic life, saved my original love for academia and finally encouraged me to become an *early scholar again*.

To be both within and without the game of academia enabled me to view the *illusory* quality and gravitational pull of the academic field that otherwise can be difficult to see for incumbents. At the same time, I argue it may work as a form of personal therapeutics against the stress of following new trends in academic life, such as publish or perish, competitiveness, or an overemphasis on advancing one's own position within the field, or the challenges managerialism poses upon the once taken-for-granted academic ideals. At the conclusion of this chapter, I cannot neglect to derive from my personal experience some reflections on these new trends of academic life that are challenging the qualities of the academic field I aimed at benefiting from so much in my early PhD days.

Having spent many years following the academic games, also within universities and business schools, as *academic-cum-something else*, allowed me to see the academic field with the distance needed not to ignore that today's academia is not heaven. In the accelerated modernity we are living

(Rosa, 2010) *Homo academicus* and her existence is somehow at stake as well as the role of university in preparing students "both to understand and influence the larger social forces that shape our lives" (Izak et al., 2017, p. 5). At the same time, from my personal point of observation, I do not view universities as relics of the past. Rather, I still found universities very lively places, especially if compared with the obsessive short-termism ruling the consulting and corporate domains. The mantra of reinventing academia (Friday, 2022; KPMG, 2020) by filling the field with "armies of functionaries—the vice presidents, associate vice presidents, assistant vice presidents, provosts, associate provosts, vice provosts, assistant provosts, deans, deanlets, deanlings, each commanding staffers and assistants—who, more and more, direct the operations of every school" (Ginsberg, 2011, p. 2) seems to be driven by the urge to apply a solution at hand, that of New Public Management and managerialism, rather than by a deep understanding of the current challenges of higher education institutions. Interestingly, I observed the same urge to apply available solutions in the other fields of consulting and management I inhabited in the personal experience. This reminded me of my PhD reading of Cohen et al. (1972) seminal piece on the Garbage can decision-making model.

As a conclusion, I would like to build on a personal issue that can open to hopefully fruitful generalizations. Along the trajectory of my professional life, I can say that I was taken in and by the game of each field I crossed. In this sense, I had the privilege to reflect upon the *illusio* of academia, consulting, and management. My feelings about each of the field are always good; it is like I tend to keep the good feelings and forget the tensions and difficulties I described along this chapter. I believe that staying in the liminal space of *academic-cum-something else* foster my enthusiasm toward each of the professional fields I inhabited. Therefore, I end up loving each of the fields remembering only the *belief in the interest of the game* of each field rather than the difficulties and tensions. This reminds me of a very cynical sentence from the Italian movie *Il Sorpasso* (1962), where the main character Bruno Cortona (Vittorio Gassman) argued:

> Do you know why we say that youth is the best time of our life? Because we do not remember it anymore!

I hold that this mainly depends upon the kind of stimuli moving individuals within a certain field and the *illusio* deriving from them and, in the interpretation of Wacquant (1992), the social gravity that pushes individuals to fulfill their desires by enjoying a certain field. From this perspective, to be an *academic-cum-something else* is a way to enjoy social gravity in multiple fields and multiple aspirations without worrying too much of the feeling of displacement. It allows to keep loving to belong to a field, although aware that the belonging might be temporary and that the hiatus between the belonging to the academic field and other field will be never filled completely. In other words, it allows to be enchanted by *illusio*, while also doubting the seriousness of the game and thus having reasons for experiencing disenchantment. In this sense, my personal experience reveals that the multiplicity of *illusio* and aspirations is not only possible but also desirable to relieve from the pain of stress and challenges of field transformation under strong institutional pressures. At least, it relieved me and gave the aspiration to be active again in academia although, I guess I will be always an *academic-cum-something else*. Even if this relief makes it more difficult to say what "I am" than what "I am not"; more difficult though wiser, following the verse by Vinicius de Moraes quoted at the beginning.

References

Agamben, G. (2018). *Homo sacer. Edizione integrale*. Quodlibet.

Akefe, I., Carpenter, L., Lee, G., & Leonard, J. (2023, March 27). Towards 2035: A future view of university education. *Times Higher Education*.

Arendt, H. (1958). *The human condition*. University of Chicago Press.

Bauman, Z. (2021). *Homo consumens: Lo sciame inquieto dei consumatori e la miseria degli esclusi*. Il Margine.

Bourdieu, P. (1984). *Homo academicus*. Editions de minuit.

Bourdieu, P. (2000). *Pascalian meditations*. Stanford University Press.

Bourdieu, P., & Wacquant, L. (1992). *An invitation to reflexive sociology*. University of Chicago Press.

Cohen, M. D., March, J., & Olsen, J. (1972). A garbage can model of organizational choice. *Administrative Science Quarterly, 17*(1), 1–25. https://doi.org/10.2307/2392088

Czarniawska, B. (1999). *Writing management*. Oxford University Press. https://doi.org/10.1093/acprof:oso/9780198296140.001.0001

Czarniawska, B., & Mazza, C. (2003). Consulting as a liminal space. *Human Relations, 56*(3), 267–290. https://doi.org/10.1177/0018726703056003612

Czarniawska, B., & Mazza, C. (2012). Consultants and clients from constructivist perspectives. In M. Kipping & T. Clark, (Eds.), *The Oxford handbook of management consulting* (pp. 427–446). Oxford University Press. https://doi.org/10.1093/oxfordhb/9780199235049.001.0001

De Boer, H., Enders, J., & Schimank, U. (2007). On the way towards new public management? The governance of university systems in England, the Netherlands, Austria, and Germany. In D. Jansen (Ed.), *New forms of governance in research organizations* (pp. 137–152). Springer. https://doi.org/10.1007/978-1-4020-5831-8

Delmestri, G. (2023). Are we all activists? *Organization Studies, 44*(1), 159–162. https://doi.org/10.1177/01708406221133507

De Moraes, V. (1966). Canto de Ossanha. In B. Powell de Aquino & V. De Moraes, *Os Afro-sambas*. Forma.

D. G. Research and Innovation & European Commission. (2005). *CEMP: The creation of European management practice: Final report*. Publications Office of the European Union. Belgium. https://policycommons.net/artifacts/231756/cemp/905758/. (Retrieved on October 13th, 2023)

Fleming, P. (2020). Dark academia: Despair in the neoliberal business school. *Journal of Management Studies, 57*(6), 1305–1311. https://doi.org/10.1111/joms.12521

Fleming, P. (2023). Never let a good crisis go to waste: How consulting firms are using COVID-19 as a pretext to transform universities and business school education. *Academy of Management Learning & Education, 22*(3), 425–438. https://doi.org/10.5465/amle.2022.0217

Friday, C. (2022). *Are universities of the past still the future?* EY Future of Higher Education report. https://www.ey.com/en_gl/education/are-universities-of-the-past-still-the-future (accessed online on October 16th, 2023).

Giannini, M. (2013). Prefazione all'edizione italiana. In P. Bourdieu, *Homo Academicus*. Dedalo.

Ginsberg, B. (2011). *The fall of the faculty: The rise of the all-administrative university and why it matters*. Oxford University Press. https://doi.org/10.1093/oso/9780199782444.001.0001

Gümüşay, A. A. (2023). Management scholars of the world, unite! *Organization Studies, 44*(8), 1377–1380. https://doi.org/10.1177/01708406231169425

Izak, M., Kostera, M. & Zawadzki, M. (2017). Introduction: The Future of University Education. In M. Izak, M. Kostera, & M. Zawadzki (Eds.), *The future of university education* (pp. 1-16). Palgrave-MacMillan. https://doi.org/10.1007/978-3-319-46894-5_1

Kakko, I., & Inkinen, S. (2009). Homo creativus: Creativity and serendipity management in third generation science and technology parks. *Science and Public Policy, 36*(7), 537–548. https://doi.org/10.3152/030234209X465570

Khurana, R. (2002). *Searching for a corporate savior: The irrational quest for charismatic CEOs*. Princeton University Press.

Khurana, R. (2007). *From higher aims to hired hands: The social transformation of American business schools and the unfulfilled promise of management as a profession*. Princeton University Press.

KPMG (2020). *The future of higher education in a disruptive world*. https://kpmg.com/xx/en/home/industries/government-public-sector/education/the-future-of-higher-education-in-a-disruptive-world.html (accessed online on October 16th, 2023).

Lounsbury, M., Gehman, J., & Ann Glynn, M. (2019). Beyond Homo entrepreneurus: Judgment and the theory of cultural entrepreneurship. *Journal of Management Studies, 56*(6), 1214–1236. https://doi.org/10.1111/joms.12429

Mazza, C., & Quattrone, P. (2017). Living in a world of foam: Global ideas, bubbles, and the fairy tale of business education. In M. Izak, M. Kostera, & M. Zawadzki (Eds.), *The future of university education* (pp. 111–121). Palgrave-MacMillan.

Mazza, C., Quattrone, P., & Riccaboni, A. (2008). European universities in transition: Issues, models and cases. *Edward Elgar*. https://doi.org/10.4337/9781848441415

McLuhan, M. (1962). *The Gutenberg galaxy: The making of typographic man*. Routledge & Kegan Paul.

Mintzberg, H. (2004). *Managers not MBAs*. Prentice Hall/Financial Times.

Parker, M. (2018). Shut down the business school: What's wrong with management education. *Pluto Press*. https://doi.org/10.2307/j.ctvqhtj8

Rosa, H. (2010). *Alienation and acceleration.* NSU Press.
Rottenburg, R. (2000). Sitting in a bar. *Studies in Cultures, Organizations and Societies, 6*(1), 87–100. https://doi.org/10.1080/10245280008523539
Slaughter, S., & Leslie, L. L. (1997). *Academic capitalism: Politics, policies, and the entrepreneurial university*. John Hopkins University Press. https://doi.org/10.56021/9780801855498
Tahir, T, (2010, March 30). The irresistible rise of academic bureaucracy. *The Guardian.*
Taylor, M. C. (2009, April 26). End of university as we know it. *New York Times.*
Turner, V. (1969). *The ritual process: Structure and anti-structure*. Aldine Pub.
Van Gennep, A. (1909/1960). *Rites of passage*. Routledge and Kegan Paul.
Wacquant, L. (1992). Towards a social praxeology: The structure and logic of Bourdieu's sociology. In P. Bourdieu & L. Wacquant (Eds.), *An invitation to reflexive sociology* (pp. 1–60). Polity Press.
Wacquant, L. (2002). Taking Bourdieu into the field. *Berkeley Journal of Sociology, 46*, 180–186.
Winter, R. (2009). Academic manager of managed academic? Academic identity schisms in higher education. *Journal of Higher Education Policy and Management, 31*(2), 121–131. https://doi.org/10.1080/13600800902825835
Zorn, J. (2014, November 4). *Music of John Zorn: A 35-years retrospective*. Interview by New England Conservatory on November 4th, 2014. Youtube. https://www.youtube.com/watch?v=8gA3m98eRpU (accessed online on October 13th, 2023).

7

Homo Academicus as Becoming Nomad: Reflections Through a Journey of Pregnancy and Motherhood

Maira Babri

Introduction: *Homo Academicus* as Same

In the publishing proposal for this book, the editors framed the starting point in the onto-epistemological history of management and organization studies as follows, "Once upon a time and not very long ago, the field of management and organization was permeated by the ontological and normative assumption that people are—and should be—maximisers of utility, a *Homo oeconomicus*. Facing a decision between alternatives, which each is likely to give different outcomes, *Homo oeconomicus* should calculate the pros and cons of each alternative and choose the alternative that maximizes the outcome in terms of utility. So the story went."

They then continue to mention developments which have questioned the position of *Homo oeconomicus* and suggest that a plurality

M. Babri (✉)
School of Business Society and Engineering, Mälardalen University, Västerås, Sweden
e-mail: maira.babri@mdu.se

Örebro School of Business, Örebro University, Örebro, Sweden

S. Cinque and D. Ericsson (eds.), *Debating 'Homo Academicus' in Management and Organization*, Palgrave Debates in Business and Management,
https://doi.org/10.1007/978-3-031-58195-3_7

of views has come to characterize the field. In this chapter, I draw on personal reflections as a management and organization scholar at a business school. I suggest that research and innovation funding in light of the political scope of Agenda 2030 and twin-transition (green and digitalized) have provided renewal to the norm of utility maximiser, today maybe more in the form of, the productive MAN who derives maximum utility from existing resources (Strengers, 2014). This norm is further emphasized within academia through the neoliberal context characterized by researcher, teaching, and university rankings, and has been shown to idealize a kind of "*academic performer identity*" (Gendron, 2008 in Englund & Gerdin, 2023 emphasis in original). Borrowing from Braidotti (2011, 2013), I liken this dominant position of the ideal academic and its perpetuation as a framing of *Homo academicus* as *the Same*. In contrast to this norming pressure, I argue that there is possible resistance and renewal in the form of necessary variations of this Same, albeit needing a lot of work, energy, and willpower to be realized. I suggest that a nomadic identity, building on Braidotti's Nomadic Theory, can provide an alternative subject position; a transformational becoming needed for the development and sustenance of alternative becomings, for scholars in a neoliberal academic context.

The concept of Nomadism came to me as I found myself lost, frustrated, and out of place as an academic and actively searching for a new way to relate to academia, for new places where I could be myself, find myself, and find my academic voice. As I worked on this chapter, I realized that I have experienced a profound transition in my identity as an academic during pregnancy and after giving birth. This identity finds itself in opposition to the much critiqued rational, "discourse of man" (Cixous et al., 1976) and in acknowledgment of the limitations of masculine writing practise for the production of embodied and affective accounts (van Eck et al., 2021). It acknowledges the marginalized space for women academics (Lipton & Mackinlay, 2017), yet highlights a rejuvenation in finding a new vantage point in what I call motherhood plus. Motherhood plus because motherhood came not just as a new identity or role for me, but as something which unlocked a whole repertoire of new ways of being, belonging, and hence identifying. In exploring this journey, I have been inspired by Braidotti's (2011, 2013) nomadic subject and nomadic ethics. I tell a story of transformation through the process of experiencing becoming gendered as a pregnant woman, looking for strategies to cope with this experience and decisively breaking with my own previously taken-for-granted academic norms. I reflect on and share how this allowed me to step into a new role and resulted in (a) a sense of liberation as well as (b) new anxieties, in the emergence of a somewhat new academic identity, one as the academic Mom Nomad.

Identifying as someone whose priority has always been achieving and delivering diligently at work, I knew that becoming a parent would entail a huge shift in my relationship to work. Long before I chose to become a mother, I was painfully aware that to create the needed space, time, and energy for a new relationship with a child, I would need to re-assess my relationship to work. What I did not anticipate, however, was how relationships at work, with people that I have known for a long time, would shift and change. It was during my pregnancy that I noticed this shift and could not help but wonder, why is it that when I am the one going through a transition phase in my life, my colleagues are treating me differently than they used to? Certainly, pregnancy is a fascinating experience and there is a lot happening inside the body, and I found myself consulting literatures I was previously oblivious to, books on parenting, books of child development, pregnancy and the body, breast-feeding, and family psychology. However, what kept me awake at night was my feeling of disconnect with the social world that used to be my safe place, my academic community, the people that I saw as my go-to-people, my extended family, and I cannot help but reflect on how different encounters with my colleagues have changed the way I see myself.

In the remainder of this chapter, I first present, considering Braidotti's Nomadic Subject, the phenomenon of *becoming minor*, a subject position necessary as a first step in the construction of a genuine alternative (and not just an act of resistance) to the majority or ideal. Next, I discuss pregnancy and motherhood as an example of becoming minor and relate to studies reporting on the experience of pregnancy and motherhood in relation to identity. After this I present the method I worked with. Then I present some of my own experiences, primarily encounters with academic colleagues which promoted transformational responses and an active search for a new academic sense of being. I conclude with a presentation of an alternative to *Homo academicus* as the Same with the idea of *Homo academicus* as *Nomad*.

Braidotti's Becoming Minor/Becoming Other and Creative Affirmation[1]

Rosi Braidotti's work has made huge contributions to the possibilities of conceptualizing subjectivity, an experience which for Braidotti has been explained as being material, discursive, situated, and affective (Minozzo, 2022). At the heart of Braidotti's (2013) conceptualizing of the Nomadic subject is the notion of Minor and the process of becoming minor, a philosophical lived experience of all those who come in second, are othered, unable to belong because the categories of belonging do not provide adequate space for such non-conforming. It is this particular experience and a vision of a possible generative emancipation form this position which drives Braidotti's arguments for becoming nomadic. She states that, "Becoming-nomadic means that one learns to reinvent oneself and to desire the self as a process of qualitative transformation" (pp. 344–345).

Braidotti expresses the state of the Majority, that which Minor is opposed to, insofar as this represents man, as stuck in a static orientation, taking on a schizoid character in advanced capitalism as "a 'spinning machine' that fabricated quantitative proliferations of objects, commodities, and data which leave the power structures unchanged and unchallenged" (p. 344).

[1] Braidotti's works on Nomadism has been widely cited and her concepts are often applied as a form of potent and vibrant critique toward dominant logics. For examples of applications of Braidotti's Nomadic Theory see e.g., Berjani et al. (2022) for a conceptualization of entrepreneurship as a form of affirmative critique and for an application of Nomadic Ethics see e.g., Parkes et al. (2020) for a conceptualization of a student's transformation through university and a way to question the purpose of higher education. It should also be mentioned that despite the vast spread of Braidotti's work, it is not without critique. See for example, Tamboukou (2021).

The process of becoming minor, explains Braidotti (2013), is a politically engaged, non-unitary, and ethically accountable version of the nomadic subject. She also explains that both those who identify as Majority and those who identify as minorities need to work through the dialectics of envy, what she refers to as negative desire, and domination. For those who identify as Majority, there is no other possible "becoming-other" than the undoing of the central position altogether. For minorities, however, the process is one where they must first find a fixed position, either through identifying with Majority or by identifying oneself as opposed to Majority. This is an active process of "identity politics." This is "both inevitable and necessary because... you cannot give up something you have never had (Braidotti, 2013, p. 345). Nor can you dispose nomadically of a subject position that you have never controlled to begin with" (Braidotti, 2013, p. 345). To break free from the dialectic of submission or otherhood as opposed to the Majority, the othered must actively become minor and identify as other to the Majority as a first step of eventually re-identifying oneself as something other than Other.

> Nomadic theory expresses a process ontology that privileges change and motion over stability. This is also rendered in terms of a general becoming-minority, or becoming molecular/woman/animal, and so on. The minority is the dynamic or intensive principle of change in nomadic theory, whereas the heart of the (phallogocentric) Majority is static, self-replicating and sterile. (p. 344)

Braidotti's theorization has an emancipatory tone. She is suggesting how the current status quo can be changed, and how genuine subject positions other than those which are reactionary to or perpetuating Sameness, can be fostered. She argues thus that "nomadic theory prefers to look for the ways in which otherness prompts, mobilizes and allows for flows of affirmation of values and forces which are not yet sustained by the current social and historical conditions" and that "this constructive approach transforms the negative conditions of the present into productive preconditions for affirmative practice" (p. 343).

She also wishes to dissociate political engagement from a difference of *negativity*, in psychoanalytic terms, and connect it instead with *positive* affect what she refers to as creative affirmation. Braidotti's interpretation of nomadism is closely related to her notion of "creative affirmation" as a positive politics of desire and a collective longing for plenitude in subjectivity. She asserts;

> In terms of the crucial relationship to sameness and difference, this means that the dialectical opposition is replaced by the recognition of the ways in which otherness prompts, mobilizes, and engenders actualization or virtual potentials. These are by definition not contained in the present conditions and cannot emerge from them. They must be brought about or generated creatively by a qualitative leap of the collective imaginary. (Braidotti, 2011, p. 269)

Braidotti paints pictures of differentiated possible future selves but is adamant also on the importance of the work it takes to move toward realization of such alternative future selves. An important part of this, is doing away with what she refers to as negative, and what I read as comparative and hierarchical difference. Instead, she suggests focusing on positive affect, desire, and longing, self-affirmation as a point of departure for becoming subject. Also, she highlights that this process needs to be acknowledged as "internally differentiated" (Braidotti, 2013, p. 345) as each of our starting points are different and the process will depend on where one starts from.

Braidotti asserts that "what is positive in the ethics of affirmation is the belief that negative affects can be transformed. This implies a dynamic view of all affects, even those that freeze us in pain, horror, and mourning. The slightly depersonalizing effect of the negative or traumatic event involves a loss of ego-indexed perception, which allows for energetic forms of reaction, [...]" and "Diasporic subjects of all kinds express the same insight. Multilocality is the affirmative translation of this negative sense of loss" (Braidotti, 2011, p. 278).

Building on a nomadic Deleuzian ethics, Braidotti reminds us that becoming woman is an essential part of becoming minor. Femininity is central to Deleuze's ethics and "life is not an a priori that gets individuated in single instances, but it is immanent to and thus coincides with its multiple material actualizations" (Braidotti, 2013, p. 343). This ontological outlook, she also refers to as a generative, affirmative, or creative force that constructs possible futures.

Womanhood, Pregnancy, Motherhood, Work, and Identity

Rosi Braidotti's theorization of the nomadic subject (Braidotti, 2011; Minozzo, 2022) and nomadic ethics (Braidotti, 2013) with an explicit interest in the construction of counter-subjectivities (Braidotti, 2023) has served as a basis for my conceptualization of the identity work which pregnancy propelled me into. What emerged was the embodied yet in-becoming academic self as a vantage point of resistance, possibility, and agency. The contextual backdrop which I was struggling to make new sense of as my identity as mother-to-be started setting in, was that of belonging to the academic field, organization, and management, with a lingering norm of rational masculinity and women as interlopers (Leatherwood, 2017).

As such, I realized that experiences of identity work during pregnancy and motherhood come to stand as an exemplary alternative to the epistemological stance of *Homo academicus* as the Same, typically male, or at best gender-neutral figuration of a productive (insert optional metaphor of the machine) producer of objective "gender neutral" knowledge. In a search for a renewed conception of the self, I encountered literature which contrasts the productive male to the (differently productive) female body and literature which emphasizes the transformational nature of pregnancy and motherhood, not least in relation to work and identity. Below I present some key findings from these works, specifically in relation to the female body and pregnancy.

Lipton and Mackinlay (2017, p. 33) note that: "Women; with all their leaking and flowing bodily associations with birth, breastfeeding, menstruation are seen as suspect and dangerous; as inauthentic against the construct of the 'ideal' academic subject." The coevolution of work and nonwork identities has been explored during pregnancy by for example Ladge et al. (2012) who define the experience of pregnancy as:

> a liminal period during which a professional woman is a 'threshold person' (Turner, 1969) who begins to experiment with provisional maternal and altered work identities that will take hold after the baby is delivered. We assume that many women will no longer be connected with their old professional identity in the same way after pregnancy. (p. 1451)

Ladge et al. (2012) build their seminal work on previous research indicating that pregnant women are both punished and rewarded by society, but that women are more likely to be punished/met with rudeness when they seek nontraditional roles or roles that violate gender norms (Hebl et al., 2007) and that pregnant women often receive mixed messages from co-workers and organizations regarding views on their capacity to manage conflicting demands of parenthood and profession (Halpert & Burg, 1997). Ladge et al. (2012) further find in their study that pregnancy "acts as a triggering event that evokes cross-domain identity uncertainties" (p. 1457). Three distinct reactions were found to the prospect of actualizing multiple identity changes, i.e., rejecting, delaying, or actualizing these felt uncertainties as identity changes. They also find that the personal as well as the organizational context shapes the vision women build of identity change and that cross-domain identity transitions are iterative, i.e., women cycle through the transition process repeatedly. Additionally, Gatrell et al. (2024) suggest that employers valorization of the mythical figure of an "ideal worker" (compare with *Homo academicus* as Same) disadvantages pregnant workers.

There is also a burgeoning literature in organization studies, related specifically to academic motherhood. Huopalainen and Satama (2019) e.g., provide a good review of the literature on academic motherhood and highlight the dual challenge in the setting of academia in that new mothers must tackle becoming mothers but also tackle a neoliberal academic setting. They further point out three tensions which they felt they needed to negotiate as they became mothers (i) the tension between the mobile researcher and the "immobile" (m)other at home, (ii) the tension between fleshy motherhood and brainy research, and (iii) committing to motherhood and academic work simultaneously.

While bio-physical difference between men's and women's bodies are a point of differentiation worthy of exploring in their own right, the experience of pregnancy and motherhood is not only a bio-physical bodily experience but, as I argue, perhaps more importantly a unique psychosocial-epistemological process, a kind of intensive, intertwined sociomaterial knowing-in-being and knowing-in-becoming (Barad, 2003) vantage point, which questions the validity of models based particularly on patriarchal knowledge-forms. As such, the unique bodily experience of both identifying as an academic and becoming a mother through pregnancy (including but not limited to the experience of becoming a parent which both men and women, and adoptive mothers would share) opens up for a different form of sensemaking through a lived experience which witnesses the limited ways in which we typically tend to conceive the academic subject, or *Homo academicus*, if you will.

Method

This paper deals with my personal experiences as an individual working in the field of management and organization and builds on autoethnographic reflections and recollections of the onto-epistemological nature of the lived experience during pregnancy and early motherhood while being employed at a business school in Sweden. I made short notes on encounters with academic colleagues which I found strange or provocative during my pregnancy and early motherhood (both while I was on leave and when I returned to work). These notes were taken between one and two years prior to finalizing this chapter and were taken specifically to be able to go back and reflect over these encounters. However, they were sporadic and related mostly to writing down what others had said to me and how it made me feel. In this book chapter I utilize an iterative process of reading literature, recollecting my experiences both through my notes and further through introspection, and writing these out. The empirical material thus consists of recollections (reconstructed based on notes) of interactions between me and colleagues as well as my current sensemaking of these. The encounters described should therefore be seen as moments of provocation and impetus for transformation rather than isolated events. As I reflect on encounters with close colleagues, therefore, my intention is not to point out individuals or exactly what was said but rather to focus on my lived experience in these encounters with others to make sense of my shifting academic identity. As the intention is not to pinpoint others' sayings per se, but rather my understanding and sensemaking of these, you will find hence that I have given my counterparts in the described settings pseudonyms. Methodological inspiration is here drawn from several sources. I borrow from Cozza and Gherardi (2023) particularly their conception of becoming with a research agencement, i.e., seeing the researcher as "immersed within the material-discursive research practices they perform" (p. 61) and both affecting and being affected as researcher.

I am making sense of my journey of pregnancy and motherhood as a form of embodied sensemaking or doing-being (Enang et al., 2023), as reflected in the awkwardness (Koning & Ooi, 2013) emerging in encounters between academic colleagues and myself. These encounters are in different ways reminders of how I am not fitting the ideal of *Homo academicus* as Same. By reading-writing this experience through Braidotti's stages of becoming nomadic, I argue for a more plural subject positioning of *Homo academicus* in Organization and Management Studies.

Personal Reflections on Collegial Interactions Spurring Transformation

I had been a scholar and lecturer in the field for over a decade before my pregnancy and believed strongly that my academic identity, as an ambivalent outsider, and in practice attempting to engender an at best androgynous identity, was rather fixed. As I reflect here over how I relate to my job during the transition phase of becoming a mother, I realize that quite a lot has changed drastically. As I became more acutely aware of patriarchal constructs, I also understood better what was holding me back and gained what has felt like a genuine access to a previously less known source of bodily knowledge and self-acceptance which has inspired new motivations for how to make use of those insights in my role also as a management and organization scholar.

Upon prompted reflection on the case of academic identity, I have maintained a shy, curious, and androgynous approach to my work for most of my decade-long academic life. This has, in my opinion, in many ways served me well career-wise, as I have often found myself in meeting rooms where I was the only woman present, I have often also been the only non-white person. However, I have mostly been serving others' agendas. Using this androgynous, non-gendered identity has not always been easy, but it has been a strategy I needed to deploy to make me feel comfortable in the environment where I work. This has entailed dressing in a certain way, primarily supressing color, multiplicity, and femininity. Also, moving around in the body of a non-white person, I have learned several coping strategies to deal with a largely white social world that has not always been very accommodating of difference. My strategy of choice, whenever I noticed others becoming uncomfortable, was often to make a joke or to start a conversation to break the awkwardness. However, as I became pregnant, my strategies felt unappealing. I did not want to hide anymore. I was bringing a new life into the world, another person whom I needed to teach how to be in the world. I found that I wanted, and needed, more than anything, spaces where I could be genuine to the plurality which I carry within. This entailed particularly, being focused on my work when I was at work and on being a mother when I was with my son. An inability to feel like I was able to maintain a good professional relationship to my colleagues who had seen me go through pregnancy, I felt I needed new ways to relate to my surroundings, I needed a shift in my academic identity.

Several encounters with academic colleagues made me feel unable to maintain focus on my work, as meeting with people seemed to prompt them into wanting to talk about my pregnancy and about parenthood instead of work. Although I appreciated being able to be seen as both mother and academic, I felt the focus was only on motherhood. This is not what I was looking for with my academic colleagues. I wanted to work when I was with my colleagues but felt as if I was seen as someone incapable of focusing on and delivering at work. I also experienced the opposite, particularly the coming together of myself and another pregnant colleague, on a writing project which perhaps otherwise would not have materialized.

Some Encounters with Academic Colleagues

Below I present, in the form of short reconstructions of notes and recollections, some encounters between myself and fellow academic colleagues during my pregnancy and upon my return to work after my maternity leave of nine months. All these encounters were to me at the time they occurred, hurtful, awkward, strange, or confusing in some sense. This was both because they differed so drastically from my previous experience of encounters with the same people, but probably also because both my peers and I were seeing things differently than we previously had. As I was in a process of transformation, I realize now that the relationships I mention were probably also changing. At the time that I encountered these events, however, I sensed that people were seeing me differently than they did before, and this new gaze of the outside world unto me was unfamiliar and uncomfortable for me. I was then grappling with making sense of this and spent quite some time trying to figure out what I was feeling and consequently, how to respond. I was far from unaffected.

One work-relationship that I feel changing drastically as I became pregnant is one with someone, I considered not only a close colleague, but also an academic friend. I call him Patrick for purposes of anonymity. From being in a relationship where I felt we were peers and could speak about anything, constantly sharing ideas and literature tips, I noticed this person gravitating away from me. I would make the usual calls, asking if we should meet for lunch or have a coffee and would be met by excuses of a busy schedule and no suggestions for new arrangements to meet. This person is someone I have worked closely with for a long time. I felt I was being rejected, particularly for young female colleagues without a pregnant belly or young kids. Colleagues who were still interested in late evening seances and weekend get-togethers.

When I was around six months pregnant Patrick, and I were teaching together. This is a course that the two of us have designed together and previously taught on. This time around, however, it felt different. I remember how sessions between the lectures would involve us going to buy a cup of coffee, talking about how the students seemed to be responding to the course content and developing in terms of our ambitious learning goals on the course. But this time around, it was as if my protruding belly was too much of a distraction to my colleague to think about anything else during the breaks. The things he asked/said made me realize he probably has not been around a pregnant woman before. It seemed he wanted to talk about my pregnancy, but simultaneously struggled to bring himself to do so. While we were walking to the lecture hall, I told him I was unable to walk as fast as I could previously, and that I needed to adjust to walking at a slightly slower pace due to my reduced lung capacity. He did not say anything then, but when we broke for lunch, he commented in relation to me mentioning having to carry extra weight, that "one of my biggest fears is to become overweight." From someone who had always been very kind and considerate I was surprised by this comment, and it felt invalidating.

Another strange encounter I recall regards a phenomenon related to not one but two academic seniors and how their inclination to connect with me based on references to their own experience of parenting surfaced in strange and unexpected ways. I noted that, although the topic of our discussions changed, the tone and dynamic was the same. Only, in this new setting I realized distinctly, how absurd it was. Independent of each other, the two senior male colleagues were giving me their best advice on how to manage my leave and remain academically relevant by mentoring me on the intricacies of breastfeeding, hormonal changes in the body, and the like. I became in this context very aware of how they changed topic but held onto their expert "coaching" tone and role and somehow seemed to want to warn me that what I was doing might feel impossible, but with some tips and tricks from them I should be able to keep up. The awkward thing here was, they really knew very little about the lived experience I was encountering but were very adamant on advising me.

A third encounter which left me pondering was a gathering with a few colleagues around my 7th month of pregnancy, in the setting of a book club. I found myself hurt when a senior female colleague interrupted me while I was speaking about how I relate the content of the book to my current situation, and demanded the word goes to the next person around the table. This is a colleague that I respect and look up to. Normally, I would respond to situations like this, say that I was not done speaking but flabbergasted in the moment by this encounter, I found myself unable to respond to the situation with anything other than a feeling of guilt. A feeling that, she wants me to shut up, as if the pregnant woman is not worthy of listening to or being taken seriously. The same colleague, despite knowing that I together with another junior colleague arranged and started up these gatherings, mentioned later during the evening how this book club community felt like "coming to visit [my male colleague] who started the book club together with me." As I ponder over this moment, I feel that this was an odd encounter, I have never felt physically as enormous as I was at this time, and simultaneously I felt more invisible than ever. As if the words coming out of my mouth were suddenly less than those of others around the table.

It is strange, I feel. When I speak of my pregnancy and share something related to it, it sparks feelings of discomfort. But when I do not speak of it and try to focus on other things, others want to talk about my pregnancy. There was something very strange about how the agency was either completely seized from me in terms of owning the experience of my pregnancy and the bodily changes that come with it, or a kind of uncomfortable curiosity where the agency was awarded to me in small glimpses, but it seemed obvious that it was difficult for some of my colleagues to embrace me as a whole subject, equally worthy of voice.

A fourth set of encounters entails communication with one of my bosses at the time during my pregnancy, and just the awkwardness of having to deal with things he would say. As I arrived at a scheduled management council meeting during my final month of pregnancy, he greeted me at the door to the conference room with a "Wow, you're huge!" Luckily, I at this point if my pregnancy felt that I had encountered so many strange comments, that I was able to respond with a neutralizing comeback saying, "I see you've made some changes too. Nice hairstyle!" Nonetheless, this comment was strange to get from my boss and I did not know what he really meant, was he surprised to see me at work, at a scheduled council meeting because he was expecting me to call in sick or not show up? Or was he trying to connect with me in some way and trying to make a superficial comment, which came out the wrong way? I don't know. Maybe someday I can ask him.

As a final encounter I would like to mention different accounts of a more general, newfound, gravitation toward women, and other non-ideal academics, particularly those with competencies in or lived experiences of having given birth and experienced both pregnancy and motherhood. This might sound straight forward but this experience was for me also awkward, probably because I had never felt a sense of collective with women based on the exceptional experiences of pregnancy and childbirth. Also, because even among women, talking about the body has become taboo. Although I will not explore this encounter in more detail here, this gravitation toward women was a longing both for connection in the acknowledgment of being othered, rejected by the Majority which I apparently had identified with previously, but also a search for competence. I wanted to better understand what my body was going through both during and after pregnancy. I felt immensely grateful to my midwives and doctor who supervised my delivery and postpartum healing. These were people who knew things no one in my highly educated, academic community had any knowledge about. Perhaps this was because they were mostly men belonging to a generation when gender roles meant that all things pregnancy, childbirth, and breastfeeding were strictly outside their domains of experience, even if they themselves were fathers. Having spent most of my time in business schools, environments dominated and controlled by men of above-said generation, I realized I was myself a novice at the pregnancy and postpartum body. I was amazed and in awe over my body's resilience, its capacity, its generative power, and I began to want to seek out those who were masters of this knowledge. I was inspired and happy to learn that so many nursers and midwives dedicate their lives to caring for the pregnant and newly born child, but also surprised by how low the mainstream knowledge in society seems to be regarding the pregnant and postpartum body. Half of the population is female and most of these biologically capable of pregnancy, yet the general knowledge and willingness to speak about these phenomena is startlingly low, at least in my community. I find that odd. Every single one of us has once been attached through an umbilical cord to the placenta formed in our mothers' wombs. The very coming to life of our bodies, ourselves to be, the first becoming of anything human. Yet this process and everything that surrounds it still seems taboo.

Academically, in terms of ideas I have wished to explore, I felt that whatever time to myself I had during my maternity leave, I wanted to put on pursuing those projects. I re-visited feminist literatures which place the body at the center of knowledge creating and I learned about a method conference open for such methodological perspectives, which I financed personally and attended. My husband came along and helped with the baby who was then three months old (acknowledging this privilege like Huopalainen & Satama, 2019). I am glad I did this, and I am grateful for all who encouraged me and treated me as any other conference attendee, despite having a baby strapped to me. This was also the time when a desired collaboration with a female fellow colleague began to take concrete shape, a method paper which had long been an idea became here something I began to believe in. I presented a version of the paper at above conference and gained great confidence in our ideas.

Previously, quite embedded in a predominantly masculine collaborative environment, I was now finding pleasure and joy in connecting with other women. Perhaps these previous colleagues now saw me as a full woman, understanding of the struggles of women as they attempt to combine their conspicuously leaking bodies with facades of a body-mind disconnect, and a body-free cognitive astuteness (Lipton & Mackinlay, 2017) and thus worthy of collaboration? Perhaps I was no longer seen as an ally of the patriarchal order. Perhaps I was just more open to being myself and less concerned about fitting in.

I also began, as part of this gravitation toward something else, applying for academic jobs at other departments. I wanted more research prerequisites in my position, and I longed for an environment with a feeling of larger plurality than where I was currently working. I was applying for jobs all over the world. The above encounters together acted as a catalyst for my compilation of a portfolio which served as a basis for several job applications. I felt I needed to be in a place where I was seen as a competent researcher, not "just a mother" or "someone who's slowed down" or the like, things I was feeling became a natural development of how I was viewed in an environment which idealized "The Same." This process of seeking new academic jobs was humbling and exciting and landed me a tenure track position where I felt I was being invited to join a university because of my competencies and what I brought to the table. Simultaneously I was able to negotiate terms for working on a distance several days a week to accommodate my responsibilities and aspirations as a mother and co-parent. This was it! Liberation! This was doing academia differently, in a way that works for me.

However, in retrospect I also realize that much of what happened during my pregnancy was also aided by past experiences. I knew since before that academic environments differ and that researchers as well as university management are pressured under neoliberal demands to produce output. I was acting on a combined need for a different way to work, and the conviction that I was unable to achieve that differentiation at my current academic institution. I might have been wrong about the latter, but I am glad I acted. Also, should be mentioned, to not make this story rosier than it is, that a permanent position at my current workplace, allowing me a leave of absence made this transition exceptionally easy. Switching institutions might not be an option before you have a certain level of base employment security.

Finally, I would like to mention that I also realize that my pregnancy came at a time which was special in many ways, academic institutions were beginning to face budget-cuts and demands on recovering student numbers which have been falling since after the 2019 Covid-pandemic. There is high inflation in Sweden, rising interest rates, and stagnating salaries. I understand that people around me have had their own stress to deal with and their own challenges to handle. To bring a child to the world in this kind of a context and to be proud of it perhaps, in such a setting, more easily becomes a provocative act.

Reflecting with Curiosity as an Affirmative Academic

In retrospect, reflecting over these encounters in light of Braidotti's constant becoming and, in an attempt, to be positively affirmative (Braidotti, 2011) in my sensemaking of the above encountered, I realize that the story does not end here; all the people who I mention in the encounters, are still people that I am in touch with, and people that I essentially like. They are still my academic peers. I have had to spend some time thinking through these encounters and trying to find compassionate explanations for the reactions to knowledge of my pregnancy, or to my protruding belly, and to me as a new mother with my new outlook of the world. I did this primarily by formulating these encounters as curious questions to myself, questions which I could reflect over to try to engage with and understand what I was experiencing, but also to give these experiences an additional reflective dimension. These questions were often in the form of, why would s/he say this? Or can I understand his/her point of view? This led me to several new curiosities including that (i) perhaps there are still many men out there with a repressed need to speak about their experiences of parenting and co-parenting and that (ii) there are women out there who project their own unhealed pains onto others. They too must be given the spaces to liberate themselves. This dimension of posing questions to myself in my inner dialogue is as much about who I am and who I am becoming but also who I wish to be in a collective. Such reflections have been paramount in my ability to emerge strengthened, more empowered and most importantly, ready to start contributing to the field of management and organization from a place of renewed confidence in myself as knowledgeable, and capable of contributing not despite but from the basis of my subjective position(s) in the web of interrelations that constitute our academic field.

I realize that what I describe in this chapter is my "becoming woman" (see Braidotti, 2013, pp. 344–348, and specifically her references to Deleuze) moment in life. It is not just at work, though, it is the first time I am allowing the world to see me so blatantly in womanhood. I did not shy away or little down. I showed up, both in pregnancy and postpartum and kept showing up with my protruding belly in places people, to my surprise, seem not to be expecting me; advisory boards, seminar sessions, doctoral defenses. I realize that I needed these encounters to begin reflecting on the ways in which I will go from being a conformist in terms of abiding the norms of the masculine, or at best gender-neutral academic to becoming non-conformist on several levels. I am imagining a future where I will not be working full time, I will not be working weekends, and I will not be working evenings. I will have to say no a lot more often. This is something I have rarely ever done in my 13 years in academia. The first step on this journey was to spend time on the application of jobs to several academic institutions before I gave birth. During my maternity leave I interviewed for several positions, not because I needed a new job, but because I wanted to gague respective institutional representatives' views on hiring a new mother. This process resulted in a new job within academia and a negotiation to start after I had finished my responsibility as head of division at my current job. This, however, was not just a shift in job titles for me, this was necessary in order to find a place from which I could imagine myself as an alternative future academic, who is also mother, and daughter, and yogi, and lover, and dreamer, and believer (that a different world is possible) so many more things (rather than feeling stuck in a place of resistance toward an ideal I no longer wished to pursue).

Reframing Possibilities: *Homo Academicus* as Becoming Nomadic

"The nomadic or intensive horizon is a sexuality 'beyond gender' in the sense of being dispersed, not binary, multiple, not dualistic, interconnected, not dialectical and in constant flux, not fixed." (Braidotti, 2013, p. 350).

Braidotti (2011) emphasizes the famous feminist slogan, that the personal is political, and stresses the everyday lived experience as central for the understanding of the nomadic subject, but she also argues that the real issue at hand is conceptual, "how do we develop a new post-unitary vision of the subject, of ourselves, and how do we adopt a social imaginary that does justice to the complexity?" (2011, p. 285). I argue that while the conceptual issue indeed continues to be a relevant humanistic quest, for our understanding of ourselves among other selves; our academic selves, it is more relevant to note the interpersonal ethics that emerge and evolve because of reflection based on encounters with others in everyday academia. I believe that in genuine meetings and acknowledgment of difference and multiplicity, perhaps lies a form of relief for both Majority and Minor, from the chains of the strait-jackets that static identifications shackle upon us. For indeed, I realize that the encounters I had were not only with men (in themselves seen as unitary subjects) lacking the experience of interacting with a pregnant woman, but also (at least in potential) themselves subjects in becoming who, at least sometimes, seemingly showed curiosity, awkward concern, and a certain uncomfortability. Perhaps the nomadic subject could hence allow us collectively as management and organization academics to break free from the restraints of dominant logics of theory as well as practice (not least productivity indulged practices of doing and showing off such doings rather than being an academic).

I note thus, that within all the awkward, strange, uneasy encounters that I had with colleagues during both my pregnancy and early motherhood, should lie an equal potential for reflection for my counterparts to embrace a broader subject position. Both for themselves, and for others around them. This kind of reflection is an example of the becoming and ongoing, the endless possibilities for evolution of the becoming subject but also a very practical, interpersonal ethics, only possible through deep engagement in new encounters with others, through acknowledgment of the awkward (see e.g., Koning & Ooi, 2013) and through creating conditions for endurance (Braidotti, 2011, p. 285) of the uncomfortable, the painful, the strange, that to which we are unaccustomed.

In this book chapter I have explored my experience of pregnancy and becoming a mother through my encounters with academic colleagues and peers. I conclude through this reflective exercise that being an academic self, like any other selves the nomadic subject might temporarily or more permanently encompass, is always bio-sociological and thus materializes in relation to self, the body, and others and their bodies. Such reflective exercises, with an interest in simultaneously exploring both self and others, a form of phenomenological approach to the human subject, if you will, could have the potential to strengthen interpersonal ethics between peers in academia, but also serve to highlight new possibilities for subject positions from which to explore the world, write, and theorize.

As I explore elsewhere together with a colleague, there is great potential in opening up that which has typically been deemed to belong to the personal sphere, not least that which we label as emotional experiences (Rosales & Babri, 2023) for continued reflection on and thus the evolution of the self, which in turn creates possibilities for an evolution of ontological and epistemological constructs of future management and organization theorizing and not least a continued interest for the methods (see e.g., Gherardi, 2019; Katila et al., 2023; van Eck et al., 2021) that make such theorizing possible.

It should be noted however that although I present my becoming nomad journey as a path toward liberation, identification as Nomad comes not without its own inherent troubles and anxieties. It is both a position of possibilities, and yet one of displacement, of being in many places at once. It is a position that requires strengthened self-esteem, belief in a basic level of self-sufficiency as academic (as opposed to the large groups of successful researchers' resilience who often work together, show up at conferences together, publish together). The modern predicament of hybrid working conditions, again allows for both possibilities and new challenges for the Nomadic academic, both in thought and in practice. Digital meeting technologies today allow the academic nomad to work from anywhere and be affiliated with several universities as well as other academics (rather than being confined to only socialize with those who happen to be part of ones' proximal physical academic milieu). The nomad is in movement, has multiple belongings and has at least in theory, the possibility to contribute to academia from places, both mental and physical, where she can best combine academic work and the joys and responsibilities of motherhood plus, or any other differentiated way of doing academia (see Robinson et al., 2023 for a refreshing collage of different ways of being an academic). The challenge constantly lies in daring to form alliances with both people and technologies in service of an empowering academic identity rather than succumbing to identifications with ideal forms which might generate success in terms of the ideal, but restrict academic difference, possibility, and agency; crucial, in my opinion, to the very joys of being a creative thinker and contributor to the knowledges we as academics make possible.

References

Barad, K. (2003). Posthumanist performativity: Toward an understanding of how matter comes to matter. *Signs: Journal of women in culture and society, 28*(3), 801–831. https://www.journals.uchicago.edu/doi.org/10.1086/345321

Berjani, D., Verduijn, K., & van Burg, E. (2022). Enacting (New) possibilities of living: Entrepreneurship and affirmation. In R. N. Eberhart, M. Lounsbury & H. E. Aldrich (Eds.), *Entrepreneurialism and society: Consequences and meanings* (*Research in the sociology of organizations*) (Vol. 82, pp. 149–159). Emerald Publishing Limited. https://doi.org/10.1108/s0733-558x20220000082007

Braidotti, R. (2011). *Nomadic theory: The portable Rosi Braidotti.* Columbia University Press.

Braidotti, R. (2013). Nomadic ethics. *Deleuze Studies, 7*(3), 342–359. https://www.euppublishing.com/doi.org/10.3366/dls.2013.0116

Braidotti, R. (2023). Valedictory lecture: We are rooted but we flow. *Future Humanities.* https://doi.org/10.1002/fhu2.4

Cixous, H., Cohen, K., & Cohen, P. (1976). The laugh of the Medusa. *Signs: Journal of Women in Culture and Society, 1*(4), 875–893. https://doi.org/10.1086/493306

Cozza, M., & Gherardi, S. (2023). Posthuman feminism and feminist new materialism: towards an ethico-onto-epistemology in research practices. In S. Katila, S. Meriläinen, & E. Bell (Eds.), *Handbook of feminist research methodologies in management and organization studies* (pp. 55–71). Edward Elgar Publishing. https://doi.org/10.4337/9781800377035.00011

Enang, E., Sminia, H., Gherardi, S., & Zhang, Y. (2023). Unpacking researchers' embodied sensemaking: A diffractive reading-writing of Mann Gulch disaster. *Scandinavian Journal of Management, 39*(4), 1–10. https://doi.org/10.1016/j.scaman.2023.101299

Englund, H., & Gerdin, J. (2023). The neoliberal university and its effects on academic researchers–Survey evidence from Sweden. In M. Benner & M. Holmqvist (Eds.), *Universities under neoliberalism: Ideologies, discourses and management practices* (pp. 86–109). Taylor & Francis. https://doi.org/10.4324/9781003246367-6

Gatrell, C., Ladge, J. J., & Powell, G. N. (2024). Profane pregnant bodies versus sacred organizational systems: Exploring pregnancy discrimination at work (R2). *Journal of Business Ethics, 192*(3), 527–542.

Gherardi, S. (2019). Theorizing affective ethnography for organization studies. *Organization, 26*(6), 741–760. https://doi.org/10.1177/1350508418805285

Halpert, J. A., & Burg, J. H. (1997). Mixed messages: Co-worker responses to the pregnant employee. *Journal of Business and Psychology, 12*, 241–253. https://link.springer.com/article/10.1023/A:1025078319958

Hebl, M. R., King, E. B., Glick, P., Singletary, S. L., & Kazama, S. (2007). Hostile and benevolent reactions toward pregnant women: Complementary interpersonal punishments and rewards that maintain traditional roles. *Journal of Applied Psychology, 92*(6), 1499–1511. https://doi.org/10.1037/0021-9010.92.6.1499

Huopalainen, A. S., & Satama, S. T. (2019). Mothers and researchers in the making: Negotiating 'new'motherhood within the 'new'academia. *Human Relations, 72*(1), 98–121. https://doi.org/10.1177/0018726718764571

Katila, S., Meriläinen, S., & Bell, E. (Eds.). (2023). *Handbook of feminist research methodologies in management and organization studies*. Edward Elgar Publishing. https://doi.org/10.4337/9781800377035.00007

Koning, J., & Ooi, C. S. (2013). Awkward encounters and ethnography. *Qualitative Research in Organizations and Management: An International Journal, 8*(1), 16–32. https://doi.org/10.1108/17465641311327496

Ladge, J. J., Clair, J. A., & Greenberg, D. (2012). Cross-domain identity transition during liminal periods: Constructing multiple selves as professional and mother during pregnancy. *Academy of Management Journal, 55*(6), 1449–1471. https://doi.org/10.5465/amj.2010.0538

Leathwood, C. (2017). Women academic researchers: Still interlopers in the UK academy? In H. Eggins (Ed.), *The changing role of women in higher education: Academic and leadership issues* (pp. 227–242). https://doi.org/10.1007/978-3-319-42436-1_12

Lipton, B., & Mackinlay, E. (2017). We only talk feminist here: Feminist academics, voice and agency in the neoliberal university. *Springer*. https://doi.org/10.1007/978-3-319-40078-5

Minozzo, A. C. (2022). Rosi Braidotti's Nomadic Subjects. In S. Frosh, M. Vyrgioti, & J. Walsh (Eds.), *The Palgrave handbook of psychosocial studies* (pp. 1–21). Springer International Publishing. https://doi.org/10.1007/978-3-030-61510-9_49-1

Parkes, S., Benkwitz, A., Bardy, H., Myler, K., & Peters, J. (2020). Being more human: Rooting learning analytics through resistance and re connection with the values of higher education. *Higher Education Research & Development, 39*(1), 113–126. https://doi.org/10.1080/07294360.2019.1677569

Robinson, S., Bristow, A., & Ratle, O. (Eds.). (2023). *Doing academic careers differently: Portraits of academic life* (1st ed.). Routledge. https://doi.org/10.4324/9781003267553

Rosales, V., & Babri, M. (2023). Harnessing Emotions for Embodied Reflexivity in Organizational Ethnography. *International Journal of Qualitative Methods, 22*, 1–11. https://doi.org/10.1177/16094069231196460

Strengers, Y. (2014). Smart energy in everyday life: are you designing for resource man? *interactions, 21*(4), 24–31. https://doi.org/10.1145/2621931

Tamboukou, M. (2021). Feeling the real: The non-nomadic subject of feminism. *Theory, Culture & Society, 38*(3), 3–27. https://doi.org/10.1177/0263276420942803

Turner, V. (1969). *From ritual to theatre: The human seriousness of play*. Paj Books.

van Eck, D., van Amsterdam, N., & van den Brink, M. (2021). Unsanitized writing practices: Attending to affect and embodiment throughout the research process. *Gender, Work & Organization, 28*(3), 1098–1114. https://doi.org/10.1111/gwao.12651

8

"*Dragged in the Opposite Direction*": Identity Tensions Facing Women Academics in Management and Organisation

Kate Black, Malgorzata Ciesielska, and Dawn Whitton

Introduction

This chapter offers reflexive-reflective accounts of three women management and organisation (hereafter "management") academics on different career journeys within differing UK Business Schools. An inward-looking approach to our experiences allows us to "inquire from the inside" (Humphreys & Brown, 2002, p. 426), and listen to our hearts rather than our minds as we consider the assumptions about who we are; assumptions held by ourselves and those held by others. In "writing

K. Black (✉)
Northumbria University, Newcastle Upon Tyne, UK
e-mail: kate.black@northumbria.ac.uk

M. Ciesielska
Sheffield Hallam University, Sheffield, UK
e-mail: G.Ciesielska@shu.ac.uk

D. Whitton
University of Durham, Durham, UK
e-mail: dawn.whitton@durham.ac.uk

S. Cinque and D. Ericsson (eds.), *Debating 'Homo Academicus' in Management and Organization*, Palgrave Debates in Business and Management,
https://doi.org/10.1007/978-3-031-58195-3_8

differently" (Gilmore et al., 2019) so we question the assumptions underpinning who we think we are, and should be, as management scholars, and to what extent we are who we want to be. Adopting a social-constructionist perspective on identity, we examine whether we have agency to construct our identities as "a" management academic, or whether our identity has been, or is at risk of being, regulated or corrupted by others holding greater power than ourselves; that we are willingly duped into taking on a particular self. We thus examine the tensions that exist between our assumptions about who we are, our idealised self-constructions, and the gendered bureaucratic societal norms and structures that we perceive to regulate and reinforce who we are and who we become. Through reflexively examining our stories we illustrate how the role of the management scholar—as with many social scientists—is based on the tensions between submission to pressures and trends in who we should be, and the power we hold to be who we want to be. We suggest that this tension is perhaps more prevalent within management and organisation studies than in business more generally, in other disciplines and workplaces, and is more urgent for female scholars, who might typically find themselves "dragged in the opposite direction" as they make efforts to live and work within a context that was traditionally the male preserve (Wittenberg-Cox, 2020).

Management and Organisation Academics' Careers Within UK Business and Management Schools

The nature of academic careers within UK Business and Management Schools has changed significantly over time. From their origins through to the 1980s these Schools were designed to provide postgraduate and executive education for practising managers which were achieved through relationships they developed with the corporate sector (Louw, 2019). Management was, within this context, understood as a practice-based craft. Thus, the large majority of Business-Management School academics were, or had been, managers, business owners or entrepreneurs and the focus of their craft was in providing tools and techniques grounded *for* management, grounded in their experience (e.g. Schoemaker, 2008; Warhurst & Black, 2022).

Over the past three-to-four decades, the prestige of a Business-Management School has instead been derived from its research credentials. Academics are now doctorally qualified researchers rather than current, or ex-, practitioners and educators, and their career success is assumed sought through securing research funding and highly ranked research outputs (Alajoutsijarvi et al., 2015; Kitchener & Delbridge, 2020) rather than through practice experience and educational excellence. The focus has, thus, become *about* management.

Academic careers are though changing, and within UK universities especially. Data over the past decade from the Higher Education Statistics Authority (HESA) illustrates the growing importance of alternative career pathways within the contemporary UK university. What in the past was an assumption of an academic-researcher now opens new pathways and opportunities. These changing career opportunities are seen more prevalently within the pre-92, traditionally research-focused,[1] Universities that have acknowledged the strategic significance of other key areas beyond traditional research, rather than the post-92s formerly teaching-focused polytechnics.

Informed by such work as Boyer's (1999/2016) "priorities of the professoriate", many of these institutions have appointed Professors of "Practice and Engagement" and of "Education", and such promotion paths are especially important in Business-Management Schools (Anderson & Mallanaphy, 2020) and other vocational disciplines. Some institutions have also awarded Chairs for excellence in institutional Leadership. This route is often though not a formal academic pathway (Grajfoner et al., 2022), but it is expected that individuals would concurrently excel in one of the three main pathways (research, education, or practice and engagement) alongside. As such, progression through

[1] The UK university sector constitute of two large groups of institutions. Traditional research institutions, often referred to as "red-brick" (or pre-92s) are those universities who were established as such and were always academic institutions. Post-92 Universities refer to the group of universities, formerly known as "Polytechnics", that started as vocational establishments and around 30 years ago were transitioned into a university structure.

Leadership necessitates significant juggling of different agendas and the meeting of implicit assumptions in how these are juggled—and, in consequence, few women secure such roles (Cotton et al., 2021). Our assumption that we should be able to create academic environment that is supportive, fair, and appreciative of differences, although core to academic ethos, is still an unsolved problem.

The need to recognise and reward other facets of a UK university's role and purpose beyond research follows increasing marketisation of the sector, with the introduction of fees and simultaneous reduction in government funding streams (Marginson, 2018). Concurrent performativity metrics in the UK, such as the Teaching Excellence Framework (TEF) which directly informs the levels of permitted tuition fees, and the Knowledge Exchange Framework (KEF), have aimed to "increase efficiency and effectiveness in the use of public funding" (UKRI, 2023). Universities in the UK now have the characteristics of both public sector organisations in, for example, costly staffing, and the characteristics of private sector organisations as they compete in a global marketplace for students. Engagement with this global marketplace has inherently brought with it changing student expectations as customers (Calma & Dickson-Deane, 2020; Guilbault, 2016, 2018), consumers or service-users (OfS, 2023; Tomlinson, 2017). Such marketisation and performativity have thus established new frameworks to govern academic work and academic lives (e.g. Rosewell & Ashwin, 2019), and these frameworks bring with them ever-rising levels of bureaucracy which is regulating and corrupting who we are as management academics. This context also poses a larger question of how much agency we have as academic in choosing a particular career pathway, how much we are dragged in different directions as dictated by organisational needs, and how this affects our assumed professional identity.

A socio-cultural approach to understanding identity can help explain the effect of these changes to academic careers (e.g. Anderson, 2011; Black & Warhurst, 2019). From such perspective, identity is not established and fixed (e.g. Hutchins & Rainbolt, 2017), but is understood as an ongoing re/crafting of the self, influenced by various factors. The self is thus "reflexively understood" (Sveningsson & Alvesson, 2003, p. 53) through dialogue within specific context/s (e.g. Brown, 2019, 2022;

Brown et al., 2021) and organised in efforts to produce a "degree of existential continuity and security" (Alvesson & Willmott, 2002, p. 622). Our assumed or preferred academic identities can though be regulated by others, by social structures (Alvesson & Willmott, 2002), threatening who we think we should be, and want to be as academics (Brown et al., 2021). As women academics do we face alternative assumptions about who we are that place us more at risk from this identity regulation? (e.g., Romero-Hall et al., 2018). Are we though also inadvertently condemning ourselves, allowing our academic identity to be regulated and controlled by others to a less valorised, feminised career path? That is, are we complicit in disadvantaging our own careers? In what follows, we present three individual reflexive-reflective vignettes examining our experiences and our identity-work within the field of management studies within both post-92 and pre-92 institutions. We acknowledge upfront that we did not each necessarily anticipate following the research-focus that is assumed of contemporary management academics. Have we though willingly found an alternative academic career, or were we dragged *in*, or *from*, another direction?

Vignette One: Kate's Account—Dragged into Education?

I am Professor of Management Learning and Education at a "post-92", previously teaching-focused but now research-focused, university. My Chair was secured through "excellence" in education and "good standing" in research and leadership-citizenship. I am not a career academic. I did not complete my Ph.D. until I was in my 40s, having had a somewhat varied career largely outside of the Business School context. My career has comprised, environmental education, secondary high-school teacher, learning and development manager within the retail sector, professional manager within a university School of Education, and an associate academic within a university geography department. Indeed, it was within this geography department that I was offered a fixed-term academic contract on the same day as I was offered a permanent academic contract in the Business School. Fearing the risk of uncertainty on a fixed-term contract, I took the latter.

Despite this eclectic and sinuous route, a key theme through my career has been education and learning. That I have embraced such a career focus, assuming an "educator identity" is though interesting given that, aged 7, I announced to my family that "when I grew up, I wouldn't be a teacher!" At that time, several of my family members were then working, or had worked, in education. Later, aged 17, when perceived to be underperforming in my mock A-level exams, I was taken aside by my form teacher and advised "perhaps you forget about entering university? Go to teacher training college instead". My response, maybe their intention, was that "I'd show them" and I successfully progressed to my university and programme of choice, studying Physical Geography, then securing a scholarship for a Masters in Ecology and Countryside Management.

It is perhaps not unexpected that I have become an educator, despite my assertions to the contrary. I strongly believe in the transformational power of education for changing people's lives. However, that I am an educator within the field of management is perhaps more questionable. Did I sacrifice my "true" self as a geographer and ecologist through the lure of a permanent contract in a discipline within which I feel less comfortable?

After securing my academic post, I completed my Ph.D.—in Education and, upon its completion, I had every intention of following an expected research-focused career, changing universities to support this trajectory. It was not though, to be. While I do research, and I do publish, this assumption that I would craft such identity has not come to fruition.

I am though lucky that I've had the opportunity to progress at a time when alternatives to a research-focused pathway have gained prominence and credibility and thus the assumptions underpinning what it means to be a management scholar have "on paper", although perhaps not for all, evolved. Yet, that I hold the title "Professor" is still something that I find it hard to come to terms with, and this imposter feeling has been intensified by a male Professor who swiftly pointed out, that I am not "a proper Professor". I still usually use "Dr" instead.

What I do though notice is that there is an unspoken assumption that women will take on such education-focused roles. Yet, as educational innovation, pedagogy and a genuine focus upon students' experiences is replaced by increasing bureaucracy, as universities make belts-and-braces responses to regulatory body legislation, so this bureaucratic burden is thus falling disproportionately upon female academics. This burden is, in turn, potentially corroding who they are, blocking opportunities for them to become what is expected of them by the academy, and/or to craft an identity that fulfils their ambitions and identity as an educator. Indeed, I still find myself regularly expected to "make up the numbers" on recruitment and promotion panels. Being the "token" woman is an expectation of me even when I might have other priorities or deadlines.

I do though sometimes question myself, as Head of Education and in accepting an education-focused Professorship, am I complicit in upholding the administrative yoke? Do my actions in fact contradict my own principles and values of learning but do they also inherently present a barrier to others' learning?

Vignette Two: Dawn's Account—Dragged Along into Academia?

I never set out to be an academic, it was an unplanned career but something which appealed while undertaking an undergraduate degree. I joked to the lecturers that I was going to join them one day; it looked like a fun and flexible job. Ten years later after a successful career as a Chartered Surveyor, I was head-hunted to join my former tutors, at a post-92 university seeking practitioners from industry. My transition to an academic was unfolding as I became a Senior Lecturer. I was probably quite naïve at this point, or maybe avoiding what I unconsciously knew, but research never really featured on my agenda, it was briefly mentioned in my interview, but the focus was very much on teaching, and I wanted to teach, share my knowledge and experience as a surveyor. I did not really see myself as an academic, I was a Chartered Surveyor employed as a Senior Lecturer, and so I threw myself into teaching and a leadership role. The only qualifications I possessed were my undergraduate degree and professional qualification, and it soon became evident from discussions with colleagues that I should start thinking about research and was encouraged to undertake a master's degree. To support my leadership role, I opted to study part-time for a MBA, and it was during this time that my interests started to shift, and this led to my next significant transition in my career, I moved to a different Faculty to focus on Business and Management programmes. During my first year in a Business School, I struggled to find my identity, I was no longer a surveyor or a specialist in a subject area and at first felt rather discombobulated. A prerequisite of this move was to undertake a Ph.D. or Professional Doctorate, I had already started to undertake a part-time DBA, the focus of which was on employability, and I therefore focussed much of my teaching around career development, employability, and academic skills with the Business School. Perhaps this focus resulted from the tension I was facing in wanting to prioritise my support of learners to "become", but having to take on a revised identity of what it meant to be an academic. But still I did not really relate to the term Academic; was I resisting this assigned identity? I still referred to myself as Senior Lecturer, with the emphasis being upon "lecturer", my interest lay still very much on teaching. Research was really just like a dull ache there in the background, but it wouldn't quite go away. I tried all I could to resist what others were trying to ascribe to me by just trying to ignore the dull ache, focusing on everything but research. This resistance was something which I soon began to regret. I was a reluctant researcher, possibly because I lacked confidence in undertaking it and found teaching and leadership more rewarding, and very much within my comfort zone. The dull ache, however, soon developed into a right pain, the lack of research was holding me back in terms of career development. I could not climb the academic ladder, and while I enjoyed teaching, I was driven to achieve more for both financial reward and a strong desire to undertake a leadership role as I wanted to contribute at a higher level. I was able to undertake interim and deputy leadership roles, but the lack of credible outputs and research income was limiting my progression. I had naively believed that in being loyal, hard-working, and good at my job as an educator and leader I would be successful and able to secure promotion to an Associate Professorship. This was not, however the case, the university was focussed on a strategy where research took primacy and thus considered academics only for their contribution to research. Little consideration was made of the educators and leaders who had built the university to be what it was, nor did they acknowledge personal constraints that might face individuals in writing highly ranked journals. Concurrent with this, the University changed academic job titles. My title of "Senior Lecturer" became that of "Assistant Professor". After a number of unsuccessful attempts at promotion, both in terms of grade and responsibilities, and despite 17 years as an academic through which I had held a number of interim leadership roles, I was reminded that I was "just an early career researcher" and thus "I lacked necessary gravitas". Although working within a vocational discipline in which students were hungry for real-world insights and, despite applying for posts that necessitated managing the department team, my organisational practice and leadership experience apparently did not count. My academic self that I had built up was severely threatened. Arguably, "gravitas" is a gendered word, and interestingly it was a male colleague that secured this specific promotion.

This rejection enabled me to recognise that I would never be valued within that university unless I became a research-focused academic. However, this was not how I saw myself as a management academic. Research was not the basis of who I am, of my personality and my being. It was not why I left industry and took an academic role. While I recognise change within organisations, I know my strengths, and that my true self lay in an education-focussed role. While I could see value in pedagogic research this would not, in itself, enable me to meet the exacting identity of researcher that was being prescribed.

To be true to myself, it was time to move on and I was offered that aspired-for promoted post at a "pre-92" (Russell Group) university on an education-focussed career track. Yet in applying for the role, I was nervous. My confidence was shattered by the previous comments that I "lacked gravitas" and that I was "just an early career researcher". Would another university really value the knowledge, skills and experience I could bring in terms of my education and leadership capabilities? During my time at the pre-92 university, I considered myself as a Chartered Surveyor and Senior Lecturer and managed the tensions that emerged between these two identities, especially the ever-present "imposter syndrome". Since becoming an Associate Professor at the pre-92 and holding an identity that is valued by the institution, this imposter syndrome is starting to diminish and, for the first time in my academic career, I would perhaps now refer to myself as "an academic".

Vignette Three: Gosia's Account—Dragged from Leadership?

I grew up within the harsh Polish education system and so I learned early on how to work hard. After a 5-year consolidated degree in Management and Marketing, which I selected as I was interested in the significant political and economic transformation that my country was going through, I started working with a government agency. At the time, I was one of few people with good English language skills and so I was sent to participate in multiple different European Union meetings. What this job taught me was not only what working life looks like, but specifically, how *not* to manage people and how *not* to push top-down onto your teams. I promised myself that if I ever moved into a managerial position, I would find a better way of translating strategy to operation and vice versa. Ultimately, I gave up this public sector job to start a small business while simultaneously enrolling on a Ph.D. in Management. I thought I could manage both at the same time; little did I know how hard that would be!

Through running my own company, I discovered that I work effectively with people and I used this opportunity to develop my own distinctive leadership style. I felt the need to demonstrate that I could run a successful business, acting as a role model for new staff, and so I ensured that I was able to step into any role within the business as needed. However, unconsciously that led me to delegate less and place a closer grip on staff. A typical entrepreneurial dilemma you could say.

In part because of my business endeavours, and in part due to other external factors, it took me 7 years to complete my doctorate and I changed my institution twice before I defended my thesis. At this time,

I decided to close the business and move to the UK where I took a fixed-term research associate contract before securing employment as Senior Lecturer elsewhere. I held a full-time academic position for 4 years before I considered taking a leadership role—as postgraduate research director. Arising from my doctoral supervision activity, this was perhaps one of the most enjoyable roles I've held. This enjoyment was perhaps because there were many problems to fix so I could see my work was making a difference. Yet, while enjoyable, I felt that this role equated to only a small part of our operations and I wanted more of a challenge; I wanted a role to which I could bring value but also learn from. The Business School then needed a Research Excellence Framework (REF) coordinator and so I took on that role. It was in this role though that I encountered difficulties through the exposure to university politics. To be frank, the role really scared me initially as I lacked the network at that level and had no history of working with these people. I felt out of my depth. I remember clearly shortly after taking on the role, I was to present the mock REF exercise outcomes. The results were poor, and I reported them accordingly. One of the Deputy Vice-Chancellors then came to me, patted me on the back, and said that "I shouldn't worry about my presentation; that it wasn't my fault". This really shocked me. How could anyone think this could have been my fault in the first place? I then realised that the expectation of delivering quality outcomes was high and that I was being scrutinised quicker than I thought!

I changed jobs at this point as despite my leadership contribution, and despite a good publication record, I had been unable to secure promotion to Associate Professor. I was apparently "only 98% there"! By moving institutions, I was able to secure this level of role with an associated leadership position as Director of Learning and Teaching (Quality Assurance) focused upon accreditations. At this point, I discovered that some UK Universities have a leadership-based promotion pathway. Such a pathway necessitates a credible research or education contribution alongside the leadership skills and knowledge of the business activities of the university. Some academics are of course able to "play" such a promotion pathway very effectively, negotiating their responsibilities effectively to secure a sought-after knowledge-base, for example relating to national excellence frameworks or business school accreditations.

Shortly after, I secured a Departmental Deputy Head role. This was the most substantial operational role that I'd held, managing 80+ academics—and a role that on paper equates to 50% workload, but in reality, could be 150% some weeks. I knew though that I was good at organising and that the department needed a rethink regarding many of its processes and practices. I wasn't aware, though, that it would be so demanding of my time and that it would take a good 12 months before I felt confident in what I was doing.

A Deputy Head role is a strange role as it is expected that you fulfil everything that the Head does—except that you aren't invited to the meetings where the decisions are being made and so you are not able to influence but also don't always know the context of instructions sent down. This caused me significant frustrations! Perhaps not surprisingly, I felt relieved and really encouraged to subsequently step in as interim Head. This role gave me an opportunity to finally have a "seat at the meetings table", to be able to contribute to the ways things were done, and to advocate for the department. The role also revealed the full spectrum of departmental, faculty and university politics, and I had to learn, fast, how to navigate them. For much of the time in this role, I was the only woman in the room and on reflection, I think it created, albeit maybe unintentionally, an environment where I felt I had to fit into the setting rather than be myself. I felt that I had to conform to the expectations that have emerged from there being a persistent gender imbalance at the higher level of academic management. I remember one meeting with a new university director who looked at me with surprise on his face and commented, "I thought you were a man!" My name is foreign and so my gender may not be obvious, but needless-to-say that episode said a lot about "model academic leaders!"

Nevertheless, being Interim Department Head was the most rewarding and satisfying role I have performed so far. Quickly I learned that the role wasn't about efficiency and skills, but about building teams, selecting the right person for the right job and supporting everyone to achieve their potential. I developed a really good working relationship with colleagues, and I learned how to rely on them in order to make progress as a department. Unfortunately, though, my focus upon leadership had been at the cost of my research and when the permanent Head role was advertised, with an accompanying Chair, I was not appointed. I was advised that my outputs were not commensurate with being a "Professor". This really highlighted the struggle that I, and indeed many leaders, face in navigating the requirements and expectations of differing academic workstreams, while, in my case and similarly for many other female leaders, also supporting a young family.

I therefore sought promotion elsewhere to achieve my Professorship, moving institutions (again!). I now lead a research team, while focusing on developing my publication and funding portfolio, in efforts to build a case for my next career step. Unsurprisingly this too requires a lot of investment and enthusiasm but also allows me to make progress on collaborative projects. For sure it is much easier than managing a whole department! I hope to go back to substantive academic leadership at some point in the future as this gave me the most professional fulfilment. I am good at doing research, I am a decent academic teacher, but my best skills are in people management and development.

Understanding Academic Identities Through an Identity Lens

How then can we make sense of these experiences? Taking a sociocultural approach to understanding our "selves" as academics, we acknowledge that we are constantly working on, crafting, our identity/ies. That is, we are constantly reasserting our "subjective claims" of "who I am" (Caza et al., 2017, p. 5) as we seek a "degree of existential continuity and security" (Alvesson & Willmott, 2002, p. 622) within the academy. Yet we do not craft our identities in isolation but rather, intersubjectively in interaction and dialogue (Watson, 2008) with others in specific social contexts at specific times (Alvesson et al., 2008). This might necessitate us invoking certain positioning tactics in relation to others (McInnes & Corlett, 2012), for example, to manage the assumptions of who we are to others we might choose to disassociate our self from others or, conversely, to emphasise our similarity with them (e.g. Tajfel & Turner, 2004; Turner & Reynolds, 2012).

While we might like to think that we have full agency in positioning our selves, in "becoming" and "being" who we are, we must necessarily recognise that our identity is also positioned, often regulated and controlled, by others (Alvesson & Willmott, 2002). That is, differing meanings may be ascribed to us by others. Consequently, our assumed, or asserted, identity might be contested, suppressed or rejected (Alvesson & Willmott, 2002) and/or an alternative identity might be imposed upon us (Winkler, 2013) by, for example, by our university, department or discipline and/or by political structures externally. Moreover, since who we "become" is constructed dialogically, crafting a new identity involves us drawing upon the available social and cultural resources of language and discourse, weaving these into our identity narratives. Our identity can thus be unconsciously "colonized" (Brown, 2017, p. 299), positioned and distorted by the dominant discourses available (Thornborrow & Brown, 2009) which may then discipline who we become (McInnes & Corlett, 2012) both in our eyes and in the eyes of others.

In order to achieve a sense of meaning and coherence for our selves, and thus a personal security through aligning with our assumptions of who we should be, we need to continuously work on our identities (Bardon et al., 2017; Knights & Clarke, 2014). This identity-work, the process of "forming, repairing, maintaining, strengthening or revising" desired identity constructions (Sveningsson & Alvesson, 2003, p. 1165) is especially pertinent during periods of change or threat. In such periods, identity crises can be provoked as our established self-understandings are challenged, and a sense of self-doubt, insecurity, and anxiety is brought to the fore (Nicholson & Carroll, 2013; Winkler, 2013). Through identity-work we then strive to re-craft and re-build or reinvent a coherent sense-of-self (Ibarra, 1999; Learmonth & Humphreys, 2012).

Yet significantly, identity-work is not only necessary for establishing "who I am", but also "who one is not" (Watson, 2008, p. 134) and this latter state may involve us "undo[ing]" (Nicholson & Carroll, 2013), and "disidentifying" (Elsbach, 1999) with an established identity, such as that associated with a previous career position, to then engage in aspirational identity-work (Thornborrow & Brown, 2009) to become a different type of person. This identity-work typically involves conscious crafting to align our self with a desired, perhaps distinctive, or prestigious, identity

(Learmonth & Humphreys, 2012). Yet if such identity-work is rejected or regulated by others (Alvesson & Willmott, 2002) an aspirational identity might not be achieved or indeed, be achievable. This rejection or regulation of our identity may result in a tension between who we are able to be/become and the assumptions we hold of our identity and resolving this tension might necessitate significant remedial or restorative identity-work (Knights & Clarke, 2014) often drawing upon resources from outside of the immediate context.

Understanding Our Management Academic Identities

Our vignettes that articulate our reflexive-reflective accounts of our experiences as academics illustrate the identity tensions we have faced through our academic careers. They also raised questions as to the extent we have had agency over our careers, crafting a true[2] self that is, we are who we think we should be as academics, and the extent to which our identity has been structurally and socially crafted for us whether consciously or unconsciously by the sector, our own institutions, our managers, and our peers.

The Agentic Academic Self

Perhaps most significantly, we all made a conscious decision to pursue a different form of academic career, to position ourselves (McInnes & Corlett, 2012) as educators and leaders foremost which is different to the contemporary "norm" of "research above all else".

In Dawn's account (Vignette 2), a significant professional career before joining academia gave her the strength of professional identity as a Chartered Surveyor. Although having aspired to be an academic when completing her original degree, this academic identity remained that of

[2] We have, throughout, referred to our "true" self rather than our "authentic" self, due to the proclivity of the latter term to assert a gendered form of control, contributing to the reproduction of gendered work and organising (Zaeemdar, 2024).

primarily educating the next generation of professionals, at least until the jaws of managerialism, notably those of the Research Excellence Framework [REF], started to bite. The changing nature of the academy that she experienced, and that coincided with her transition into the Business School, placed a threat upon this secure sense-of-self. We see evidence of her ensuing identity crisis as she tried to secure promotion and administrative leadership-management roles, to be told that she lacked the necessary "gravitas" to take on such roles. The identity she assumed as an academic remained misaligned with that expected of her. The rejection of her identity by others, combined with the change of role title from "Senior" to "Assistant", created a threat to her extant, and previously secure, identity as educator and resulted, whether consciously or unconsciously, in a process of identity-work as she sought resources from outside of that institution to engage in the necessary remedial and restorative identity-work (Knights & Clarke, 2014) in the form of a promoted post elsewhere where her experience and expertise held value and thus her chosen identity, how she saw herself as an academic, could be reasserted.

Similarly, in Kate's account (Vignette One), her education-focused identity was deeply ingrained; this was how she saw her academic self. She asserts this to be a career choice, albeit perhaps unconscious, due to her strong belief "in the transformational power of education" (e.g. O'Sullivan, 2023). This choice was despite her aspirations at an earlier stage of her university academic career to "be" a different kind of academic—a researcher—and of her moving institutions in pursuit of that dream. Then, rather than adopting the assumptions of the self that are embedded within the discourse of "research-above-all-else" she instead employed positioning tactics (McInnes & Corlett, 2012), working on and asserting her identity as an educator. This intention was achieved through her securing promotion on the grounds of educational "excellence" (albeit with the necessary "good standing" in research). Interestingly, and by contrast to Dawn, this identity claim as an education-focused Professor was not challenged by others and she would seem therefore to have been successful in agentically identity-re/crafting, despite the male colleague who questioned her over being a "proper

Professor". Concurrently though she finds it hard to accept her promotion, tending to disassociate from the title due to the assumptions that she un/consciously knows underpin it. She primarily uses "Dr" instead. Such disassociation is perhaps down to her recognition that education is still seen as second-class within the academy (Denny, 2023).

Gosia (Vignette Three) has also seemingly had significant agency to become who she wanted to become as a management scholar—an academic leader-manager—but also the agency to be the type of academic leader-manager that she wanted to be, as learned from her first working experiences of how *not* to lead! However, more recently, as her vignette suggests, this agency has been to some extent regulated and controlled by others, by the assumed norms of what it is to be a Professor as held by the predominantly male incumbents of such titles, and the perceived credibility that is now required to be allowed to perform an academic leadership position.

Our Ascribed and Regulated Identities as Management Academics

Did, and do we, therefore really have agency in crafting our academic selves or are the identities we have crafted for ourselves really the result of regulation by others, and rejection of alternative identities by others with greater power (Alvesson & Willmott, 2002)? That is, have our assumptions of who we are as academics been brought into question by the assumptions held by others causing us to feel, albeit unconsciously, a sense of imposter syndrome (Addison et al., 2022)? Perhaps unconsciously we have understood that our assumptions of who we should be are misaligned with those sought and valued by a contemporary academy where research has primacy. Have we crafted an identity with which we had confidence and/or capability thus seeking recognition from elsewhere through being "different"?

We have shown how Dawn's transition to an academic role within the Business School met with a resistance to adopt the academic identity that was being ascribed to her (Humphreys & Brown, 2002). Yet the tensions she faced through the more recent threat to her identity, that of being considered an early career academic without the "gravitas" to be promoted to a leadership role, was, consciously or unconsciously, the trigger for further identity-work, as she repositioned herself, crafting an alternative and aspired identity that was valued elsewhere. Dawn now suggests that she has re-secured her sense-of-self, holding tight to her true self of supporting nascent professionals rather than capitulating to the imposed identity of academic-as-researcher. That is, there is alignment between who she assumes she should be, and what others are assuming of her. Yet inherently, in transitioning to a new identity as an Associate Professor, "for the first time in my academic career, … [identifying] as an academic", has she succumbed herself to the managerial grasps of the new institution (e.g. Shams, 2019), her true identity lost and replaced by a regulated self? Moreover, in repositioning as an education-focused academic has she capitulated to assumptions held by others of who she should now be, accepting the gendered role of educator and administrator in lacking the supposed "gravitas" associated with research? (e.g. Cardel et al., 2020; Górska et al., 2021).

Similarly, in Vignette One, Kate's school experiences of "not being good enough for university" perhaps unconsciously pushed her to accept assumptions made about who she should be, crafting an identity that has supported her success—at least objectively. This success has been crafted, for example, through securing a permanent academic contract (even if that was not within her favoured area), in securing an education-focused Professorship, surrendering to the neoliberal discourse of striving to be "better". But in doing so, so she "sacrifice[d]" her more true identity within environmental and earth sciences, and of achieving the hard-to-craft identity of "researcher". Her identity has thus arguably been regulated by the powerful neoliberal discourses of "success above all else", and to achieve this success she has been pushed, perhaps dragged into crafting an alternative self as a management educator, inherently a more feminine role (Brommesson et al., 2022). Yet as she reflects, in achieving this success, is she complicit in the managerialism that corrodes our identities (Mansfield, 2023; OfS, 2022)? Moreover, is it really success to be ascribed an identity as "token woman" on panels, to take on the gendered role of nurturing "educator" (Cooper, 2019; Westoby et al., 2021)?

Although on the face of it, Gosia (Vignette Three) has been able to craft an agentic self as an academic leader, at least until very recently, so, too, her assumptions of who she is have arguably been shaped and regulated, socially and structurally. She asserts at the outset that she is not afraid of hard work having been schooled within the harsh Polish education system, and as a result her assumptions of who she is, and should be, are underpinned by the need for hard graft, running a business while pursuing her doctorate, giving "150%" as Deputy Head, while also raising a child. This assumption of continuous grafting has arguably encouraged her to keep on pushing for a never-satiated success, even when enjoying the role that she held (Black & Warhurst, 2019). As Gosia secured more senior roles so she experienced a need to craft a "less true" self as a female leader adopting the assumptions that she held of who she should be. She notes how she felt the need to "fit into the setting rather than be myself" a sense of having "to conform to the expectations" and this was then further asserted by an explicit rejection of her identity by a senior manager who noted his surprise that she was female. This assumption made is perhaps though not entirely surprising given how few senior leaders within UK institutions, and Business Schools, are women (Cotton et al., 2021; UCU, 2022). Yet, that Gosia saw herself an academic leader, might be understood from a more critical perspective, not as a true desire but as an outcome of the neoliberal imperative to develop skills, notably leadership and communication, that have value as productive labour (e.g. Urciuoli, 2008)?

Conclusions and Implications

Who then are we as academics, as women scholars in the field of management and organisation? As we have seen, as management scholars we are faced with multiple identity pressures and expectations that emerge from within our institutions but also more widely, for example, from our discipline, neoliberalist politics and economics, student expectations and so on. Within this chapter, in drawing upon a socio-cultural identity lens, we have examined the tensions between these structural constraints and our own agency to craft who we think we should be. Have we been dragged into becoming what/who others within our discipline assume we are? Has who we are been determined by the outcome of maximum utility as characterises *Homo oeconomicus*? Or have we been true to our hearts and become who *we* think we should be?

We also question whether we have felt these tensions more intensely as women academics, and women within management and organisation studies? Each of us has experienced our identity as we understand ourselves as management scholars being rejected, and having an alternative identity ascribed to us; an identity that we have accepted to varying degrees. Yet we have continued to craft, to re-craft, to use necessary positing tactics to make-the-most of who we can/have become, associating, and disassociating with others, as necessary, in efforts to craft some sense of security for ourselves; to be who we think we should. As we have navigated these tensions there is though evidence to suggest that we have simultaneously disciplined ourselves, being complicit in constraining who we can become as women academics. In taking on the more caring, education-focused, or leadership-focused, roles, supporting our learners and colleagues to achieve their aspirations, we have undoubtedly reinforced structural assumptions of who we should be, contributing significant invisible labour to this end, but we have also potentially curtailed how we are perceived by others within the academy while potentially corroding our own identities (Sennett, 1998).

Have we experienced these tensions, the rejections, and ascriptions, dragged *to* and *from* the opposite direction more strongly because we are women academics within a context that is conventionally masculine (Whittenberg-Cox, 2020)? The evidence we present, of a male colleague's surprise of being a woman (Gosia, Vignette Three), of lacking "gravitas" (Dawn, Vignettes Two) and of a questioned Professorship (Kate, Vignette One), would suggest this may well be the case. That management and organisation are, by contrast to more general business, dominated by conflict and power relations, positions that women tend to avoid (Mease & Neal, 2023; Schneider et al., 2016), further support our experiencing such tensions.

Such tensions in who we are, who we can be, and how others perceive us are though not only apparent within the academy. Issues of power and conflict are evident across the very large majority of contemporary organisations and thus we are not in this way, distinct or "special". Indeed, such examples as these could undoubtedly be found in the life-worlds of many managers and employees. Yet, the level at which these tensions are experienced by women is, we suggest, far greater within the academy and thus the situation of women academics is perhaps more precarious than most.

What then are the implications of this situation for women academics within management and organisation? How then can such precarity be created through unresolved tensions between who we see ourselves to be and how we are assumed by others to be? Each of us must consciously take a stand on whether to assert greater agency to become the management academic we want to become or become the product of those with the power, forever assigned to those roles that are perceived to be more feminine such as those that underpin education-focused careers, and excluded from those perceived to be more masculine: the Leadership or research-focused careers. Standing against structural and cultural inequalities has never been an easy task and will certainly take a lot of effort but gives an opportunity to build solidarity among women academics. Asserting greater agency over our identity, ensuring greater inclusion and diversity within the academy will necessitate women academics making active efforts to resist the identities assigned to us, to collectively stand up for who we really want to be as management academics. At the same time, we must necessarily raise awareness across Management and Organization of the implications and shortcomings of assigning such identities upon their women academics. We also hope that our narratives and analysis will help senior academic leaders to understand the burden of identity tensions in today's academia and to support rebuilding the sense of solidarity and collegiality.

References

Addison, M., Breeze, M., & Taylor, Y. (Eds.). (2022). *The Palgrave handbook of imposter syndrome in higher education*. Springer Nature.

Alajoutsijarvi, K., Juusola, K., & Siltaoja, M. (2015). The legitimacy paradox of business schools: Losing by gaining? *Academy of Management, Learning and Education, 14*(2), 277–291. https://doi.org/10.5465/amle.2013.0106

Alvesson, M., Ashcraft, K., & Thomas, R. (2008). Identity matters: Reflections on the construction of identity scholarship in organisation studies. *Organization, 15*(1), 5–28. https://doi.org/10.1177/1350508407084426

Alvesson, M., & Willmott, H. (2002). Identity regulation as organizational control: Producing the appropriate individual. *Journal of Management Studies, 39*(5), 619–644. https://doi.org/10.1111/1467-6486.00305

Anderson, L. (2011). Time is of the essence: An analytic autoethnography of family, work, and serious leisure. *Symbolic Interaction, 34*(2), 133–157. https://doi.org/10.1525/si.2011.34.2.133

Anderson, L., & Mallanaphy, C. (2020). *British academy of management MKE white paper—Education focused career tracks in UK Business and Management Schools current practice and recommendations for progress.* https://www.bam.ac.uk/bam-community/management-knowledge-education/white-paper.html

Bardon, T., Brown, A., & Pezé, S. (2017). Identity regulation, identity work and phronesis. *Human Relations, 70*(8), 940–965. https://doi.org/10.1177/0018726716680724

Black, K., & Warhurst, R. (2019). Career transition as identity learning: An autoethnographic understanding of human resource development. *Human Resource Development International, 22*(1), 25–43. https://doi.org/10.1080/13678868.2018.1444005

Boyer, E. (1999/2016). *Scholarship reconsidered: Priorities of the professoriate.* Jossey-Bass.

Brommesson, D., Erlingsson, G., Ödalen, J., & Fogelgren, M. (2022). "Teach more, but do not expect any applause": Are women doubly discriminated against in universities' recruitment processes? *Journal of Academic Ethics, 20*(3), 437–450. https://doi.org/10.1007/s10805-021-09421-5

Brown, A. (2017). Identity work and organizational identification. *International Journal of Management Reviews, 19*(3), 296–317. https://doi.org/10.1111/ijmr.12152

Brown, A. (2019). Identities in organisation studies. *Organization Studies, 40*(1), 7–22. https://doi.org/10.1177/0170840618765

Brown, A. (2022). Identities in and around organizations: Towards an identity work perspective. *Human Relations, 75*(7), 1205–1237. https://doi.org/10.1177/0018726721993

Brown, A., Lewis, M., & Oliver, N. (2021). Identity work, loss and preferred identities: A study of UK business school deans. *Organization Studies, 42*(6), 823–844. https://doi.org/10.1177/0170840619857464

Calma, A., & Dickson-Deane, C. (2020). The student as customer and quality in higher education. *International Journal of Educational Management, 34*(8). https://doi.org/10.1108/IJEM-03-2019-0093

Cardel, M., Dhurandhar, E., Yarar-Fisher, C., Foster, M., Hidalgo, B., McClure, L., & Angelini, C. (2020). Turning chutes into ladders for women faculty: A review and roadmap for equity in academia. *Journal of Women's Health, 29*(5), 721–733. https://doi.org/10.1089/jwh.2019.8027

Caza, B., Moss, S., & Vough, H. (2017). From synchronizing to harmonizing: The process of authenticating multiple work identities. *Administrative Science Quarterly, 63*(4), 703–745. https://doi.org/10.1177/0001839217733972

Cooper, O. (2019). Where and what are the barriers to progression for female students and academics in UK higher education? *Perspectives: Policy and Practice in Higher Education, 23*(2–3), 93–100. https://doi.org/10.1080/13603108.2018.1544176

Cotton, E., Beauregard, T., & Keles, J. (2021). Gender equalities: What lies ahead. *Work, Employment and Society, 35*(4), 615–620. https://doi.org/10.1177/09500170211034659

Denney, F. (2023). A glass classroom? The experiences and identities of third space women leading educational change in research-intensive universities in the UK. *Educational Management Administration & Leadership, 51*(6), 1440–1460. https://doi.org/10.1177/17411432211042882

Elsbach, K. (1999). An expanded model of organizational identification. In R. I. Sutton & B. M. Staw (Eds.), *Research in Organizational Behavior, 21*, 163–199.

Gilmore, S., Harding, N., Helin, J., & Pullen, A. (2019). Writing differently. *Management Learning, 50*(1), 3–10. https://doi.org/10.1177/1350507618811027

Górska, A., Kulicka, K., Staniszewska, Z., & Dobija, D. (2021). Deepening inequalities: What did COVID-19 reveal about the gendered nature of academic work? *Gender, Work & Organization, 28*(4), 1546–1561. https://doi.org/10.1111/gwao.12696

Grajfoner, D., Rojon, C., & Eshraghian, F. (2022). Academic leaders: In-role perceptions and developmental approaches. *Educational Management Administration & Leadership, 0*(0), 1–28. https://doi.org/10.1177/1741143222109595

Guilbault, M. (2016). Students as customers in higher education: Reframing the debate. *Journal of Marketing for Higher Education, 26*(2), 132–142. https://doi.org/10.1080/08841241.2016.1245234

Guilbault, M. (2018). Students as customers in higher education: The (controversial) debate needs to end. *Journal of Retailing and Consumer Services, 40*, 295–298. https://doi.org/10.1016/j.jretconser.2017.03.006

Humphreys, M., & Brown, A. (2002). Narratives of organizational identity and identification: A case study of hegemony and resistance. *Organization Studies, 23*(3), 421–447. https://doi.org/10.1177/0170840602233005

Hutchins, H., & Rainbolt, H. (2017). What triggers imposter phenomenon among academic Faculty? A critical incident study exploring antecedents, coping and development opportunities. *Human Resource Development International, 20*(3), 194–214. https://doi.org/10.1080/13678868.2016.1248205

Ibarra, H. (1999). Provisional selves: Experimenting with image and identity in professional adaptation. *Administrative Science Quarterly, 44*(4), 764–791. https://doi.org/10.2307/2667055

Kitchener, M., & Delbridge, R. (2020). Lessons from creating a business school for public good: Obliquity, waysetting, and wayfinding in substantively rational change. *Academy of Management Learning & Education, 19*(3), 307–322. https://doi.org/10.5465/amle.2019.0195

Knights, D., & Clarke, C. (2014). It's a bittersweet symphony, this life: Fragile academic selves and insecure identities at work. *Organization Studies, 35*(3), 335–357. https://doi.org/10.1177/0170840613508396

Learmonth, M., & Humphreys, M. (2012). Autoethnography and academic identity: Glimpsing business school doppelgängers. *Organization, 19*(1), 99–117. https://doi.org/10.1177/1350508411398056

Louw, J. (2019). Going against the grain: Emotional labour in the face of established business school logics. *Studies in Higher Education, 44*(6), 946–959. https://doi.org/10.1080/03075079.2017.1405251

Mansfield, I. (2023, February 16). Providers must submit to regulation—And the OfS to proportionality. *Times Higher Education.*

Marginson, S. (2018). Global trends in higher education financing: The United Kingdom. *International Journal of Educational Development, 58*, 26–36. https://doi.org/10.1016/j.ijedudev.2017.03.008

McInnes, P., & Corlett, S. (2012). Conversational identity work in everyday interaction. *Scandinavian Journal of Management, 28*(1), 27–38. https://doi.org/10.1016/j.scaman.2011.12.004

Mease, J., & Neal, B. (2023). Paradox as resistance in male dominated fields and the value of (sur)facing enthymematic narratives. *Gender, Work & Organization, 30*(4), 1334–1353. https://doi.org/10.1111/gwao.12991

Nicholson, H., & Carroll, B. (2013). Identity undoing and power relations in leadership development. *Human Relations, 66*(9), 1225–1248. https://doi.org/10.1177/0018726712469548

O'Sullivan, K. (2023). *Poor*. Penguin Books.

OfS [Office for Students]. (2022). *Regulatory framework for higher education in England*. https://www.officeforstudents.org.uk/media/1231efe3-e050-47b2-8e63-c6d99d95144f/regulatory_framework_2022.pdf

OfS [Office for Students]. (2023). *Protecting students as consumers*. https://www.officeforstudents.org.uk/publications/protecting-students-as-consumers/

Romero-Hall, E., Aldemir, T., Colorado-Resa, J., Dickson-Deane, C., Watson, G., & Sadaf, A. (2018). Undisclosed stories of instructional design female scholars in academia. *Women's Studies International Forum, 71*, 19–28. https://doi.org/10.1016/j.wsif.2018.09.004

Rosewell, K., & Ashwin, P. (2019). Academics' perceptions of what it means to be an academic. *Studies in Higher Education, 44*(12), 2374–2384. https://doi.org/10.1080/03075079.2018.1499717

Schneider, M., Holman, M., Diekman, A., & McAndrew, T. (2016). Power, conflict, and community: How gendered views of political power influence women's political ambition. *Political Psychology, 37*(4), 515–531. https://doi.org/10.1111/pops.12268

Schoemaker, P. J. (2008). The future challenges of business: Rethinking management education. *California Management Review, 50*(3), 119–139. https://doi.org/10.2307/41166448

Sennett, R. (1998). *The corrosion of character: The personal consequences of work in the new capitalism*. Norton.

Shams, F. (2019). Managing academic identity tensions in a Canadian public university: The role of identity work in coping with managerialism. *Journal of Higher Education Policy and Management, 41*(6), 619–632. https://doi.org/10.1080/1360080X.2019.1643960

Sveningsson, S., & Alvesson, M. (2003). Managing managerial identities: Organizational fragmentation, discourse and identity struggle. *Human Relations, 56*(10), 1163–1193. https://doi.org/10.1177/00187267035610001

Tajfel, H., & Turner, J. (2004). The social identity theory of intergroup behavior. In J. Jost & J. Sidanius (Eds.), *Key readings in social psychology* (pp. 276–293). Psychology Press.

Thornborrow, T., & Brown, A. (2009). 'Being Regimented': Aspiration, discipline and identity work in the British Parachute Regiment. *Organization Studies, 30*(4), 355–376. https://doi.org/10.1177/0170840608101140

Tomlinson, M. (2017). Student perceptions of themselves as 'consumers' of higher education. *British Journal of Sociology of Education, 38*(4), 450–467. https://doi.org/10.1080/01425692.2015.1113856

Turner, J. C., & Reynolds, K. J. (2012). Self-categorization theory. In P. A. M. Van Lange, A. W. Kruglanski, & E. T. Higgins (Eds.), *Handbook of theories of social psychology* (pp. 399–417). Sage. https://doi.org/10.4135/9781446249222.n46

UCU (2022). *Higher education: A workforce in crisis.* https://www.ucu.org.uk/media/12532/UK-higher-education---a-workforce-in-crisis/pdf/UK_HE_Report_24_Mar22.pdf

UKRI (2023). *Knowledge exchange framework.* https://www.ukri.org/what-we-do/supporting-collaboration/supporting-collaboration-research-england/knowledge-exchange-framework/

Urciuoli, B. (2008). Skills and selves in the new workplace. *American Ethnologist, 35*(2), 211–228. https://doi.org/10.1111/j.1548-1425.2008.00031.x

Warhurst, R., & Black, K. (2022). Professionalising education in organisation studies and human resource management. In K. Black & R. Warhurst (Eds.), *Organisation studies and human resource management: An educators handbook.* Routledge. https://doi.org/10.4324/9780429262937-1

Watson, T. (2008). Managing identity: Identity work, personal predicaments and structural circumstances. *Organization, 15*(1), 121–143. https://doi.org/10.1177/1350508407084488

Westoby, C., Dyson, J., Cowdell, F., & Buescher, T. (2021). What are the barriers and facilitators to success for female academics in UK HEIs? *A Narrative Review. Gender and Education, 33*(8), 1033–1056. https://doi.org/10.1080/09540253.2021.1884198

Winkler, I. (2013). Moments of identity formation and reformation: A day in the working life of an academic. *Journal of Organizational Ethnography, 2*(2), 191–209. https://doi.org/10.1108/JOE-11-2011-0001

Wittenberg-Cox, A. (2020, March 2). Business schools are balancing, at last. *Forbes.*

Zaeemdar, S. (2024). Postfeminist technologies of authenticity: Examining the construction of authentic feminine selves in the neoliberal workplace. *Organization*, Online First, https://doi.org/10.1177/13505084231224363

Part III

Homo Mutatus

9

Homo academicus and Gender: The Cracking Assumptions of Rationality

Anna M. Górska

Introduction

Academia is traditionally assumed to be rational, meritocratic, and fair, so alike the academic scholar is assumed to be rational, efficient, and altruistic (Acker & Armenti, 2004; Bourdieu, 1984). Particularly, in the disciplines of management and organization, where the prevailing academic narrative often assumes the rationality of organizations and the maximization of utility and efficiency as the foremost objectives, scholars are implicitly guided by this strong ontological assumption. This assumption posits that the primary purpose of a worker aligns with the principles of *Homo oeconomicus*, where economic self-interest and efficiency are predominant. This perspective deeply influences how these academics perceive and define their roles and contributions within the realm of academia.

A. M. Górska (✉)
Department of Human Resource Management, Kozminski University, Warsaw, Poland
e-mail: amg@kozminski.edu.pl

S. Cinque and D. Ericsson (eds.), *Debating 'Homo Academicus' in Management and Organization*, Palgrave Debates in Business and Management,
https://doi.org/10.1007/978-3-031-58195-3_9

The paradigm of New Public Management (NPM) and its focus on marketization, significantly strengthens these assumptions as well as the roles, responsibilities, and expectations of academics, with far-reaching implications for the quality and purpose of education. As this transformation continues, it is critical to understand its impact on the ontological assumptions that have implications for daily lives and careers of academics, and how it shapes the broader academic environment. Because the transformation of academia is not just about increasing performance metrics or competition, it also involves the "human" aspect: who as academics we think we are, which results in daily work, well-being, and sense of purpose. In this context, a particular attention should be paid to gender aspects, as women often treated as "others" experience additional hurdles in an already demanding environment (Górska, 2023).

This chapter specifically examines the ontological assumptions underlying the dual pressures faced by women in academia within the fields of management and organization, as they navigate the clashing assumptions between the traditional intellectually driven *Homo academicus* and the efficiency-focused *Homo oeconomicus*. Rather than a complete transformation, there exists a persistent internal and institutional conflict: while market-driven metrics increasingly dictate academic success, the enduring pursuit of knowledge for its own sake continues to influence scholarly values, aspirations, and the assumptions they make about themselves. This internal struggle is reflective of broader challenges within academia, where diverse voices often grapple with the mismatch between existing norms and the idealized, yet outdated, assumptions of the academic worker. Through a gendered lens, I aim to deepen the understanding of how these two assumptions coexist and contend within the modern academic landscape.

To accomplish this, I interpret the lived experiences of 54 women working in the fields of management and organization. The study is based in the Central and Eastern Europe (CEE), a region with its distinct socio-political history. By examining the gendered dimensions of *Homo economicus* and *Homo academicus*, my aim is to reveal the underlying assumptions and biases that not only their academic work but also how they understand themselves. To my mind, this is a crucial step toward building more inclusive and equitable academic spaces, where all individuals can thrive and contribute to the advancement of knowledge.

This chapter is structured in the following manner: following this introduction, which sets the stage by discussing the rise of NPM and its impact on academic life, I delve into the evolving ontological assumptions underpinning the identities of academics, particularly in the fields of management and organization. The core of the chapter examines the specific gendered implications of these shifts, utilizing in-depth interviews with women academics to highlight the disparities and challenges they face in the NPM-influenced academic environment. Finally, I conclude by synthesizing the findings, discussing their broader implications for academic practice and policy, and offering recommendations for addressing the identified challenges within the context of management and organization.

Literature Review

Unintended Consequences of New Public Management in Higher Education

In exploring the shifts in the ontological assumptions of academics in management and organization, and the consequences in their roles and identities, it is vital to understand the changes in Higher Education Insitutions (HEIs) environment and changing paradigms. The transformation in HEIs across CEE has brought significant shifts in management paradigms, moving from the Soviet model to Weberian Public Administration (PA) model, and now to NPM, which emphasizes neoliberal principles and market-driven approaches (Dobija et al., 2019; Górska et al., 2022; Vohlídalová, 2012).

The Soviet model, characterized by heavy bureaucracy, high levels of centralization, and a command-and-control culture, was the dominant paradigm across the CEE region. The relationships between the bureaucracy and political power under this model (Pollitt & Bouckaert, 2004), however, were fundamentally different from those in Western liberal democracies. Following the collapse of Soviet-style communism, the inefficiencies inherent in an all-encompassing administrative system became starkly apparent, catalyzing a shift in the management approach of HEIs in the region. The subsequent paradigm, the Weberian PA model, began to transition into the NPM model in recent years, marking a pivotal evolution in the governance of HEIs in the CEE region.

This transition has introduced elements like performance metrics, competition, and a private-sector management style, increasingly shaping HEIs into business-like entities. While aimed at enhancing efficiency and competitiveness, this shift, with its focus on quantifiable outputs and marketization, often undermines the intrinsic values of academia (Halligan, 2010; Parker, 2012). Particularly in management and organizational fields, this trend is more pronounced due to their closer alignment with the private sector. These disciplines are often expected to mirror business practices, reflecting the managerial principles and objectives they teach. As such, the adoption of a business-like approach in these areas is not only a reflection of broader trends in higher education but also a natural consequence of the fundamental principles of management and organization that underpin their academic and pedagogical frameworks.

NPM, as conceptualized by Hood (2000), encompasses several key components, including hands-on professional management in the public sector, explicit standards and measures of performance, a greater emphasis on output controls, disaggregation of units in the public sector, competition in the public sector, and a focus on private-sector styles of management. Additionally, the NPM model stresses discipline and parsimony in resource use. This shift embodies the infusion of neoliberal ideologies into public sector reforms, as illustrated by the incorporation of business-type managerial and market principles from the private sector into HEIs (Hood, 2000; Sułkowski, 2016).

A fundamental aspect of the NPM logic is the increased reliance on markets, competition, and contracts for resource allocation and service delivery within public services (Osborne, 2006). This competitive and market-driven approach underpins the operational structure and strategic orientation of current HEIs in the CEE region.

This transition in higher education, driven by a desire to increase performance and competitiveness and orient the sector more toward market demands, reflects a profound shift in the ontological assumptions about the nature and purpose of academic work. Rooted in NPM principles of "value for money" and "management by objectives", this paradigm shift places a strong emphasis on the performativity of academics and institutions, subtly redefining their roles from educators and researchers to performers in a market-driven environment (Parker et al., 2021; Pollitt & Bouckaert, 2004). This emphasis on efficiency and measurable outcomes creates a framework where women academics, often grappling with additional responsibilities such as domestic duties and caregiving, are perceived as "riskier" investments (Burkinshaw, 2015; Fox et al., 2017). The insistence on performance and competition among institutions has led to a deep-rooted accountingization, economization, and marketization of HEIs (Parker, 2012; Parker et al., 2021). This evolution toward neoliberal values and practices signifies a fundamental change in how universities are perceived and valued, moving away from traditional educational ideals to a model where university outputs are commodified, and institutions are expected to meet governmental and market needs with utmost efficiency.

Universities are increasingly being modeled after private-sector businesses, with academics being redefined as CEOs, managers, and employees with corporate boards. As I argued above, business schools and management and organization faculties in particular are more predisposed to adopt these private-sector approaches. The introduction of NPM has led to the rise of an audit culture in academia. This culture is focused on quantified measurements, evaluations, and productivity, leading to the commodification of academic performance (Power, 1997). Metrics such as quality of research, teaching, journals lists, and rankings have become the definition of academic performance, replacing academic value or societal impact (Martin-Sardesai et al., 2017; Shore & Wright, 2015). Moreover these quantified measures became a goal itself.

Contrary to the belief that performance evaluations are rational and unbiased, research indicates that our judgments are often influenced by an effortless, rapid, and unconscious mode of cognition, as shown in studies by Conway et al. (1995), Dane and Pratt (2007), and

Evans (2008), influencing on how we evaluate people, which also has its gendered consequences. Gender status beliefs lead to double standards in performance evaluations, affecting how women and men are assessed differently, especially in academic contexts. This bias is evident in the evaluation of women for grants, scholarships, awards, and even in double-blind peer-review processes, where women face stricter scrutiny and more critical evaluations (Biernat et al., 1991; Biernat & Manis, 1994; Foschi, 1996, 2000; Fox, 1991; 2019; Fox et al., 2017; Górska, 2017; Hengel, 2017; Moss-Racusin et al., 2012; Trevino et al., 2017). This also leads to different fundamental beliefs of "who am I" as an academic between women and men.

Under the constant evaluations, universities managers have to think strategically about their employees and their performativity, and who will generate the highest "value" under the NPM ideology, they promote and strengthen the existing power structures. As the career progress in academia rests on evaluation of outcomes, measured in the form of publications, grants, citations, teaching hours, and student's evaluation, academics often pursue these outcomes strategically, focusing on "what counts" rather than "what matters". This trend not only undermines workplace morale but also reflects a shift in the ontological assumptions of academics, where the intrinsic values of education and knowledge creation are overshadowed by a market-driven rationale, gradually eroding the fundamental purpose of the higher education sector (Halligan, 2010).

The prevailing focus on metrics and performance evaluations in academia not only limits the recognized scope of research and teaching but also signifies a fundamental shift in the ontological assumptions about what constitutes valuable academic work. As highlighted by Archer (2008), this trend, with its bias toward quantitative and objective measures, inadvertently elevates research activities over more relational and communal forms of academic engagement, such as teaching and mentoring. These latter aspects, often associated with feminized roles within the academic framework, are undervalued and less recognized. This emphasis contributes to a gendered division of labor, where women are disproportionately engaged in and often confined to these less esteemed yet crucial areas of academic practice (Górska et al., 2021;

Morley, 2003). Such a dichotomy in the valuation of academic activities reflects a deeper ontological shift, where the market-driven metrics overshadow the broader, more inclusive understanding of academic contributions and roles.

At the same time NPM logic creates a myth of rationality and meritocracy, as it is to be based on measurable values that are the same for everyone (Fleming, 2017). However, despite claims of objectivity and meritocracy, NPM criteria tend to favor existing power structures (Ball, 2012; Parker et al., 2021), predominantly male-dominated, thereby exacerbating gender inequalities in academia (Acker & Armenti, 2004; Altbach et al., 2009). This system often penalizes women, whose career paths may not align with the male-centric norms of mobility, research focus, and uninterrupted career trajectories (Garforth & Kerr, 2010; Gonzalez Ramos et al., 2015). The performance-based culture, premised on a rationality and meritocracy, often fails to recognize the unique challenges faced by female academics, disregarding the varied life experiences and challenges. The neoliberalism of higher education has fostered the belief that gender is irrelevant and that the culture of HEIs is gender-neutral.

While NPM purports to be objective and meritocratic, it actually exacerbates gender biases in academia (Acker & Armenti, 2004; Altbach et al., 2009; Fox et al., 2017; Górska, 2023; Trevino et al., 2017). Studies showcase that women in academia are treated differently by their peers, subordinates, supervisors, and even students (Burkinshaw, 2015; Fox et al., 2017; Hengel, 2017; Spoon et al., 2023; Van den Brink and Benschop, 2012). Implicit biases and gender-based stereotypes create situations where women are treated as "the other", leading to isolation and a reduced sense of belonging.

Another drawback of focusing on metrics and performance evaluations in academia is that it can lead to a culture of overwork and burnout. The unrelenting pressure to publish and produce measurable outcomes can be overwhelming for both men and women. However, since women tend to have more caregiving responsibilities outside of work, it is even more difficult for them to meet the expectations set by the system (Górska et al., 2021; Morley, 2003). This scenario reflects a fundamental assumption in academia that equates academic worth with continuous, measurable productivity, disregarding the diverse life circumstances of academics, particularly affecting women with dual roles. This leaves less room for diversity and for those who "stick out" from the default expectations become "risky employee" or "the other". This tendency is rooted in an assumption that views deviation from the "ideal academic"—often implicitly modeled on a male, uninterrupted career path—as a liability or a divergence from the norm. This affects women and men differently, as women in neoliberal HEI where quantified measures have become a goal in itself, may be seen as riskier employees, due to their second shift at home, the possibility of taking maternity leave, and their caring duties. Thus, the realities of women and men academics differ under the logic of NPM (Ball, 2012), highlighting the need to reconceptualize these ontological assumptions to embrace a broader and more inclusive understanding of academic contributions and career trajectories.

Homo academicus and *Homo oeconomicus*

The transition toward NPM in academia, with its emphasis on market-oriented efficiency and quantifiable outputs, cascades down onto academics and represents a paradigmatic shift from the values embodied by *Homo academicus* to those of *Homo oeconomicus*. This shift toward a utilitarian approach prioritizes economic gains and productivity in academic institutions. Consequently, the ideals of academia—rooted in the pursuit of knowledge and humanistic values—are increasingly overshadowed by pragmatic, profit-driven imperatives. This reflects a significant shift in the ontological assumptions within academia, where the intrinsic purpose and values of academic work are being redefined in terms of market utility and economic efficiency, challenging the very essence of the ontological assumptions, academic identity and mission. This tension not only redefines the operational dynamics of higher education but also reflects a fundamental philosophical conflict within the academic sphere.

This dilemma between the academic ideals and pragmatic imperatives was described by Bourdieu. In his 1984 book "*Homo Academicus*", Pierre Bourdieu presented two distinct and opposite constructs—*Homo academicus* and *Homo oeconomicus*—rooted in contrasting notions of values and operational dynamics within the university environment. *Homo academicus* represents humanistic values, the search for truth, and the creation and dissemination of knowledge. Conversely, *Homo oeconomicus* is market-oriented, relentlessly driven by efficiency, and aims to maximize utility. Bourdieu's constructs provide a critical lens through which to examine the evolving ontological assumptions in academia, especially how the shift toward NPM is altering the fundamental nature and purpose of academic work, pushing it away from its traditional ethos toward a more market-driven identity.

In the eyes of Bourdieu *Homo academicus* and *Homo oeconomicus* coexist within the academic sphere but represent a modern embodiment of the timeless struggle between David and Goliath (Czerepaniak-Walczak, 2014). Yet, in this narrative, David's humanistic values, represented by *Homo academicus*, seem to have lost ground to Goliath's market-oriented efficiency, embodied by *Homo oeconomicus*. Current academic institutions mirror this power shift, where universities, governed by economic imperatives, are shaped by competitiveness and profit-driven logic. This fierce competition extends to academics who, like their institutions, compete for grants, scholarships, publications, and positions. The systemic pressure cascading onto academics compels them to adopt the norms of *Homo oeconomicus* to remain relevant.

This framework as proposed by Bourdieu, however, overlooks the gendered experiences in academia. Women, facing unique challenges such as balancing professional and caregiving roles, encounter additional hurdles in this environment. This situation reveals a deeper ontological oversight in Bourdieu's framework, where the nuanced realities of gender dynamics and their impact on academic roles and identities are not adequately considered. The pressure to conform to *Homo oeconomicus*, while navigating societal expectations and structural biases, disproportionately impacts female academics. This discrepancy underscores an implicit notions within the academic milieu that does not fully account for the diverse life experiences and constraints faced by women in academia, thereby perpetuating gender disparities in a system increasingly aligned with the principles of *Homo oeconomicus*.

In line with Bourdieu's constructs, *Homo academicus* position within the academic hierarchy was traditionally determined by scientific achievements, evaluated by peer reviewers within the academic community. In contrast, *Homo oeconomicus* is placed within the hierarchy based on economic accomplishments such as profitability and financial gains. However, the prevailing economic paradigm within academia conflates these two constructs. Institutions today are driven by the mandate to be profitable and competitive in all their functions. Full professors are deemed "too expensive" for long teaching hours, passing that burden to adjunct and assistant professors, (regardless of teaching quality), as well as onto women who are seen as natural teachers (regardless of their preferences). As a result, women often shoulder a higher teaching load, a task perceived as less prestigious under NPM framework (Ash, 2017), while at the same time women being evaluated more harshly than men (Fan et al., 2019). Research, too, is increasingly commodified, with a rising emphasis on publishing in prestigious and ranked journals to secure funding, and sometimes even monetary rewards by academics. This aspect of academic work is also gendered, as female-authored papers are subjected to more rigorous editorial scrutiny and prolonged peer-review process (Fox, 1991; Hengel, 2017).

Even the concept of research "impact" has become commodified (Dobija et al., 2019; Smith et al., 2013), whereas academics are expected to measure and report, the societal impact of their work, based on which often funds are granted. This shift suggests that the idea of research that doesn't immediately or visibly contribute to economic development or industry progress is less likely to receive funding. Thus, academics are held hostage to a utilitarian mindset that requires quantifiable, economically beneficial research outcomes. Under this systemic influence, academics are judged based on their economic output, while these judgements as argued before are not gender-neutral. Today's academia welcomes these principles, enforcing a constant assessment of academics' measurable outputs that can be compared to others, as these become the goal in itself. This paradigm shift is evident in academia's increasing reliance on metrics of productivity, efficiency, and rationality—principles firmly rooted in the construct of *Homo oeconomicus*. Hence, to sustain their careers, academics are urged to think strategically about their measurable outcomes and act as *Homo oeconomicus*.

The landscape of modern academia presents a complex image where the ideals of Bourdieu's *Homo academicus* are not eclipsed but haunted by the pragmatic approach of *Homo oeconomicus*. Both constructs are entangled within the institution and, more significantly, have cascaded down to individuals, who themselves may experience an internal conflict. This situation reflects a profound ontological dilemma in academia, where the deep-seated beliefs and values about the nature and purpose of academic work are being challenged and reshaped by market-driven imperatives. Although the contemporary academic environment increasingly embodies the principles of *Homo oeconomicus,* suggesting a dominance of this paradigm, there remains a persistent presence of *Homo academicus*. This juncture represents a pivotal shift in academia's philosophy, where the scholarly mission is under pressure from economic imperatives, engendering a professional dichotomy that continues to define and complicate the academic experience.

Finally, as women and men face different challenges in academia, the pressure of *Homo oeconomicus* is particularly intertwined with societal expectations for women. This interplay further accentuates the ontological struggle, where the gendered experiences in academia are shaped not only by philosophical conflicts between *Homo academicus* and *Homo oeconomicus* but also by societal norms and biases. Thus, the dichotomy between *Homo academicus* and *Homo oeconomicus* is not only a philosophical struggle but also a reflection of gendered realities in the academic world, highlighting an urgent need to reconsider and broaden the ontological assumptions that underlie the academic profession.

Doing Gender in Academia

As discussed above, the transition to NPM and the framework of *Homo academicus* and *Homo oeconomicus* has a different impact on women and men. Gender dynamics in academia are not simply a mirror of societal gender biases but are integral to the perpetuation and consolidation of male dominance (Acker, 1990, 1992). This dynamic is deeply rooted in the ontological assumptions of academic institutions, where traditional male-centric models are often the default, shaping the expectations and evaluations within these environments.

Gender is a core concept for distinguishing our lives and understanding how people encounter organizations. It is both performed and performative, shaping our perceptions, practices, and attitudes. Although gendered structures, processes, and practices are presented as gender-neutral, they in fact perpetuate and preserve gender inequalities. The persistence of these gendered practices reflects an underlying ontological assumption that academic success and validity are predominantly defined through a male lens, often marginalizing or overlooking the contributions and challenges of women in academia.

As organizational culture is reflected in what is done, how it's done, and who is doing it; therefore, it has both instrumental and symbolic value (Acker, 1992; Stainback et al., 2016). Organizational cultures, processes, structures, and daily behaviors constitute an ideal or typical employee, while these images often fall under the image of masculinity. Despite the increase in female representation among students and faculty, academic environments often uphold masculine norms as the benchmark for success, while women remain "the other" (Burkinshaw, 2015; Górska, 2023). These gender dynamics are deeply rooted in ontological assumptions about the academic profession and who the "perfect academic" is, often excluding or diminishing the experiences and achievements of women in academia.

Moreover, as under NPM, HEIs present themselves as gender-neutral meritocracies, the realities are inherently gendered and gendering (Fox et al., 2017; Savigny, 2014). The criteria and objectives of measuring performance are based on a default, male-dominated model, penalizing women whose career paths do not fit this model (Garforth & Kerr, 2010; Gonzalez Ramos et al., 2015; Savigny, 2014; Trevino et al., 2017). The idealized academic worker norm is often seen as male, with the focus on mobility, research, and uninterrupted career, and the penalization of any departures from these standards, prioritizes individual rather than collective merits. This principle of excellence, rooted in traditional male-centric ontological assumptions, not only holds women in academia to a double standard but also reflects a broader ontological misalignment, where the diverse realities and contributions of women are consistently underrecognized and undervalued.

This misalignment presents a profound challenge for women, who face systemic inequalities in research, teaching, and administrative roles. For example, women academics frequently find themselves shouldering a disproportionate burden of administrative and teaching tasks, assignments perceived under NPM as less prestigious, and which do not directly contribute to their career advancement (Górska, 2023). This allocation often results from systemic pressures and inherent biases within the academic structure, revealing an ontological discrepancy where the value of different academic roles is unevenly distributed, often to the disadvantage of women. These tasks, though crucial for the functioning of the institution, often consume a significant amount of time and energy that could otherwise be channeled into research and publication efforts, potentially hindering the professional development and recognition.

Studies have shown that women face tougher standards, their qualifications and abilities are underestimated, and evaluations in teaching, administrative work, and research are biased against them (Barres, 2006; Fox, 1991; Moss-Racusin et al., 2012; Scott, 2020). In research, for example, female-authored papers are often held to stricter editorial standards and longer peer reviews than male-authored papers, despite studies showing that female-authored papers tend to be better written (Fox, 1991; Hengel, 2017). This "publishing paradox" is a manifestation of the deeply entrenched ontological assumptions within academia that undervalue the contributions of women, reinforcing gender disparities under the guise of objectivity and meritocracy.

Moreover, although teaching is seen as a "natural" domain of women in academia, studies in this regard are also not optimistic and have shown that women are often evaluated less favorably than their male colleagues, regardless of their actual performance in the classroom (Fan et al., 2019). This bias against women teachers could harm their careers, as universities often use student evaluations to make decisions about hiring, tenure, and promotions.

In administrative work, women tend to be tasked with "institutional housekeeping", which is seen as "women's work" (Górska, 2023).

However, despite the critical nature of this work, it is often unappreciated, invisible, and uncompensated, pulling academics away from their primary responsibilities (Ash, 2017), as performing these administrative tasks rarely result in women being promoted to leadership positions (Burkinshaw, 2015). This reflects an ontological bias in academia, where the value of different types of work is hierarchically ordered, often to the disadvantage of women, perpetuating systemic gender inequalities.

The issue of gender inequality in HEIs extends beyond these issues to everyday interactions, attitudes, and behaviors that create a hostile environment for women. As Fisher and Kinsey (2014) argue, one contributing factor to gender discrimination is the prevailing masculinity in HEIs. Masculinity invisibly shapes social relations; however, its significance is concealed by its constitution as the default, neutral, and universal, revealing an ontological assumption that normalizes and privileges male perspectives and experiences in academia. This masculine bias, often institutionalized in the form of an academic "boys' club", reinforces gender discrimination, making the academic journey more demanding for women (Dixon-Reeves, 2003; Garrett, 2006).

In the context of NPM and the *Homo oeconomicus* paradigm, academic institutions' focus on excellence and quantifiable measures intensifies gender disparities. This framework, emphasizing efficiency and measurable outcomes, disproportionately affects women academics, reflecting an ontological bias where the academic model is tailored to a male-dominated perspective, often disregarding the unique challenges and contributions of women. Although NPM values, with the ethos of *Homo oeconomicus* promise fairness, objectivity, and equity, what we have witnessed is rather a stratification and intensification of competition, which tends to favor those already privileged and compound inequalities for women and other disadvantaged groups. This situation underscores the need to critically examine and challenge the ontological assumptions that underpin current academic practices, fostering an environment where diverse experiences and contributions are recognized and valued equally.

Method

To better understand how women perceive their role as academics, the expectations from universities and stakeholders and their own lived experiences, I conducted a qualitative research study based on semi-structured interviews with 54 women academics from CEE. The choice of method was based on the desire to prioritize women's voices in constructing the narrative of their own experiences. Qualitative research was also deemed appropriate as it is context-sensitive and allowed for a deeper understanding of the phenomenon in its natural context (Parsons & Priola, 2013). Semi-structured interviews balanced structure with flexibility. While they ensured coverage of the research questions and desired topics, they also allowed gave interviewees the leeway to express their opinions and actions candidly.

The sample for the study was selected using purposive sampling, which entailed recruiting respondents based on their experience, position, career stage, and country. All interviewed women were academics from college of business and management or from business schools, specifically working in the field of management and organization. Purposive sampling ensured the inclusion of a diverse group of respondents, which helped to elicit a broad range of perspectives. Because of COVID-19 restrictions, all interviews were conducted in English via Microsoft Teams or Zoom. A total of 54 interviews were conducted for this study. While the majority of these interviews were recorded and transcribed for analysis, there were instances where interviewees did not consent to be recorded. In such cases, the analysis relied on comprehensive notes taken during the interviews.

The coding and analysis of the interviews were conducted using MAXqda computer software, which supports researcher in the coding process (Kuckartz, 2014). Firstly, open coding was used to code the raw data that allowed to emerge themes (Corbin & Strauss, 2014). This inductive approach allowed for the identification of recurrent patterns, sentiments, and concepts from the participants' narratives.

Next, axial coding was used to synthesize and organize these initial codes and provide a more coherent framework that allowed to establish connections and relationships between the codes and further sort them into broader categories. Finally, the analysis involved the selective coding, where the core categories allowed for broader and theoretical schemes (Charmaz, 2014; Corbin & Strauss, 2014).

Despite the differences in national policies and internal university policies regarding performance evaluations, the analysis revealed common themes in the experiences of the female academics in this study. The NPM paradigm, with its focus on performance and metrics, the increasing weight given to publication, and the devaluation of teaching and social work were apparent throughout the interviews. Although from previous research we know that both women and men may experience similar barriers within academia, in this study I specifically prioritized the voices and experiences of women academics to showcase "who they are" under the notion of increased neoliberal values across academia.

Results

In the course of the interviews, it becomes evident that as academia in the CEE region undergoes its transformation toward NPM and marketization, there is a fundamental shift in the ontological assumptions underpinning the roles, responsibilities, and expectations of academics. This shift is marked by an intensified focus on measurable outcomes, evidenced by new requirements for publication in indexed journals, international collaboration, and heightened competition for grants, scholarships, and awards. Interviewees express concerns about the ambiguity and constant changes in expectations stemming from national regulations, accreditations, and ranking agencies, which directly influence their performance evaluations. Consequently, this evolving landscape, driven by market-oriented ontological assumptions, places academics in a state of flux, challenging their ability to effectively plan and prioritize work within the shifting paradigms of academic values and responsibilities.

> I don't know how to prepare for these [changes] (…) So, every time there are different expectations, obligations, rules. (R19)

The shifting expectations of academics, propelled by a confluence of external forces such as governments, accreditation institutions, and competitors, as well as evolving internal objectives, have led to a crisis among academics. They find themselves grappling with changing evaluations and expectations, as highlighted by the experiences of the interviewees. This rapidly evolving environment not only fosters uncertainty and inconsistency in institutional directions and priorities but also deeply affects the self-conception of individual academics. Many interviewees express a sense of disorientation and identity loss, as articulated by respondents:

> So, we actually don't know where the school is going or you know, what we are doing or why we are doing it. We are changing constantly. The management calls it "agile". I see it more as inconsistent. As a result, I also don't know where to go and what to do. (R13)
>
> I remember when the most important thing was teaching, then suddenly research, then publications in Scopus journals. Now they talk about impact. Who knows what will be in five years? (R19)

The ongoing evolution in university expectations is not just altering external demands on academics; it's fundamentally reshaping their ontological assumptions about their roles and purposes. This shift from a primary focus on teaching, to research, and now toward creating a positive societal impact, coupled with intensifying pressures to publish and compete, has introduced a profound sense of uncertainty and inconsistency into the academic sphere. Academics find themselves in a dilemma, attempting to navigate this shifting terrain where the benchmarks for success and recognition are constantly changing. As a result, the interviewees underscore the necessity to adapt and strategize their professional endeavors in a landscape where the very essence of "what counts" as academic achievement is in a state of continuous evolution. This situation not only challenges their practical approaches but also leads to deeper introspection and questioning of their identity and values as academics, reflecting the complex interplay of changing ontological assumptions in academia.

Publishing: Goal for All and Privilege for Few

The increasing importance of research and active publishing is evident from the interviews. However, despite this heightened emphasis, HEIs seem to provide only limited support for academics in terms of release time, lighter teaching quotas, fewer administrative responsibilities, and research funding. Consequently, many academics are left to conduct research in the little "free" time they have, often on weekends or late at night.

> And that the pressure was really big in the last years, but they didn't reduce our teaching loads, so we don't really have enough time to do research. And so that was a problem. (…) We do research during the weekends, holidays and late at night. (R24)

Moreover, it seems that these additional teaching and administrative work loads are gendered and often seen as "female work", which I argue in the next section. At the same time the interviewees expressed growing frustration that even though the university has assigned them teaching and administrative responsibilities, research remains a determining factor in their performance evaluations.

> I see that all this teaching and admin side are viewed as kind of like an unnecessary thing we have to do and then research is the main thing, focus, basis of all the evaluations and everything. But research side is demanding in the sense that I constantly feel that I'm expected to do more than I'm able to do. (R13)

This dilemma has led to a focus on fulfilling publication requirements just for the sake of job security, rather than producing meaningful research that has academic and societal value. It seems that academics are acutely aware of the tension between managerial demands reflective of *Homo oeconomicus* and their own commitment to conducting meaningful and significant research, an embodiment of the *Homo academicus* ideal.

> To do good, valuable research, you need time and space. But now all we are doing is what is expected to fulfil the requirements and keep our jobs (...) we publish meaningless shitty (sic.) research just to publish anything and keep the job. (R51)

At the same time academics who publish are "rewarded" with lighter teaching loads on the one hand and "punished" with more administrative work on the other. Moreover, interviewees said that they are often forced to subsidize their own research, as the competition for grants is too intense and the university will not provide sufficient funding. Ultimately, the ability to conduct research becomes a privilege reserved for those who have the financial means and time to do so, further exacerbating gender disparities within academia.

Balancing Acts: Research, Teaching, Administrative and Invisible Work

Interviewees insist that the focus on research has relegated teaching to a secondary obligation, even though it is the most time-consuming of their professional responsibilities. Its value is diminishing in the eyes of the academics, leading to a decline in motivation among faculty to advance their teaching skills. Furthermore, the additional work and emotional labor associated with teaching often go unrecognized and unappreciated by university management.

> Well, honestly, it doesn't really matter how well I teach. It's not recognized much here. Good or bad teacher, it really doesn't matter. Sometimes I ask myself, what's the point? What's the difference? (R8)
>
> No one really wants to teach anymore because research is the only thing that counts. And then you want to do teaching on this very minimum level in terms of your own effort, in terms of how good it is to the students. You just teach well enough not to get into trouble basically, but nobody cares. (R48)

This shows that academics *have* to consider and strategize what "counts" further in evaluations, rather than what matters. There is a visible tension between their professional actions and personal convictions, often manifesting as a profound sense of doubt and a waning sense of purpose, encapsulated in "What's the point?" This doubt into the purpose of academic work as well as themselves was expressed in one of the interviews:

> At this point I don't know why to do it well anymore. My boss cares only about the research, students care only about passing [the course]. (…) I think I'm losing a meaning (…) but never feel like I'm doing enough. (R24)

This internal discord underscores the struggle between the economic imperatives of *Homo oeconomicus* and the scholarly values of *Homo academicus*. At the same time, it seems that interviews not only lose a sense of "mission" of academia, but also have signs of self-doubt. The notion of not doing enough was echoed by many women interviewees, who expressed feelings of inadequacy, reflecting a deeper ontological challenge in aligning with the evolving expectations of academia. The conflict between pursuing what is quantifiably recognized versus what is intrinsically valuable appears to erode their sense of integrity as scholars, as they navigate a landscape where their traditional academic values are often at odds with the prevailing market-driven criteria. Furthermore, the issue of teaching highlights another ontological disconnect in academia. Teaching, which involves a substantial amount of "invisible work"—including class preparation, assignment administration and grading, and office hours—is often undervalued and unacknowledged by university management. Despite the significant workload, the institutional evaluation of teaching is frequently reduced to mere teaching hours, neglecting the quality of teaching and the additional time and effort invested by educators. This oversight reflects a deeper ontological misalignment in academia, where the comprehensive role and contribution of teaching are overshadowed by a narrow focus on quantifiable metrics, failing to recognize the full spectrum of efforts that constitute effective pedagogy. Consequently, faculty members who feel discouraged and undervalued seek ways to cut corners and save time, often at the expense of the quality of their classes. As one interviewee shared:

> Each year I'm trying to cut my time spend on preparing for class and grading students. I no longer ask students to write reports; these are time consuming to check and evaluate. Now they got computer exams that automatically grade them. (R24)

The devaluation of invisible work has consequences for both educators and students. For teachers, it can cause frustration and burnout. This can erode their dedication to teaching, potentially undermining their students' educational experience. Female faculty also mentioned the additional challenge of students being more demanding and disrespectful. In the words of one faculty member:

> I had students commenting on my looks, the way I dress (…) others tried to intimidate me. This doesn't happen to my male colleagues. (R15)

This is the example of how women feel objectified by students. Women cope with this by dressing "appropriately" when going to classes and even meeting with men. This necessitates a conscious adaptation in their appearance and behavior, as shared by one of the respondents:

> I have studied some psychology, so I adjust even body language. I think it's also important like the way how you speak, the way how you are dressed, all this should be kind of appropriate. (R14)

This adaptation goes beyond mere surface-level changes. It involves a deeper transformation where women feel compelled to "fit in" to the prevailing masculine norms of academia. This is not just a matter of changing dress or demeanor but adjusting their very identity to survive and succeed in a gendered environment. Another respondent shared:

> And I have built a really strict aura around myself to fight to those sexist things. (R17)

This indicates a profound psychological and ontological dilemma for women in academia, as they navigate a landscape dominated by masculine expectations. This phenomenon represents a form of invisible and emotional labor that is uniquely experienced by women in academia.

They are forced to engage in this additional work to be accepted and respected in their professional spheres.

Paraphrasing Faulkner's (2009) findings about women engineers: women academics are simultaneously highly visible as women yet invisible as academics. This duality of being both visible and invisible adds a significant burden, stemming from gender biases, which affects not just their professional trajectory but also their personal sense of self. Consequently, women in academia find themselves in a constant process of renegotiating their identities, struggling to assert their scholarly value in a space frequently influenced by gendered perceptions.

From another perspective, this study echoes previous findings that female faculty experience a heavier burden of invisible or undervalued labor in the forms of mentoring, committee work, and administrative tasks. This extra workload takes their time and focus away from the research that is a decisive factor in their productivity and career advancement. In their interviews, women mentioned the work that they did for the university, supporting students and shouldering uncompensated and unacknowledged administrative obligations that are not considered in the performance evaluations that are so crucial under the NPM logic. Nevertheless, this type of work keeps the university functioning:

> I don't think that even the leaders are aware of how much [administrative] work I do. Still, no one cares, I have to publish and teach as usual. (R6)

The interviews revealed that administrative work is "women's work", not only because it is more likely to be assigned to them, but also because it was assumed to be normal and natural role of women.

> When we have some administrative stuff at our department, it is always women doing it. (…) It is normal, no? (R7)

The gendered nature of administrative work in academia not only reflects but also reinforces deep-rooted ontological assumptions about gender roles in the academic environment. This disparity has profound consequences for the career progression and job satisfaction of women academics. The additional workload from administrative tasks often detracts from the time and focus they can dedicate to research and teaching. These latter activities are typically more valued in academic performance evaluations, thus affecting women's opportunities for career advancement and recognition. Moreover, despite their substantial contribution to administrative work, women seldom see this involvement translate into higher representation in leadership or senior academic positions. This perpetuates a systemic gender imbalance in the academic hierarchy and highlights an ontological misalignment in how contributions are valued and rewarded in academia. Women in academia, therefore, face a double bind: their extensive administrative responsibilities, essential for the functioning of academic institutions, are undervalued, while their underrepresentation in leadership roles continues to uphold the gender disparities in academic power structures.

Gendered Aspects of *Homo academicus* in Academia of *Homo economicus*

Under the NPM both academics and their institutions are being transformed. With the intense pressures to publish, internationalize, and compete with other institutions, academics have become more focused on doing what counts, rather than what matters. This leads to the situation in which academics simply "play the game" by neglecting their teaching to produce the research that will be the basis of their performance evaluations.

> I do what I have to do. If it's research that counts, well someone's gotta pay, and in most cases it's students. (R4)

The lack of fit between university expectations reflected in the performance evaluations and teaching and administrative tasks, leads to academics feeling burned out, unmotivated, and frustrated.

> On the one hand I keep hearing that research is all that matters, but then I look at the scope of my responsibilities and there is no time for research in my day, week and sometimes even a month. (…) This is frustrating. (R17)

As a result of the NPM-driven emphasis on publication metrics, academics find their motivation to engage in socially valuable work, effective teaching, or conference organization diminishing, primarily because such contributions are often undervalued by their managers. This growing focus on quantifiable outputs coerces academics into embodying the role of *Homo oeconomicus*, where rational choices aimed at career advancement take precedence. This paradigm shift is particularly impactful for those who deviate from the stereotypical and idealized academic model. Academics who do not fit this mold find themselves in a position where they must continually legitimize and strengthen their standing within the academic community. They face an ontological challenge, navigating an environment that narrowly defines academic success and worth, compelling them to prioritize activities that align with these constrained metrics over broader scholarly pursuits.

> So, it is not a fair system, I think, because if only publication counts and if you don't have time either because you have so many teaching obligations or because you organize something, an event, a conference together with your students, it is taken as your private issue and it is not really included into the evaluation (...) so what is the point of this additional work? (R37)

It should be also emphasized that interviewees notice that women are expected to take on additional administrative and invisible work, more teaching obligations and contend with the masculine culture of academia. Moreover, with their caring duties and family obligations, women have less time and energy to devote to the research that is so valuable for university managers.

The frustration as seen by one of the interviewees echoed in the following citation:

> I can't win, no matter what we do it is not enough. I think that even if you'd focus only on research and have the great publication record, then they would say that it's not impactful enough or that you don't do admin work, or that students don't like you. (R24)

This statement captures the profound disillusionment and self-doubt experienced by women academics, reflecting a broader sense of inadequacy stemming from the multifaceted challenges they encounter. This feeling seems to be the reflection of all the above-shown challenges: it is not just about being overlooked or objectified, but also about constantly shifting evaluation criteria and the burden of additional, often unpaid, administrative work. While male academics may face similar challenges, for women, these are compounded by the "otherness" they experience within the academic setting.

In management and organization, where the ethos of academia meets corporate efficiency, women are often perceived as riskier hires and expected to manage additional domestic responsibilities alongside their professional duties. This intersection of gender stereotypes, objectification, and the expectation to conform to masculine norms within these specific academic fields represents a persistent struggle. As Monroe et al. (2008) observed, women in academia, particularly in management and organization, find themselves navigating a unique predicament: they must balance the traditional academic values of *Homo academicus* with the market-driven imperatives of *Homo oeconomicus*, all while contending with entrenched gender biases.

Unlike their male counterparts, women must consider not only their personal values and academic aspirations but also the prevailing societal norms about what it means to be a woman in academia. This complex interplay of gendered expectations and professional ambitions highlights the unique challenges that women face in what is often perceived as a meritocratic and fair academic environment. The pursuit of what "counts" for evaluations gains even greater urgency as they endeavor to establish their worth within a traditionally male-dominated academic landscape. This necessity to focus on quantifiable achievements to "catch up" does not always align with the scholarly integrity they seek to maintain, resulting in a conflict that underscores the complex interplay of gender and professional identity in the academic realm.

Discussion

This chapter underscores that the evolving demands in universities, especially within management and organization disciplines, reflect deep-seated ontological shifts in academic identities. The rise of NPM has not only changed structural aspects of academia but has fundamentally altered the self-concept and professional identity of scholars in these fields. These changes have forced academics to reevaluate their ontological beliefs resulting shift of their roles, responsibilities, and expectations within the university setting, leading to a conflict between traditional academic values of *Homo academicus* and the new corporate-like norms of *Homo oeconomicus* (Ball, 2012). The findings of this study align with and extend the literature on the impact of NPM on HEIs and the academic profession, particularly in terms of the growing emphasis on research and publishing, and the gendered aspects of academic work (Acker & Armenti, 2004; Altbach et al., 2009).

Central to this discussion is the transformation of the academic self under NPM. This model prioritizes research output and economic efficiency, compelling scholars to adopt a persona more aligned with *Homo oeconomicus*, characterized by a focus on individual achievements and metrics. This shift represents a significant departure from the communal and collegial ethos traditionally associated with *Homo academicus*. The findings from the interviews with women academics in the management field highlight this tension, revealing how gendered expectations further complicate their professional identities and roles. The pressure to conform to a more economically driven identity, while also struggling with systemic gender biases, exemplifies the complex ontological negotiations that academics, particularly women, navigate.

As the interviews reveal, the lack of support from HEIs in terms of time, resources, and funding has forced many academics to conduct research during their limited free time, often leading to burnout and a decline in the quality of their teaching and research output. As a result, it seems that academics lose their sense of purpose and meaning of the work, as fulfilling requirements becomes the goal on its own. This finding supports the argument that the rise of NPM principles compels scholars to adopt a persona resembling *Homo oeconomicus*, prioritizing career-centric achievements over the erstwhile communal academic ethos of *Homo academicus* (Ball, 2012). Under the NPM model, the current academic landscape is characterized by *Homo academicus* in academia of *Homo economicus*. Yet, it isn't a complete metamorphosis; both identities coexist in tension. Academics recognize the dissonance between the prevailing NPM-enforced norms and their intrinsic academic values. They are aware that this shift toward a more self-serving paradigm isn't inherently right. They criticize it, yet they find themselves compelled to "play the game", these two forces are at odds: institutional pressures push toward a more economically driven identity, while personal and professional values resist, favoring the traditional academic virtues. Such a conflict is deeply felt within the academy; there's an awareness that the status quo "should" be challenged, yet the harsh realities of the current academic landscape demand conformity.

Moreover, this study highlights the gendered nature of academic work under NPM, echoing the findings of Acker and Armenti (2004). Within the competitive ground of academia, where the idealized worker is often unconsciously modeled on a male archetype, women academics confront additional layers of complexity. The pressure to align with what is quantitatively evaluated—citations, grants, and publications—becomes amplified for women striving to establish their legitimacy and "catch up" in an environment that does not always acknowledge their starting point to be further back due to systemic biases (Savigny, 2014).

The interviews reveal a sense of frustration among women academics, who feel that no matter their achievements, it is never deemed enough. This frustration is indicative of a deeper sense of purpose loss and self-doubt, exacerbated by being overlooked, objectified, and burdened with unpaid work, while also facing changing evaluation criteria. These challenges, though faced by all academics, are particularly pronounced for women who must also navigate the gendered expectations of academia.

Although, while the phenomenon I've outlined affects all academics regardless of their gender, the focus on women is deliberate. Firstly, by foregrounding women's perspectives, I illuminate facets of academic life that may remain unseen in more gender-neutral analyses. Secondly, I offer a platform for their experiences and perceptions, which can often be overlooked in the largely male-dominated narratives of academia.

Lastly, as women academics are disproportionately affected by certain structural inequalities within academia, their experiences provide a valuable lens through which we can examine these systemic issues. Despite the supposed objectivity of academia, gender bias still permeates many aspects of academic life. Women often face unique challenges such as balancing family responsibilities and academic careers, experiencing subtle or overt forms of discrimination, or encountering barriers to progression due to gender stereotypes. The adoption of NPM principles and the rise of *Homo oeconomicus* in academia, though affecting everyone, often amplify these issues for women.

Furthermore, this study's focus on the management field brings to light the specific ontological challenges faced by scholars in this discipline. The pressures of NPM and its implications for academic identity are particularly acute in management and organization, where the balance between economic efficiency and academic integrity is often most challenged. The necessity for academics in this field to align their self-perceptions and professional practices with the evolving demands of NPM highlights the need for a critical reassessment of the values and goals that define academic work in management and organization.

To display a true commitment to meritocratic values, HEIs managers must stop ignoring the lived realities of academics and rectify the factors that make it more difficult for some groups to conduct and publish their research. HEIs and policymakers must therefore reevaluate the criteria used for performance evaluations and ensure that the full scope of academic work—teaching, administrative, and support roles—is acknowledged and valued. This would help create a more equitable and supportive environment for all academics, male and female alike.

By recognizing the varied ontological assumptions that underpin academic identities, especially in the fields of management and organization, institutions can better support the diverse needs and aspirations of their faculty. Such an approach would not only address the gender disparities highlighted in this study but would also reinvigorate the academic ethos, bridging the gap between *Homo academicus* and *Homo oeconomicus* in the contemporary academic landscape.

Finally, it is crucial to create an environment where what "counts" also aligns with what truly "matters" for both academics and society at large.

References

Acker, J. (1990). Hierarchies, jobs, bodies: A theory of gendered organizations. *Gender and Society, 4*(2), 139–158. https://doi.org/10.1177/089124390004002002

Acker, S. (1992). New perspectives on an old problem: The position of women academics in British higher education. *Higher Education, 24*, 57–75. https://doi.org/10.1007/bf00138618

Acker, S., & Armenti, C. (2004). Sleepless in academia. *Gender & Education, 16*(1), 3–24. https://doi.org/10.1080/0954025032000170309

Altbach, P. G., Reisberg, L., & Rumbley, L. E. (2009). Trends in global higher education: Tracking an academic revolution. *UNESCO*. https://doi.org/10.1163/9789004406155

Archer, L. (2008). The new neoliberal subjects? Young/er academics' constructions of professional identity. *Journal of Education Policy, 23*(3), 265–285. https://doi.org/10.1080/02680930701754047

Ash, S. A. (2017). Part of the discussion? Gendered role of support staff in higher education. In P. L. Eddy, K. Ward, & T. Khwaja (Eds.), *Critical approaches to women and gender in higher education* (pp. 136–162). Palgrave MacMillan. https://doi.org/10.1057/978-1-137-59285-9_7

Ball, S. J. (2012). Performativity, commodification and commitment: An I-spy guide to the neoliberal university. *British Journal of Educational Studies, 60*(1), 17–28. https://doi.org/10.1080/00071005.2011.650940

Barres, B. (2006). Does gender Mmatter. *Nature, 442*(13), 133–136. https://www.nature.com/scitable/content/does-gender-matter-by-ben-a-barres-10602856/

Biernat, M., Manis, M., & Nelson, T. E. (1991). Stereotypes and standards of judgment. *Journal of Personality and Social Psychology, 60*, 485–499. https://doi.org/10.1037/0022-3514.60.4.485

Biernat, M., & Manis, M. (1994). Shifting standards and stereotype-based judgments. *Journal of Personality and Social Psychology, 66*, 5–20. https://doi.org/10.1037/0022-3514.66.1.5

Bourdieu, P. (1984). *Homo academicus*. Stanford University Press.

Burkinshaw, P. (2015). *Higher education, leadership and women vice chancellors. Fitting into communities of practice of masculinities*. Palgrave
Charmaz, K. (2014). *Constructing grounded theory*. Sage.
Conway, J. M., Jako, R. A., & Goodman, D. F. (1995). A meta-analysis of interrater and internal consistency reliability of selection interview. *Journal of Applied Psychology, 80*(5), 565–579. https://doi.org/10.1037/0021-9010.80.5.565
Corbin, J., & Strauss, A. (2014). *Basics of qualitative research: Techniques and procedures for developing grounded theory* (4th ed.). Sage.
Czerepaniak-Walczak, M. (2014). Homo academicus w świecie Homo oeconomicus. O obszarach i przejawach zmagań z akademickim zniewoleniem. *Pedagogika Szkoły Wyższej, 1*, 11–24. https://doi.org/10.18276/psw.2016.1-01
Dane, E., & Pratt, M. G. (2007). Exploring intuition and its role in managerial decision making. *Academy of Management Review, 32*(1), 33–54. https://doi.org/10.5465/amr.2007.23463682
Dixon-Reeves, R. (2003). Mentoring as a precursor to incorporation: An assessment of the mentoring experience of recently minted Ph.D.s. *Journal of Black Studies, 34*(1), 12–27. https://doi.org/10.1177/0021934703253680
Dobija, D., Górska, A., Grossi, G., & Strzelczyk, W. (2019). Rational and symbolic use of performance measurement. Experience from Polish universities. *Accounting, Auditing & Accountability Journal, 33*(3), 750–781. https://doi.org/10.1108/aaaj-08-2017-3106
Evans, J. S. B. T. (2008). Dual-processing accounts of reasoning, judgment, and social cognition. *Annual Review of Psychology, 59*, 255–278. https://doi.org/10.1146/annurev.psych.59.103006.093629
Fan, Y., Shepherd, L. J., Slavich, E., Waters, D., Stone, M., Abel, R., & Johnston, E. L. (2019). Gender and cultural bias in student evaluations: Why representation matters. *PLoS ONE, 14*(e0209749), 1–16. https://doi.org/10.1371/journal.pone.0209749
Faulkner, W. (2009). Doing gender in engineering workplace cultures. II. Gender in/authenticity and the in/visibility paradox. *Engineering Studies, 1*(3), 169–189. https://doi.org/10.1080/19378620903225059
Fisher, V., & Kinsey, S. (2014). Behind closed doors! Homosocial desire and the academic boys club. *Gender in Management: An International Journal, 29*(1), 44–64. https://doi.org/10.1108/gm-10-2012-0080
Fleming, P. (2017). *The death of Homo Economicus. Work, eebt and the myth of endless accumulation*. Pluto.

Foschi, M. (1996). Double standards in the evaluation of men and women. *Social Psychology Quarterly, 59*, 237–254. https://doi.org/10.2307/2787021

Foschi, M. (2000). Double standards for competence: Theory and research. *Annual Review of Sociology, 26*, 21–42. https://doi.org/10.1146/annurev.soc.26.1.21

Fox, M. (1991). The outer circle: Women in scientific community. In H. Zuckerman, J. Cole, & J. Bruer (Eds.), *The outer circle* (pp. 188–204). Norton.

Fox, M. (2019). *The transition from dissertation student to publishing scholar and professional* (pp. 6–16). Scholarly writing and publishing, Routledge.

Fox, M., Linková, M., & Bunker-Whittington, K. (2017). Gender, (in)equity, and the scientific workforce. In U. Felt, R. Fouché, C. A. Miller, & L. Smith-Doerr (Eds.), *The handbook of science and technology studies* (pp. 701–732). The MIT Press.

Garforth, L., & Kerr, A. (2010). Let's get organised: Practicing and valuing scientific work inside and outside the laboratory. *Sociological Research Online, 15*(2), 11–26. https://doi.org/10.5153/sro.2146

Garrett, R. U. (2006). Effects of mentoring on the quality of the doctoral experience at historically black colleges and universities: Results of groundwork investigation. *Race, Gender & Class, 13*(3/4), 311–327. https://doi.org/10.4135/9781412971928.n141

Gonzalez Ramos, A., Navarrete, C., & Cabrera Moreno, E. (2015). Dancers in the dark: Scientific career according to a gender- blind model of promotion. *Interdisciplinary Science Reviews, 40*(2), 182–203. https://doi.org/10.1179/0308018815z.000000000112

Górska, A. (2017). Perception of women in top managerial åositions in Poland. *Journal of Management and Business Administration Central Europe, 25*(1), 16–32. https://doi.org/10.7206/jmba.ce.2450-7814.187

Górska, A. (2023). *Gender and academia: Experiences of women in Central and Eastern Europe*. Routledge.

Górska, A., Kulicka, K., Staniszewska, Z., & Dobija, D. (2021). Deepening inequalities: What did COVID-19 reveal about the gendered nature of academic work? *Gender, Work and Organization, 28*(4), 1546–1561. https://doi.org/10.1111/gwao.12696

Górska, A., Pikos, A., Dobija, D., & Grossi, G. (2022). Autonomy without accountability in resource allocation reforms: Blending old and new logics in universities. *Central European Management Journal, 30*, 43–82. https://doi.org/10.7206/cemj.2658-0845.75

Halligan, J. (Ed.). (2010). *The Australian public service: New agendas and reform.* ANU EPress.

Hengel, E. (2017). Publishing while female. Are women held to higher standards? Evidence from peer review. *Cambridge Working Papers in Economics* 1753. Faculty of Economics, University of Cambridge. https://doi.org/10.1093/ej/ueac032

Hood, C. (2000). Paradoxes of public-sector managerialism, old public management, and public service bargains. *International Public Management Journal, 3*(1), 1–22. https://doi.org/10.1016/S1096-7494(00)00032-5

Kuckartz, U. (2014). *Qualitative text analysis: A guide to methods, practice and using software*. Sage.

Martin-Sardesai, A., Irvine, H., Tooley, S., & Guthrie, J. (2017). Organizational change in an Australian university: Responses to a research assessment exercise. *The British Accounting Review, 49*(4), 399–412. https://doi.org/10.1016/j.bar.2017.05.002

Morley, L. (2003). *Quality and power in higher education, Maidenhead*, Society for Research into Higher Education & Open University Press.

Moss-Racusin, C. A., Dovidio, J., Brescoll, V., Graham, M., & Handelsman, J. (2012). Science faculty's subtle gender biases favor male students. *Proceedings of the National Academy of Sciences of the United States of America, 109*(41), 16474–16479.

Osborne, S. P. (2006). The new public governance?. *Public Management Review, 8*(3), 377–387. https://doi.org/10.1080/14719030600853022

Parker, L. D. (2012). Qualitative management accounting research: Assessing deliverables and relevance. *Critical Perspectives on Accounting, 23*(1), 54–70. https://doi.org/10.1016/j.cpa.2011.06.002

Parker, L., Martin-Serdesai, A., & Guthrie, J. (2021). The commercialized Australia public university: An accountingized transition. *Financial Accounting and Management, 39*(1), 125–150. https://doi.org/10.1111/faam.12310

Parsons, E. & Priola, V. (2013). Agents for change and changes agents: the micro- politics of change and feminism in the academy. *Gender, Work and Organization. 20*(5). https://doi.org/10.1111/j.1468-0432.2012.00605.x

Pollitt, C., & Bouckaert, G. (2004). *Public management reform: A comparative analysis*. Oxford University Press.

Power, M. (1997). *The audit society: Rituals of verification.* Oxford University Press.

Savigny, H. (2014). Women, know your limits: Cultural sexism in academia. *Gender and Education, 26*(7), 794–809. https://doi.org/10.1080/09540253.2014.970977

Scott, L. (2020). *The double X economy. The epic potential of women's empowerment*. MacMillan.

Shore, C., & Wright, S. (2015). Governing by numbers: Audit culture, rankings and the new world order. *Social Anthropology. Anthropologie Sociale, 23*(1), 22–28. https://doi.org/10.1111/1469-8676.12098

Smith, K. M., Crookes, E., & Crookes, P. A. (2013). Measuring research 'impact' for academic promotion: Issues from the literature. *Journal of Higher Education Policy and Management, 35*(4), 410–420. https://doi.org/10.1080/1360080X.2013.812173

Spoon, K., LaBerge, N., Wapman, H., Zhang, S., Morgan, A. Galesic, M., Fosdick, B. K, Larremore, D. B., & Clauset, A. (2023). Gender and retention patterns among U.S. faculty. *Science Advances, 9*(42), 1–12. https://doi.org/10.1126/sciadv.adi2205

Stainback, K., Kleiner, S., & Skaggs, S. (2016). Women in power: Undoing or redoing the gendered organization? *Gender and Society, 30*(1), 109–135. https://doi.org/10.1177/0891243215602906

Sułkowski, Ł. (2016). Accountability of university: Transition of public higher education. *Entrepreneurial Business and Economics Review, 4*(1), 9–21.

Trevino, L., Balkin, D., & Gomez-Mejia, L. (2017). How "doing gender" leads to gender imbalances in the HigherRanks in colleges of business [and how to "undo gender"]. *Academy of Management Learning & Education, 16*(3), 439–453. https://doi.org/10.5465/amle.2015.0053

Van den Brink, M., & Benschop, Y. (2012). Slaying the seven-headed dragon: The quest for gender change in academia. *Gender, Work and Organization, 19*(1), 71–92. https://doi.org/10.1111/j.1468-0432.2011.00566.x

Vohlídalová, M. (2012). Early-career women academics: Between neoliberalism and gender conservatism. *Sociological Research Online., 26*(1), 27–43. https://doi.org/10.1177/1360780420914468

10

Beyond Conventional Leadership: On *Homo academicus (dux)* and Ontological Assumptions in Academia

Mattias Jacobsson and Anders Söderholm

Introduction

To understand the question of "who we are" as scholars, we must look at ourselves in the mirror and examine what shapes our reflection. After all, "who we are" is influenced by "where we are" and the taken-for-granted assumptions in that specific setting (Morgan, 1980). In this chapter, the focus is on *Homo academicus* and his/her habitat, i.e., the University setting. The aim of the chapter is twofold. First, we aim to challenge some taken-for-granted assumptions of this setting by discussing three conditions that, we argue, better explain the essence of

M. Jacobsson (✉)
Umeå School of Business, Economics and Statistics, Umeå University, Umeå, Sweden
e-mail: mattias.jacobsson@umu.se; mattias.jacobsson@ju.se

School of Engineering, Jönköping University, Jönköping, Sweden

A. Söderholm (✉)
KTH Royal Institute of Technology, Stockholm, Sweden
e-mail: soderholm@kth.se

S. Cinque and D. Ericsson (eds.), *Debating 'Homo Academicus' in Management and Organization*, Palgrave Debates in Business and Management,
https://doi.org/10.1007/978-3-031-58195-3_10

"where we are". The three conditions are *reversed hierarchy*, *lateral independence*, and *community-based belonging*. Our discussion takes its basis in how these conditions deviate from standard assumptions in organisational theory and leadership practices regarding *how power is distributed*, *the role of dependencies among units and practices*, and *how a sense of belonging is formed*. Second, based on these alternative assumptions, we intend to discuss the consequences thereof for *Homo academicus* and *Homo academicus dux* (i.e., the academic practitioner and the academic leader). We propose that the conditions we outline not only shape *"who we are"* but ultimately explain *why* and *how Homo academicus* and *Homo academicus dux* acts the way (s)he acts. By that, we advance the understanding of everyday practice and leadership in the academic setting, in general, and within management and organisational sciences, specifically.

Background

Being an academic citizen—or as referred to in this book chapter, a *Homo academicus*—requires a solid understanding of what a university *is* and the assumptions on which it is formed. Assuming a leadership role in academia—becoming a *Homo academicus dux* (an academic leader)—requires even more. It requires not only an understanding of what a university is but also how it functions and how leadership can be performed in this somewhat "special" organisational context (Rowley & Sherman, 2003).

In this chapter, the initial emphasis will be on the latter, where we will start by outlining three conditions that we argue shape the practices of *Homo academicus* and *Homo academicus dux* and discuss why and how these conditions (should) impact academic leadership and practice. By that, we follow in the footsteps of Bourdieu (1988) in the way he analyses how the academic world operates and how it impacts its practices. However, the conditions we are to outline are at odds with some of the standard assumptions in organisational contexts and leadership practices. It challenges the "taken-for-granted" by building on an alternative ontology to what management writings and economic literature commonly build on.

The most common sets of assumptions in management theory have been labelled *Homo oeconomicus* (or economic man), emphasising economic rationality and decision-making based on maximising utility, and later as an *Administrative man* (Simon, 1957) seeking satisfying outcomes of decision-making and thus acting differently in reaching decisions. While these two sets of assumptions are idealisations of human agency in decision-making, they are both more than this. These idealisations hold assumptions about ambiguity and cognitive capacities and how such assumptions may impact behaviour and everyday practice. Furthermore, assumptions about *"man"* are also connected to the organisational context and organisational properties. Cyert and March (1963) made this argument in their seminal contribution *A Behavioral Theory of the Firm* and developed these ideas further in several later publications, for example, in March and Olsen (1976) and March (1994).

Over the years, many scholars have presented additional sets of assumptions to replace the *economic man* as the protagonist of human rationality. For example, Haustein (1981) introduced *Homo ludens* to emphasise the playful and creative nature of human rationality, Nyborg (2000) underscored the political dimensions of rationality through the conceptualisation of *Homo politicus*, and Redmalm and Skoglund (2020) delve into the darker aspects of rationality where individuals may be marginalised or excluded from societal norms in their paper on *Homo sacer*. Recently, Jacobsson and Söderholm (2022) also included the consequences of temporality in their essay on *Homo projecticus*, highlighting the action-driven rationale and bracketing of time and space to create purposeful areas to get things done.

The lessons learned so far is that ontological assumptions such as *Administrative man, Homo projecticus* or *Homo academicus* need to include knowledge and analysis of the organisational context where they act. Consequently, it is an interplay between conditions shaping individuals' decision-making capabilities (and practice) and the properties or conditions under which they operate in their organisations. However, it is also important to remember that, for obvious reasons, organisations and individuals are not separate entities. Organisations are made up of individuals where individual capacity and institutional conditions constitute a complex web of relationships, impacting everyday life as well as long-term development regarding how decisions are made and how leadership is executed (Hwang & Colyvas, 2020).

When discussing *Homo academicus,* it is thus relevant to understand the university setting, or the business school, in terms of the interactive relationship between individuals and organisations. One does not exist without the other, and any set of assumptions defining *Homo academicus* is dependent on a parallel set of assumptions on the organisational or institutional context.

Before we move over to the somewhat unique characteristics of the university setting in terms of governing ideals, it is necessary to point out that our use of the "man" in this text is solely to us trying to be true to the (conceptual) tradition but should in all aspects be interpreted as "human". Ontological assumptions are thus, in every way, gender-neutral.

Homo academicus and the University Setting

Sahlin and Eriksson-Zetterquist (2016) provide a starting point and source of inspiration for the discussion as they point out that management and bureaucracy models exist in parallel with more traditional collegial governing models in academia (see also Bleiklie & Kogan, 2007). Management tends to be viewed as a modern contemporary governing model opposed to, or even replacing, a more conventional and conservative collegial model. Since collegial models are challenging to understand from a management or bureaucracy point of view, management theories and bureaucratic governing mechanisms may be over-emphasised in importance when designing university governance structures.

Consequently, leadership training and practice will focus on management roles, bureaucratic organisational models, and how to work as efficient managers, inspired by new public management ideas and general reforms in the public sector. However, collegial issues, collegiality as a culture and working environment, and the benefits of a solid collegial organisation are not a strong focus in leadership training or discussions on how to design a university organisation.

Sahlin and Eriksson-Zetterquist (2016) stress that a university needs all three: an efficient bureaucracy, good management practice, and collegial governance to meet those tasks facing universities today. The point is that even though all three are needed, there is much more understanding and focus on management and bureaucracy and much less on collegial forms of governance.

The core of collegial governance models is to produce sound science output in terms of high-quality research and teaching. Collegial discussions are based on scientific arguments, and a solid collegial culture includes seminars with open discussions as well as mentorship and network activities where peers continuously meet to discuss content and quality of research or education. A structure of collegial decision-making mechanisms is also part of a collegial organisation.

From another perspective, management, bureaucracy, and collegial models are different sets of ontological assumptions to understand and shape the organisational context in which they are deployed. In a context built on management and bureaucracy, such assumptions are the belief in hierarchy and a leadership practice where those at the top need to understand and control the organisation, where the organisation is believed to be integrated and mutually dependent among its various parts and where identity and sense of belonging are closely attached to the organisation as such. In other words, there are inherent assumptions about *how power is distributed*, *the role of dependencies among units and practices*, and *how a sense of belonging is formed.* Managerial ontological assumptions of this kind are then used to design leadership practices, organisational structures, routines, and expectations in a way that may be far from what is appropriate. Over time, universities risk being more of a burden than a facilitator for *Homo academicus* to do exemplary research and education. Our assumptions to be presented can, in other words, be understood as ontological assumptions based on "the fact" that universities are populated by many *Homo academicus* and thus explain what *Homo academicus* require in terms of management and leadership to deliver high-quality work.

When discussing *Homo academicus,* it is vital to understand that collegial culture and leadership practice may differ within a university. Traditions in natural sciences are different from those in business.

Fine arts are different from engineering. Building a career, academic autonomy and searching for academic excellence are essential aspects of all scientific disciplines, but the methods and practices may vary. Patterns of cooperation are also different, and societal engagement is organised in various ways depending on how the relationship to practice is maintained within the discipline. We will build our discussion on practice within business schools, and our discussion is maybe most relevant for understanding *Homo academicus* in this particular part of the university, even though we argue that these discussions are also valid for a broader understanding of universities in general.

In the following, we will look more deeply into three ontological assumptions, or conditions, of the collegial culture, which need to be understood by *Homo academicus* and addressed when acting as *Homo academicus dux*. The three conditions partly also explain why bureaucracy and management models might not work or how they must be adjusted to fit a university.

We have two parallel themes in the following discussion. The first is to outline the core assumptions on which *Homo academicus* build his or her work and how the organisation, in terms of the university, is understood. Based on these assumptions, it is also a discussion on how academic excellence is strived for and achieved.

The second theme is the practices of *Homo academicus dux,* in other words, how leadership should be formed in an organisation populated by *Homo academicus.* It is a call for an understanding that traditional leadership models based on theories in management sciences and bureaucracy need to be replaced by a leadership and management approach based on the core assumption of *Homo academicus.*

The first theme is descriptive. It is "who we are" (*Homo academicus*) based on centuries-old institutional arrangements and a shared understanding which has been passed down through generations of academic citizens.

The second theme is prescriptive. It is "how academic leadership should be" when there is pressure on university leadership to be so many things, from loyal state bureaucrats to academic role models, in the crossfire between budget constraints, competitive talent recruitment, outside evaluations, and faculty requirements. Now, let us introduce and discuss our three alternative sets of conditions.

Reversed Hierarchy

The first condition is what we have chosen to call a *reversed hierarchy*, and it challenges the traditional notion of how power is distributed. Management models and theories usually build on the ontological assumption that the top of the organisational pyramid has a profound knowledge of what subordinate units do. Knowledge about the content of the organisation's operations increases as you move up the organisational ladder. Each unit, consequently, can only overlook a slice of the knowledge base on which the organisation's existence is built (see e.g. Mintzberg, 1980).

Traditional manufacturing operations may be the most obvious example of where these standard assumptions hold true. Those cutting and welding do not necessarily know the facts about the product to which they contribute. Even though you could take the cutting and welding people out of the factory and look at the content of what they know as a separate professional knowledge base, it will still be hard to see the use of it unless you combine it with other knowledge bases which are outside the cutting and welding sphere. The same applies to painting, assembling, developing manufacturing robots, marketing, engineering, and construction. The list of examples can be made extensive.

Also, in knowledge-based firms, such as engineering consultants, public accounting, management consultants, and other lines of business where the knowledge held by the individual is the core asset of the organisation, the same assumptions hold true. Higher up in the hierarchy, people tend to know more. They are there, up the ladder of the hierarchy, to define how to use the competence of lower units and relate them to each other, what kind of external customers or stakeholders to engage with, and how to separate one knowledge area from another. Business cases are either designed or confirmed by higher levels for lower levels, and overall business models are the responsibility of higher-level managers.

This is not to say that employees cannot contribute to creating new business opportunities or enhancing corporate performance types of industries. However, as they do so, such improvements usually need to be confirmed by higher organisational levels before being implemented.

Let us compare this with the university setting, where this standard model of taken-for-granted assumptions can be challenged. Research-based knowledge is gained and developed by *Homo academicus*, may it be a professor, their peers in the same or adjacent disciplines, their post-docs, Ph.D. students, or fellow researchers. There is no need for a researcher in chemistry to ask the Dean if he or she should try to publish a new polymer discovery. Likewise, a Head of the department is not necessarily the right person to provide feedback to a professor in economics if pursuing research in the evolution of labour markets in the euro area will be a good idea, provided that the Head of the department in question is not also happen to be a labour market scholar.

Homo academicus would instead turn to their peers and colleagues in the specific research field and try to define if there is a need for research projects going this or that way—if this or that has already been done, or if there is something new to tell. *Homo academicus* will go to conferences or read journals within their disciplines to find out the latest news on how scientific knowledge develops in their area. Through peer review of publications, research applications, and promotions, there are ample tools to verify the value of their research. In simple terms, in a university, the knowledge of the core operations tends to be reduced when moving up the hierarchy rather than the opposite, which is traditionally assumed. As illustrated in Fig. 10.1, there is a *reversed hierarchy* where power is built on *Homo academicus* expertise and built from the bottom up.

Consequently, the reversed hierarchy implies that the Head of a department cannot encompass all the knowledge areas of the department, the Dean cannot overlook and govern knowledge creation in the various departments of the faculty, and the President is unable to contribute to how to design research agendas in all the faculties of the university. If the Dean is a professor in statistics, he or she would be able to take part in the discussions on research in the statistics department, but, and this is a crucial observation, this is done only because he or she, in this specific case, is a peer *Homo academicus* and not the Dean.

The *reversed hierarchy* is thus one of the main reasons why a collegial organisational nature is needed and is truly invaluable for universities. No other mechanism is available to replace the collegial nature of quality enhancement and quality control (Bennett, 1998). The management

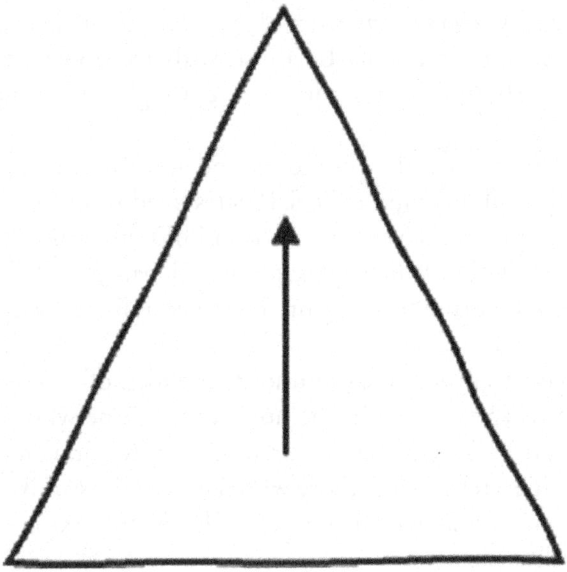

Fig. 10.1 Reversed hierarchy

task is consequently to guarantee the quality of collegial interactions, to maintain and develop its prerequisites, and to intervene when collegial mechanisms are not working as they should—when it is corrupt, dysfunctional, or not open for peer-review activities.

Implications for *Homo academicus* and *Homo academicus dux*

The first and most important implication is that *Homo academicus* is the essential contributor to the university's mission which is, in one way or another, to create and disseminate knowledge for the best of society—despite the challenges that exist (Gera, 2012). Academic autonomy in terms of defining and carrying out research, choosing scientific methods, and publication channels are core values that the university must honour. As such, it serves an essential function in upholding the principles of governmentally independent research (The Swedish Agency for Public Management, 2019). Decisions on research and educational content must be taken by *Homo academicus* based on scientific arguments and not hierarchy, and arguments by those with the most comprehensive understanding should always carry more weight than merely formal power.

A collegial nature can be promoted and improved as part of faculty members' responsibility, and collegial issues need to be considered when designing training at all levels, as well as in PhD programs and workplace development activities. When a discipline or department fails to uphold a positive collegial culture, it is essential to re-establish it from the bottom up.

At odds with traditional assumptions, the idea of a *reversed hierarchy* at universities is thus rooted in the notion that those who hold teaching and research positions (such as lecturers and professors) are at the top of the academic hierarchy, while those who have administrative and support functions (such as managerial staff and administrators) are lower down in the hierarchy.

This inversion of the traditional hierarchy is because universities are fundamentally, and in all aspects, knowledge-based organisations, where creating and disseminating knowledge is the primary goal. As such, those directly involved in creating and transmitting knowledge are the most essential contributors to the university's mission.

In addition, *Homo academicus* have traditionally been granted significant autonomy in their work, particularly regarding their research activities. This has led to a culture where faculty members are seen as the intellectual leaders of the university, with considerable influence over the direction of research and teaching.

However, it is essential to note that the assumptions of a *reversed hierarchy* are not absolute or universal. In some cases, administrative and support staff may hold positions of significant influence and responsibility within the university, particularly in areas such as finance, facilities management, and student services. Still, it should never be the case that administrators dictate the tasks for the core operations. If this happens, the *raison d'être* of the academic system can be questioned. Described differently, the tail should never be wagging the dog (Alvehus & Kastberg Weichselberger, 2023).

Overall, the idea that the hierarchy is "upside down" at universities reflects the unique nature of knowledge-based organisations, where creating and transmitting knowledge is the primary mission. While *Homo academicus* may hold a privileged position within the university, it is still essential to recognise the contributions of all members of the university community, including staff, administrators, and students, in achieving the institution's goals.

Lateral Independence

The second condition at odds with the standard ontological assumption in organisational contexts and leadership practices is *lateral independence*. It is well-established that activities in most organisations have different kinds of logical interdependencies (Thompson, 1967). One unit delivers something to another, adding value to what was done by the first unit. In some cases, these interdependencies are pooled; in others, they can be sequential. This is true for manufacturing, where raw material is worked with to comprehensive end products in lines of operations that follow one after another. Departments such as research and development or marketing are also interdependent with other departments in a logical way. Without new products, there will be nothing to manufacture in the future, and without selling efforts, there will be few or no customers.

In other business areas, the logic between parts of the organisation is different, but the interdependence is still there. The interdependence can be mutual. Consultants work together over department borders; accounting offices and public accountants need to interact, and so on. Administrators in public authorities are interdependent in the sense that one department does legal evaluations while another is responsible for the storage of data and dispatch of decisions.

Understanding and designing logical steps of interdependence between various areas of operation, or areas of competence, is necessary when building an organisation involving comprehensive and complicated deliveries, many people, and financial risks. These steps must be controlled in terms of quality and efficiency to make the best use of available resources and to survive in a competitive market. It is also evident that the organisational design is best done from the top by higher management, who can overlook the processes and hold the necessary means to coordinate and make decisions on everything from financial investments to procurement.

From time to time, an organisation merges with another, and because of the logical interconnectedness of operations, this will result in processes to integrate operations between the two organisations to increase efficiency and effectiveness. On other occasions, an organisation will outsource parts of the operations to someone more professional. Because of the interconnectedness, the challenge is, again, to integrate and overlook the cooperation between the different operations.

The university setting is different. Usually, there is no (or very little) lateral interdependence between departments at a university. What is done by *Homo academicus* in Business Administration has no immediate impact on what must be done by *Homo academicus* in the language or phycology departments. Likewise, a researcher in Economics or Industrial Engineering will not influence what is done in History or Computer science. As illustrated in Fig. 10.2, in addition to the reversed hierarchy, there is a unique lateral independence between various departments and units.

The lateral independence also explains why the struggle for more money among departments is such a vivid activity. If someone loses money, it can only be an advantage for other departments that will be able to fight for some more money. Since one department can grow independently of others, internal power struggles can be common and even rewarding. It requires a significant amount of trust in the faculty before department heads are willing to give up the continuous discussion on more resources and trust the Dean's office to do "what is best" for the faculty or university.

Still, some parts of the university will be well interconnected. Departments depend on each other through study programs where students take courses from various fields towards their final degree. For example, Business Administration departments are often interconnected with the Departments of Statistics, Economics, and Law through their Business programs, and a Department of Family Medicine can be dependent on the Department of Integrative Medical Biology through the Medical

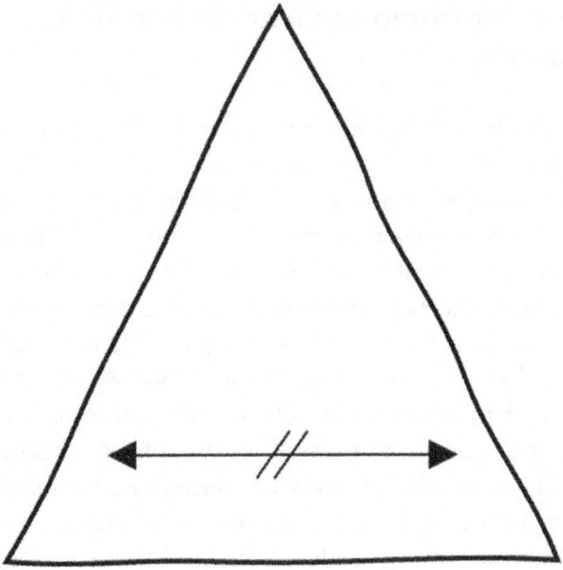

Fig. 10.2 Lateral independence

Programme. As such, this creates clusters of interdependent departments within the university where some efforts are devoted to making this integration work. Such clusters may be within broader areas such as engineering sciences, languages and humanities, business and economics, or medicine. Given that this type of interdependence is built around a specific educational program, if there are changes in curricula, established interdependencies can cease to exist, and new interdependencies can emerge.

This is usually a challenge, and the easy way out is to divide responsibilities within a program and then continue to discuss more resources for the individual departments. Alternatively, clusters of academic fields may find ways of integrating both research and education and create a common interdisciplinary agenda, a wider department, which can then continue to discuss more resources to the cluster of disciplines. Still, due to the way science is structured and organised globally, these types of clusters may come at the expense of reduced specialisation.

Implications for *Homo academicus* and *Homo academicus dux*

The most obvious implication of *lateral independence* is that *Homo academicus* have the freedom to pursue their research and scholarship interests without undue influence from their colleagues at other departments or from management. This means that *Homo academicus* can pursue their personal research agendas and collaborate with other researchers outside their departments, academic units, or university.

However, understanding the implications of lateral independence is essential for other reasons as well. First, it allows faculty members to explore new and innovative research directions that may not fit neatly within existing academic departments or disciplines. This can lead to the development of new fields of study and interdisciplinary collaborations. Through this, lateral independence nurtures a diversity of perspectives and approaches within the academic realm. Without it, there is a risk that academic departments can become too insular, stifling creativity and limiting the development of new ideas.

From the point of view of *Homo academicus,* lateral independence is essential for maintaining academic freedom and integrity. *Homo academicus* must be able to pursue their research interests without fear of retribution or interference from their colleagues or superiors. This autonomy not only upholds the principles of academic freedom but also ensures that research is conducted with integrity and impartiality, enhancing the credibility and reliability of scholarly work. Also, it enables *Homo academicus* to respond quickly to emergent empirical phenomena.

To support lateral independence, universities, through *Homo academicus dux,* should foster a culture of openness and collaboration. This includes encouraging interdisciplinary research and providing opportunities for *Homo academicus* to connect with peers outside their academic units. Universities should also develop appropriate support structures for faculty members to pursue their research interests and engage in novel ideas by, for example, providing funding for research and travel, access to specialised equipment and facilities, and enabling professional development.

Overall, lateral independence is crucial for upholding academic freedom and the pursuit of knowledge. By supporting it, universities can promote innovation, diversity, and excellence in research.

Community-Based Belonging

The third and final condition that we argue is at odds with standard assumptions in organisational contexts and leadership practices is *community-based belonging*. The standard assumption is that employees in companies and more traditional organisations are expected to honour corporate values or a shared vision in their workplace. They are expected to act as a loyal part of the organisation and to have a strong belonging in line with what the organisation stands for. It is assumed that they should act and live by the "company spirit", which is considered a key component in company success (Baumgartner, 2020). For government employees in Sweden, there are specific values on which governmental authorities should be built, such as democracy, objectivity, respect, rule of law, free formation of opinion, and efficacy and service (The Swedish Agency for Public Management, 2019). Such values or visionary statements are aligned with the core of the democratic state and aim at building a culture to which individuals can relate and contribute.

In parallel to their organisational belonging, many professions also have a strong professional belonging. Medical doctors, lawyers, nurses, and auditors have a professional knowledge base founded in specific educational backgrounds and scientific research disciplines on which their professional actions must be established. Training and lifelong learning initiatives guarantee a continuous knowledge update among those practising a particular line of work. Sometimes, there are professional associations to which they belong that safeguard the professional interest of the group, as is true for nurses or medical doctors.

For some occupations, it is necessary to have a licence from either a government agency or a professional organisation before being able to take up work in that field. Psychologists, medical doctors, lawyers, and architects are some occupations with different licencing procedures, either governed by law or as a joint professional agreement of standards.

It is easy to understand that sometimes there might be a conflict between belonging and loyalty to the employing organisation (e.g., the hospital or health care organisation) and the professional values that a particular occupation is founded upon, e.g., national associations for medical doctors or nurses (see, e.g., Monrouxe, 2010). Such conflicts can be professional in terms of deciding what kind of therapies to use, or they can involve working conditions, involvement in bureaucracy and paperwork, or accessibility to training and recovery periods. Since those who are part of the profession hold a unique competence defined in the broader community, they can claim that their expertise should be counted when making organisational decisions.

In universities, *Homo academicus* is part of a strong professional community defined not primarily by the university or department but by the peers in the academic disciplines to which *Homo academicus* belong (Jawitz, 2009). Each discipline has its own communities with established paradigms, theories, and methods that guide scholarly inquiry and determine what is considered valuable knowledge and excellence within the field (Lamont, 2009).

The previously discussed condition of lateral independence partly enables such community-based identity to develop, and as illustrated by Fig. 10.3, these communities span countless organisations, both nationally and internationally. Most of the organisations are universities, but research institutes, research-intensive industries, and public authorities can also be included depending on the type of discipline.

Homo academicus in these communities have joint training, read the same journals, go to the same conferences, spend time at each other's organisations as post-docs or guest professors, and learn the same community-specific terms and ways of expression (Jacobsson & Söderholm, 2011, 2020). The communities can be empirically or theoretically driven but do not necessarily have to follow the traditional disciplinary domains. Unifying is the shared fascination with a specific phenomenon at the community's core. It is even argued that these communities can develop into "micro-tribes" with many barriers to entry and clear downsides (Alvesson et al., 2017).

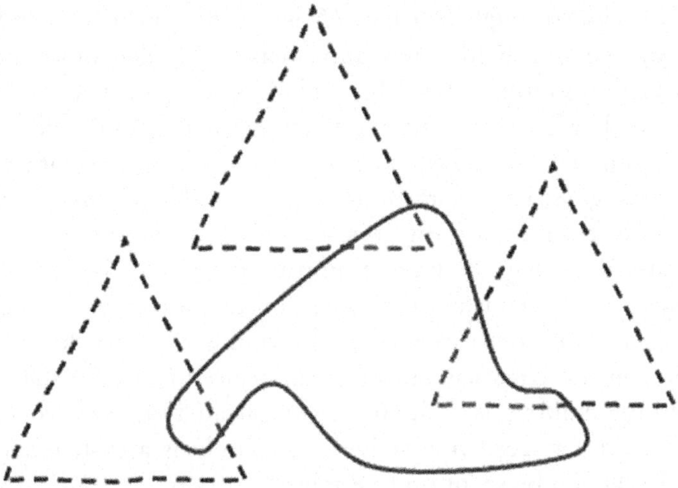

Fig. 10.3 Community-based identity

Implications for *Homo academicus* and *Homo academicus dux*

So, what are the consequences of this *community-based belonging* for *Homo academicus* and *Homo academicus dux?*

First, the university paying *Homo academicus* monthly salary is not the focal point for their profession. Instead, the university is a "convenient place" to undertake research and a necessary source of legitimacy. Still, it is not necessarily so that the university provides much to build the professional belonging for *Homo academicus* in a defined and delimited academic discipline. When professional belonging is built at the university, like in traditional industries, it is usually done within the department's walls and related to teaching programmes, not within the university as a joint organisation. Still, most professional belonging is developed within the mentioned communities through interaction with international peers at conferences and during research visits.

A notable difference between, for example, the professional identity of *Homo academicus* and other professional areas is that *Homo academicus* not only belongs to a profession but also creates and recreates the essence of its profession through research. *Homo academicus* renews and review the knowledge base before it is implemented in educational programs or published in journals. Also, they uphold shared practices and ways of thinking as they go to the same conferences, write, read, and review for the same journals, and spend time overseas at each other's organisations as post-docs, guest professors, or as exchange PhD students.

Therefore, communication policies, university vision statements, or faculty strategies have a limited impact on the daily life of *Homo academicus*. He or she is not dependent on the organisational belonging (i.e., university or department) to determine what to do or how to perform. On the contrary, university strategies or policies may be read as something making daily life more complicated or, even worse, something that hinders academic activities and only is a cost, reducing the resources that can be spent on research.

In fact, any initiative understood as defining the university as a delimited organisation with boundaries defining *who is in* and *who is out* can be perceived as threatening *Homo academicus* professional belonging. It is a threat since it does now acknowledge *Homo academicus* "real" belonging, which is a *community-based belonging* developed across organisational and national borders. Since many routines, guidelines, and strategic documents depend on the university as a cohesive unit, the university administration may become a symbol of the non-acceptance of professional academic belonging. Conflicts between the administration and the academic part of universities become more evident as administrative professions, such as human resources or communication, are reinforced as professional areas with their knowledge base.

Discussion

Having outlined the three conditions and discussed how they deviate from standard assumptions in organisational theory and leadership practices and their implications on academic leadership and practice, we now turn our attention back to the core question of the ontological assumptions of *Homo Academicus*. If "who we are" depends on "where we are", what do the alternative conditions tell us about academic rationality?

As briefly discussed in the background, two commonly adopted ideas about human rationality are the assumptions of *the Economic-* and *the Administrative man.* While the former is characterised by full rationality and an ambition to maximise utility function, the latter is assumed to be limited by its cognitive and information-processing abilities. As such, the *Administrative man* is assumed to make "satisficing" rather than "maximising" decisions (Simon, 1947, 1957).

Building on Simon's model of rationality, Jacobsson and Söderholm (2022) recently brought the temporality of contemporary society into the equation. They argued that while the idea of bounded rationality and "satisficing decisions" holds in stable organisational settings (Cyert & March, 1963), the temporality often characterising today's organised settings brings a slightly different rationality. Conceptualised as *Homo Projecticus*, they argue that "man" in such temporal settings is bounded by "brackets", more specifically time brackets and scope brackets, which they create to reduce uncertainty and facilitate action. Given the extensive projectification of contemporary society (Jacobsson & Jałocha, 2021), where academia is no exception (Dollinger, 2020), we argue that *Homo Academicus* is subject to a very similar rationality shaped by the above-described conditions.

For example, as part of the *lateral interdependence* and *community-based belonging*, *Homo Academicus* seek, define, and delimit their work as projects, often in collaboration with peers at other universities and institutions within their domain. While this, on the one hand, enables innovation and diversity of ideas, such temporal organising, on the other side, lends itself to the monitoring of tasks and financial control (Deem & Brehony, 2005). However, given the *reversed hierarchy*, the monitoring and control do not primarily stem from the academic institutions but from the government agencies (or equivalent), where the project funding has been sourced. As such, *Homo Academicus* is highly dependent on the institutional logic and subject to the pressures of the financing regimes in establishing his/her legitimacy.

Furthermore, when *Homo Academicus* engage in time- and scope bracketing, he/she does this based on the prevailing understanding of what contributes to the personal career and what is, by peers, perceived as academic excellence in the relevant academic community. At business schools, creating major management programs and building competence for students' future careers has historically been high on the agenda. The instrumental importance of building "a great CV" by, for example, being the PI of projects, attracting the "right type of money", being the first author, and systematically targeting what is currently perceived as the best-ranked journal, has become more and more emphasised over time. This is often done at the expense of cooperation with businesses as part of the curricula or developing research efforts that build academic communities where practical applications are high on the agenda.

It is thus possible to claim that *Homo Academicus*, particularly in the Business school setting, resembles what can best be described as a slightly more instrumental version of *Homo Projecticus*. Bounded by brackets, *Homo Academicus* balance the intricate challenges of normative expectations, conventions, and individual career trajectories.

Concluding Remarks

This chapter offers a fresh perspective on leadership and ontological assumptions in the academic setting by outlining three important conditions—*reversed hierarchy*, *lateral independence*, and *community-based belonging*—that are at odds with standard assumptions in organisational contexts and leadership practices. The conditions are challenging common assumptions regarding *how power is distributed*, *how dependencies are created*, and *how a sense of belonging is formed*, and, we argue, are essential in understanding leadership and everyday practice in the mentioned setting. In other words, they are vital in understanding *Homo academicus* and *Homo academicus dux*.

Reversed hierarchy emphasises that knowledge and decision-making authority reside in universities, with the men and women directly involved in research and teaching. The hierarchical structure is reversed, with *Homo academicus* holding the most knowledge and autonomy while administrators and higher-level managers are to provide support rather than control. This alternative assumption has significant implications emphasising the central role of *Homo academicus* in fulfilling the university's mission of knowledge creation and dissemination.

Lateral independence, the second condition, challenges the standard assumption about the role of interdependencies among units and practices as it recognises the lack of immediate interdependence between departments and units in universities. Unlike traditional organisations, where different units often contribute to the same output and thus depend on each other's performance, departments and units at universities most often operate independently. This independence allows *Homo academicus* to pursue their research interests and collaborate across disciplines, fostering innovation, diversity, and the development of new ideas with little or no influence from management. For *Homo academicus dux*, supporting lateral independence is crucial for maintaining freedom and integrity, which is the foundation on which academic institutions rest.

The third condition presented, *community-based belonging*, emphasises the importance of a collegial culture and a sense of belonging within the academic domain or discipline rather than the organisation. Instead of developing a firm/organization-centred belonging and adhering to organisational values, *Homo academicus* from all over the world form domain-related communities of scholars who engage in scientific discussions, peer review, and mentorship. This *community-based belonging* is essential for quality enhancement, peer control, and upholding scientific standards.

The implications of these alternative assumptions could be acknowledged both in terms of management and leadership research and academic leadership practice.

From a research point of view, and as described at the outset of this chapter, it is well-known that traditional leadership theories often draw upon hierarchical models and assumptions of interdependence among organisational units (Mintzberg, 1980; Thompson, 1967). As illustrated, the academic setting is subject to an alternative set of conditions. These conditions challenge conventional leadership assumptions beyond what is described in this chapter and thus open for the re-evaluation of existing theories and models. For instance, the notion of reversed hierarchy underscores the central role of *Homo academicus* in the process of knowledge creation and dissemination. This could lead to exploring leadership approaches that empower academics as decision-makers. *Lateral independence* suggests that traditional interdependency assumptions may not apply uniformly in academia. Future research could delve into how leadership practices accommodate the autonomy of departments and researchers, fostering interdisciplinary collaboration while respecting their independence. Furthermore, *community-based belonging* presents an opportunity to investigate how leadership strategies can utilise the strong sense of belonging beyond the prime organisation and, for example, understand how to encourage community-based influences without scientific disciplines turning into protectionist "micro-tribes" (Alvesson et al., 2017).

From a more practical academic leadership perspective, and as argued at the outset of this chapter, both *Homo academicus* and *Homo academicus dux*, first and foremost, need to recognise the alternative set of assumptions presented and engage the implications. Described differently, we need to know "who we are". To do so, leadership training in the academic setting might have to be altered or updated. For example, training must emphasise decentralised decision-making and empowering individual academics to shape their research and teaching pursuits to foster a culture of ownership and engagement. Also, by fostering an environment that appreciates diverse perspectives and promotes cross-disciplinary projects, academic leaders can harness lateral independence to advance innovation. Incorporating these practical implications and others into the practice of *Homo academicus dux* can lead to more effective leadership. Still, it requires leaders to adapt their approaches to align with the specific conditions of the academic setting, ensuring that academic institutions thrive and fulfil their knowledge-creation and dissemination missions.

References

Alvehus, J., & Kastberg Weichselberger, G. (2023, February 4). Varning för strategerna som slipper göra jobbet. *Dagens Nyheter.*

Alvesson, M., Gabriel, Y., & Paulsen, R. (2017). *Return to meaning: A social science with something to say*. Oxford University Press.

Baumgartner, N. (2020). Build a culture that aligns with people's values. *Harvard Business Review*, 3–18.

Bennett, J. B. (1998). *Collegial professionalism: The academy, individualism, and the common good*. Oryx Press.

Bleiklie, I., & Kogan, M. (2007). Organization and governance of universities. *Higher Education Policy, 20*, 477–493. https://doi.org/10.1057/palgrave.hep.8300167

Bourdieu, P. (1988). *Homo academicus*. Stanford University Press.

Cyert, R. M., & March, J. G. (1963). *A behavioral theory of the firm*. Prentice Hall/Pearson Education.

Deem, R., & Brehony, K. J. (2005). Management as ideology: The case of 'new managerialism' in higher education. *Oxford Review of Education, 31*(2), 217–235. https://doi.org/10.1080/03054980500117827

Dollinger, M. (2020). The projectification of the university: Consequences and alternatives. *Teaching in Higher Education, 25*(6), 669–682. https://doi.org/10.1080/13562517.2020.1722631

Gera, R. (2012). Bridging the gap in knowledge transfer between academia and practitioners. *International Journal of Educational Management, 26*(3), 252–273. https://doi.org/10.1108/09513541211213336

Haustein, H. D. (1981). Human resources, creativity, and innovation: The conflict between homo faber and homo ludens. *Behavioral Science, 26*(3), 243–255. https://doi.org/10.1002/bs.3830260307

Hwang, H., & Colyvas, J. A. (2020). Ontology, levels of society, and degrees of generality: Theorizing actors as abstractions in institutional theory. *Academy of Management Review, 45*(3), 570–595. https://doi.org/10.5465/amr.2014.0266

Jawitz, J. (2009). Academic identities and communities of practice in a professional discipline. *Teaching in Higher Education, 14*(3), 241–251. https://doi.org/10.1080/13562510902898817

Jacobsson, M., & Jałocha, B. (2021). Four images of projectification: An integrative review. *International Journal of Managing Projects in Business, 14*(7), 1583–1604. https://doi.org/10.1108/IJMPB-12-2020-0381

Jacobsson, M., & Söderholm, A. (2011). Breaking out of the straitjacket of project research: In search of contribution. *International Journal of Managing Projects in Business, 4*(3), 378–388. https://doi.org/10.1108/17538371111144139

Jacobsson, M., & Söderholm, A. (2020). Project studies beyond the straitjacket: An escape artist's manual. *Project Management Journal, 51*(4), 411–419. https://doi.org/10.1177/875697282092

Jacobsson, M., & Söderholm, A. (2022). An essay on 'Homo Projecticus': Ontological assumptions in the projectified society. *International Journal of*

Project Management, 40(4), 315–319. https://doi.org/10.1016/j.ijproman.2021.11.004

Lamont, M. (2009). *How professors think: Inside the curious world of academic judgment*. Harvard University Press.

March, J. G. (1994). *A primer on decision making: How decisions happen*. Free Press.

March, J. G., & Olsen, J. P. (1976). *Ambiguity and choice in organizations*. Universitetsforlaget.

Mintzberg, H. (1980). Structure in 5's: A synthesis of the research on organization design. *Management Science, 26*(3), 322–341. https://www.jstor.org/stable/2630506

Monrouxe, L. V. (2010). Identity, identification and medical education: Why should we care? *Medical Education, 44*(1), 40–49. https://doi.org/10.1111/j.1365-2923.2009.03440.x

Morgan, G. (1980). Paradigms, metaphors, and puzzle solving in organization theory. *Administrative Science Quarterly, 25*(4), 605–622. https://doi.org/10.2307/2392283

Nyborg, K. (2000). Homo economicus and homo politicus: Interpretation and aggregation of environmental values. *Journal of Economic Behavior & Organization, 42*(3), 305–322. https://doi.org/10.1016/S0167-2681(00)00091-3

Redmalm, D., & Skoglund, A. (2020). Rethinking government and its economy with Giorgio Agamben: The homo sacer in alternative entrepreneurship. *The Sociological Review, 68*(5), 948–964. https://doi.org/10.1177/0038026120914

Rowley, D. J., & Sherman, H. (2003). The special challenges of academic leadership. *Management Decision, 41*(10), 1058–1063. https://doi.org/10.1108/00251740310509580

Sahlin, K., & Eriksson-Zetterquist, U. (2016). Collegiality in modern universities–the composition of governance ideals and practices. *Nordic Journal of Studies in Educational Policy, 2016*(2–3). https://doi.org/10.3402/nstep.v2.33640

Simon, H. A. (1947). *Administrative behavior*. Macmillan.

Simon, H. A. (1957). *Models of man: Social and rational*. Wiley.

The Swedish Agency for Public Management. (2019). *Den statliga värdegrunden—gemensamma principer för en god förvaltning*. https://tinyurl.com/StadskontoretValeuBase [Downloaded 2023–06–22]

Thompson, D. J. (1967). *Organizations in Action*. McGraw-Hill.

11

From *Homo academicus activistarum* to *Homo academicus imaginatus*

Mikael Lundgren and Martin Blom

Introduction

Current reality seems abundant with pressing challenges. Global pandemics, geopolitical conflict, economic inequality, social unrest, and the ever-more alarming signs of climate change and disturbance of the Earth's fragile systems on which all of us depend dominate public debate and weigh on the minds of individuals. At the same time, faith in traditional institutions, such as governments and politics, to successfully solve these issues is declining. Universities, along with their various fields and disciplines, are no exception, as they struggle to be relevant and (re)claim their position in the institutional framework. According to Jonathan Haidt, professor at the New York University Stern School

M. Lundgren (✉)
School of Business and Economics, Linnaeus University, Kalmar, Sweden
e-mail: mikael.lundgren@lnu.se

M. Blom
School of Economics and Management, Lund University, Lund, Sweden
e-mail: martin.blom@fek.lu.se

S. Cinque and D. Ericsson (eds.), *Debating 'Homo Academicus' in Management and Organization*, Palgrave Debates in Business and Management,
https://doi.org/10.1007/978-3-031-58195-3_11

of Business and co-founder of the Heterodox Academy organisation, universities are now pursuing two alternative teloi: the search for truth, or the search for social justice or progressive change more broadly (Haidt, 2022). This is reflected in everything from university mission statements, image building, and hiring and staffing policies to research focus, education programmes and courses offered, and teaching practices. The problem, claims Haidt, is that a university can only have one telos and that elevating social justice to the telos of the university will, inevitably, interfere with the search for truth. In this bewildering state of affairs, many scholars are also struggling to find their way, caught between the ever-increasing demand to publish in the "right" journals, growing expectations to contribute to solving various social problems, and a perceived lack of public attention and respect for what academia has to offer.

Unfortunately, the field of management and organisation is no exception to this precarious state. More and more scholars in the field raise concerns about the lack of truly meaningful research which addresses the urgent issues of our time, despite—or perhaps because of—the astonishing rise in academic publications (Alvesson et al., 2017a, 2017b; Harley & Fleming, 2021; Tourish, 2019). Critical voices argue that business schools are in need of substantial change, not only to contribute better to solving current societal problems but also to make up for their alleged roles in creating the problems in the first place (Ghoshal, 2005; Hoffman, 2021; Parker, 2018). To an extent, this relates back to the so-called rigour–relevance debate (Hambrick, 1994; Nicolai & Seidl, 2010; Tushman et al., 2017; Vermeulen, 2005). According to several observers over recent years, business schools are becoming less relevant (Bennis & O'Toole, 2005; Mintzberg, 2004) as our research (Pettigrew, 2001) and teaching (Pfeffer & Fong, 2002) have become more and more detached from the world of practice. To close this gap, some (Hambrick, 1994; Susman & Evered, 1978) have argued that business school research should be more applied and closer linked to businesses and organisations. Others have criticised our research for a persistent lack of rigour, stating that "research that is not rigorous simply cannot be relevant" (Antonakis, 2017, p. 6) and that relevance vs. rigour is a false dichotomy.

This debate is, as can be expected, far from resolved. But the toilsome refinement of the classical "*Homo academicus*" is obviously not the answer for all our colleagues. Instead, some scholars who have grown weary and desperate with this whole situation have responded by turning towards activism, either integrated into their regular scholarly activities, such as research or teaching, or in activities primarily outside of university campuses (Barnett, 2021; Cox, 2015; Croog et al., 2018; Derickson & Routledge, 2015). Perhaps the most well-known example of the latter in recent years is Scientist Rebellion. Scientist Rebellion is a network of primary academics who no longer believe that regular academic practice and discourse is enough to fight "climate failure". According to them, academics are both well-suited and obliged to "rebel" if the issue is urgent enough:

> Scientists have spent decades writing papers, advising governments, briefing the press: all have failed. What is the point in documenting in ever greater detail the catastrophe we face, if we are not willing to do anything about it?
>
> Academics are perfectly placed to wage a rebellion: we exist in rich hubs of knowledge and expertise; we are well connected across the world, and to decision-makers; we have large platforms from which to inform, educate and rally others all over the world, and we have implicit authority and legitimacy, which is the basis of political power. We can make a difference. We must do what we can to halt the greatest destruction in human history (scientistrebellion.org).

Often, these scientists claim it is "their job" to try to inform the public about urgent policy matters in almost any way possible. In their "rebellion", they not only arrange public meetings and lawful demonstrations but also advocate for civil disobedience actions, such as blocking roads/bridges/airports and sometimes even sabotage in pursuit of particular agendas (Malm, 2021). It is worth noting that the activists' status as scientists, even when they are arrested for breaking the law, is emphasised by both themselves and the media covering their actions (Thompson, 2021).

It seems obvious that, for at least some academics, the urgency to actively engage in the issue(s) at hand and deliver their message to a broader public not only compels them to act but also influences how they see their role as academics. They are what we would like to call *Homo academicus activistarum*, academic activists.

Admittedly, all diligent academic work has the potential to change both society and the minds of individuals. However, in our opinion, this is a power which should be set in motion with some caution, as the consequences might be unforeseen and/or counterproductive. Nor do we deny academics the right to engage in political or social movements, including taking activist measures if they so choose. Nevertheless, we adhere to the virtue of at least trying to keep these roles and practices apart, for the sake of both individual academics and academia at large. In this chapter, we, therefore, problematise the role and practice of *Homo academicus activistarum*. As a contrast, we present and suggest what we think is a potential academic role which enables constructive engagement with current affairs and challenges while simultaneously preserving the integrity and legitimacy of academia.

Academic Activism

The societal commitments and engagement of scholars and other intellectuals in public policy debate have been discussed for a long time (Nelkin, 1977; Pielke, 2007). The idea of the *public intellectual*—an academic participating in public discourse and reaching out to a broad, intellectually interested public—has long been established (Etzioni & Bowditch, 2006). However, what is often referred to as "issue advocacy" or "science advocacy" comes in many forms, and no clear consensus has been reached on how to conceptualise advocacy (Kotcher et al., 2017; Tormos-Aponte et al., 2023). Since essentially all statements by scientists contain at least some element of normativity, it is reasonable to think of advocacy as a continuum, varying in how much, and in what form, normative judgement is communicated (ibid.). Therefore, arguing that something is the case (e.g., a changing climate) is a "lesser" form of advocacy than evaluating different policy options, which itself is a "lesser" form of advocacy than outright endorsing one specific option over any others.

What is now often referred to as "academic activism" or "scholar activism" resembles this latter form of advocacy, as it fuses academic activities and agendas with taking an active stance to create a (more or less) coherent practice (Chatterton et al., 2010).

> Intellectual activism calls you to focus not only on knowledge production as an abstract process but as part of an actual academic praxis (i.e. an embedded and embodied set of practices characterized by ideas, values, norms and theories). It additionally invites you to link your praxis directly with the questions thrown up by concrete daily justice issues and demands. (Contu, 2020, p. 738)

A common argument in relation to academic activism is that it cannot be avoided, that academics are always and inevitably advocating certain values and ideals:

> Hence, (morally loaded) activism is unavoidable *within* academia on several levels: in the choice of research questions and objects (do we investigate shareholder value or the value of shareholders for society?), in the theorizing process (is it respectful of the Other or does it violate it?), in the methods (do we objectify persons as numbers or do we engage in empathic understanding and involvement?), in the goals (do we pursue emancipation, social critique, or functional improvement of the existing?). (Delmestri, 2023, p. 3, emphasis original)

In addition, it is often claimed that even a seemingly apolitical stance is, in fact, political, since it stands in favour of the status quo (Young et al., 2010). It seems that being political cannot be avoided—but does this necessarily entail being an academic activist?

For the purpose of this chapter, academic activism is defined rather broadly as *mobilising one's academic credentials or institutional affiliation in support of a particular political position.* Here, we draw on Warren's (1999) definition of politics as "the subset of social relations characterized by conflicts over goods in the face of pressure to associate for collective action, where at least one party to the conflict seeks collectively binding decisions and seeks to sanction decisions by means of power" (Warren, 1999, p. 218).

The support can be through the promotion of their chosen political position as well as the active denigration or denial of alternative positions. Support may come in the form of research activities (from choice of research question, objects of research, and methodology to the interpretation and reporting of results), external outreach activities, and teaching. Furthermore, academic activism can be more or less explicit or implicit. Explicit academic activism entails open, outspoken, and public activities in support of or against particular issues, wherein one's academic status is utilised to enhance impact. Often, these activities are connected to social movements, or collaboration with activist organisations (Tormos-Aponte et al., 2023). Sometimes, explicit academic activism is not so much a personal choice but rather is imposed or at least characterised by strong social pressure, whereby internal or external activist groups demand universities, business schools, or individual scholars to "take sides"—with the usual argument that "not taking sides is also taking a side". Consequently, neutrality or arm's-length distance in relation to the conflict, struggle, cause, social movement, etc., in question is not possible. In contrast, implicit academic activism is more subtle and involves silently endorsing, emphasising, or ignoring certain issues, positions, and/or values in one's research or teaching.

Recent examples of explicit academic activism involving business schools and scholars include US university faculty members joining students in marches and protests against policy initiatives by then-President Donald J. Trump, or promoting Democrat candidates in Senate elections (Gee, 2017). A more implicit (or even borderline) example of activism is the Stockholm School of Economics inviting artists to put on a performance involving faculty being (voluntarily) chained outside the main entrance as an illustration of humans' climate impact. In summary, we can imagine a spectrum of various explicit–implicit activist positions and activities.

To be clear, we are not against critical research or scholars trying to inform broader publics of the results of their research, nor against scholars bringing up difficult and potentially controversial subjects in their teaching to challenge taken-for-granted norms and behaviours (Tallberg et al., 2022). On the contrary, we believe these to be essential elements of good scholarship. We are also, in general, supportive of the use of art and artistic approaches to help vitalise the field of management and organisation. However, we remain skeptical about letting explicit and/or implicit academic activism dominate one's scholarly activities, even as we honestly admit that implicit academic activism is much harder to both identify and avoid. As stated above, claims of total objectivity in social science are of course an illusion. All of us have more or less explicit assumptions, biases, and views with regard to the world we live in (Alvesson & Sköldberg, 2009). Moreover, passion for our chosen topic can be a very powerful driving force for research, helping us endure challenges such as grant applications, endless revise-and-resubmit processes, etc.

Researchers who subscribe to the arguments above usually add that as long as scholars are open and transparent about their sympathies and their potential biases, there is no problem. However, even if transparency might solve some problems, it can actually also cause new ones. In an era characterised by increased polarisation and questioning of science as a reliable producer of knowledge and a trustworthy institution, "transparency" might actually repel the people we try to reach, away from our arguments and research results (Nelson & Vucetich, 2009). A study by Kotcher et al. (2017) indicates that issue advocacy in general might not harm the credibility of scientists, but endorsing specific policies or engaging in issues of heated public debate will sometimes do so. In a polarised society where truths increasingly are regarded as "lived experiences" and publicly recognised expertise and titles can be viewed with suspicion rather than awe (Meyer & Quattrone, 2021), it becomes hard to reach "the other side" with unpopular arguments, e.g., convincing flat-earthers (Fernbach & Bogard, 2023), racists/anti-racists, etc. If we, as academics, openly and repeatedly associate with and label ourselves as something which large parts of society find controversial or extreme, we run the risk of turning people off—regardless of the logic in the argumentation or the empirical evidence (i.e., who are *you* to tell me how things are and how the world works?).

Furthermore, to be labelled as "tendentious" as a scholar is seldom desirable; this holds true regardless of whether it is a matter of type of research questions, favourite concepts, assumptions, or conclusions—with or without an activist agenda (Alvesson & Blom, 2022). The element of surprise is vital in research. We need to be open to empirical results which go against both personal and commonly held presumptions and, perhaps, our more or less ideologically loaded, deeply rooted convictions. Our audience—regardless of whether they are in-group peers, funding agencies, policymakers, or simply an interested public—expect us to be able to (at times) point to others rather than "the usual suspects" and to not repeat ourselves according to a predictable pattern. Serious academics are expected to listen to and engage with their critics' best arguments—not ridicule them, make a strawman of them, or pretend that they do not exist. Arguably, the majority of our stakeholders prefer to at least *potentially* be surprised by our research results. It is hard to imagine a more credible source than a researcher who, after extensive empirical investigations and self-reflection, changes their mind and refutes previous beliefs and truths.

Another dilemma associated with academic activism is dogmatism. It is easy to get "boxed in", tied to certain favourite theories, models, concepts, vocabulary, etc., due to career tactics, fashion, identification, or simply old unreflective habits (Alvesson & Blom, 2022; Alvesson & Sandberg, 2013). If ideological zeal is also added to this mix, the risk of dogmatism and unwillingness to question one's own assumptions tends to increase significantly. Adding conscious blinders to already-present unconscious ones might turn us into more zealous and more unwavering activists, but it will not make us better scholars. In summary, an open mind and a readiness to question our own previous beliefs are pivotal to our role as social scientists.

Homo Academicus Imaginatus: The Imaginative Scholar

To outline our idea, our image, of the imaginative scholar, we draw on and further develop a recent essay by Ali Aslan Gümüsay and Juliane Reinecke (2022) published in *Journal of Management Studies*. In this piece, Gümüsay and Reinecke discuss how we, as management scholars, can reclaim societal relevance by helping to co-create desirable futures. They argue that neither critical analysis of the present, nor prediction of probable futures, are sufficient for the management discipline to be relevant and useful in pursuit of what is desirable.

Instead, they write:

> We believe that there is another way of researching the future that goes beyond the search for existing empirical alternatives: feeding forward soci(et)al change through acts of imagination about the future. Imagination refers to the ability to form pictures in one's mind of something that cannot be immediately sensed or that has not been previously perceived: the irreal, unreal, and surreal. Imagining is making the absent present. (Gümüsay & Reinecke, 2022, p. 238)

Imagination, as "the creative ability to form images and ideas in the mind" (Patriotta, 2019, p. 3), facilitates the projection of possible future states and exploration of potentialities (Duhamel et al., 2023); it helps one, in the words of Hannah Arendt (1989), "go visiting", by considering a given issue from different perspectives and viewpoints. As Emirbayer and Mische (1998) have shown, human agency, in understanding and acting upon the world, is always temporally embedded. Therefore, projectivity is a constitutive element of agency as "the imaginative generation by actors of possible future trajectories of action, in which received structures of thought and action may be creatively reconfigured in relation to actor's hopes, fears, and desires for the future" (p. 971). According to Emirbayer and Mische (1998), human actors have the ability to distance themselves cognitively, emotionally, and sometimes practically from given structures and habits, to conceive new possibilities for thought and action, and thereby to transcend themselves into the future. In a similar vein, Mills (1959) coined the term "sociological imagination" as an approach to reconcile the individual and societal aspects of social reality. Through sociological imagination, an individual can come to understand theirself in relation to, and as part of, the societal, as well as understand the societal in relation to individuals. Fostering sociological imagination, then, could help us relate the particular to the general and the individual to the collective of not-yet-realised but imaginable and potentially realisable situations.

However, it would be a mistake to perceive imagination as mere experiments of thought and thereby neglect its transformative potential (Kostera, 2020). Especially in collective forms, imagination has performative potential, as it can bring people together and unleash alternatives to the present which might guide the collaborative co-creation of potential new social realities (Mangnus et al., 2021; Oomen et al., 2022). Gümüsay and Reinecke's (2022) suggestion for research is to embrace an explicit normative orientation by putting this performativity at the centre of theorising. This "what-if theorizing" (p. 240) explores potentialities to explore and articulate desirable futures through acts of *disciplined imagination.*

While we appreciate Gümüsay and Reinecke's (2022) effort to revitalise our field to make it more societally relevant, and we endorse much of what they suggest, we would nevertheless like to discuss and expand a few points. First, we believe that all activities tending towards utopian thinking should be pursued with care. Levitas (2003, 2013) has defined "utopia" broadly as an expression of or a desire for a better way of living. As such, utopias invite both critical engagement with the present as well as images of a better future. At the same time, with their inclination towards seeking out and pursuing "perfection", utopias often clash with the complexity and multifacetedness of reality, not the least the flaws and diversity of human beings. Even if practically unattainable, the depiction of an unequivocally desirable future makes utopias extremely prescriptive, with all alternative images, viewpoints, and desires seen as their adversary. History shows, with devastating clarity, what can happen when a diverse reality is forced to fit the idealised utopian vision, as authority and force are mobilised to alter reality—including people—in efforts to make the utopia come true (Popper, 1986; Sargent, 1982). However, open and reflexive imagination could serve as an antidote to these risks, as "imagination makes it possible to open up to the Other and try to understand the consequences that our deeds, technical solutions and social institutions may have for other people" (Kostera, 2020, p. 33).

Second, closely following our first point, we think that "questions of plurality, participation, and (re)presentation also need to be addressed" (Gümüsay & Reinecke, 2022, p. 240) to an even greater extent than the authors do in their essay. As Mangnus et al., (2021, p. 6) stated, "imagined futures have power. They coordinate and structure action in the present, thereby giving a particular shape to the future". Aiming to create more desirable alternatives to the present inevitably begs the question of *what* is desirable and *whether* everyone has the same view of this desirability. Consequently, future-making is not only a social but also a political act, as it reenacts certain sociopolitical structures and preferences (Mangnus et al., 2021). We believe that "desirable futures", plural, indicate the key approach to this issue. This entails not confining scholarly activities to one single image of what a desirable future would be, but rather embracing multiple alternatives and the constant diversity of opinions on essentially all matters of desirability. One possibility would be to include multiple groups of actors in collaborative exploration of alternatives in both research and education. This is of course hard to achieve in practice, given the extensive number of stakeholders with different views who can/should be involved. The risk of a consensus-based, abstract desirable future which is severely eviscerated—and thereby says nothing which can be questioned—must be taken into account.

Third, we also suggest engaging in imagining alternatives as part of higher-education activities, something which Gümüsay and Reinecke (2022) barely touch on. We do not reject the utility of problem-based learning (Duch et al., 2001), case study teaching (Greenhalgh, 2007; Lynn Jr, 1999), or any other mode of teaching and learning developed to enhance higher education. Nevertheless, we think that disciplined imagination also offers considerable pedagogical potential, especially if it involves actively engaging students. An illustrative example would be to explore "organisation without formal leaders" as an "alternative" mode of organising. Centuries of inherited experience—documented and theorised by classical scholars like Weber (1947) and Bendix (1956) as well as more contemporary ones like Du Gay (2000)—have established the image of at least formal organisations as hierarchical structures as more or less taken for granted. In this view of organisations, hierarchies are formally recognised (Lundholm et al., 2012) and based on vertical social relationships (Diefenbach & Sillince, 2011). However, alternatives do exist, and they are represented in, e.g., research on social and anarchistic movements (Reedy, 2014; Sutherland et al., 2014; Western, 2014), which could serve as imaginative inspiration. In this learning scenario, students could then—in teams or individually, under the teacher's guidance—address questions such as: What would an organisation without formal leaders look like, and how would it work? Are there any practical examples to be identified, current or historical? What are the conditions under which such an organisation (and its members) could possibly thrive? What are the possible benefits as well as drawbacks compared to traditional, hierarchical organisations? Imagining and investigating organisations without formal leaders could enhance the understanding of traditional modes of organising and their characterising features at the same time as expanding our thinking towards potential alternatives.

Another example is the work with *Climaginaries*—a cross-discipline, international collaboration between Lund University, Durham University, University of Warwick, and Utrecht University which aims to "advance the understanding of imaginaries as means through which to catalyse the forms of political, economic, and social responses required for transitioning to a post-fossil society" (https://www.climaginaries.org/our-impact/). This is done through a mix of techniques, including scenarios, modelling, experimentations, the creation of visions, and various cultural expressions such as films and arts. The key here is to enable imagination, in order to influence policy- and decision-making.

Practical Implications

Working as imaginative scholars has several practical implications, which we would like to briefly touch on. Emirbayer and Mische (1998) remind us that the past, present, and future are always simultaneously present in human experience, as humans draw on and try to understand the past, evaluate the present, and imagine the future. This means that when employing disciplined imagination, researchers have to be future-oriented as well as focused on the present and the past simultaneously. Beyond backtracking from the imagined future(s) to the present to depict present conditions, as Gümüsay and Reinecke (2022) suggest, all evaluations of the present state of affairs need to take alternative future developments into account. This means that the empirical data will, by necessity, be at least partly fictional, but this does not mean that anything could qualify as valid data. Instead, Gümüsay and Reinecke (2022) argue for *speculative rigour,* targeting questions such as the significance of the imagination, how the imagination arised, what the preconditions are, and potential implications for a broad range of stakeholders. As reviewers of research, we need to evaluate theory not (only) on whether it describes or explains an existing reality, but also on its potential to open up new paths of thought and action. Imaginative research which makes sense depends more on plausibility and plurality than accuracy (Weick, 1995) as it tries to provide something truly interesting and meaningful (Alvesson et al., 2017a, b; Davis, 1971).

On a general note, a more reflexive approach to our own research in terms of assumptions, findings, and conclusions is needed in order to challenge the fixed positions which might otherwise follow from an activist-attractive research agenda. Here, *reflexivity* is defined as the ambition to carefully and systematically take a critical view of one's own assumptions, ideas, and favoured vocabulary and to consider whether alternative ones make sense (Alvesson et al., 2017a, b; Alvesson & Sköldberg, 2009), hence, it is a vital element in the protection against stubborn dogmatism, regardless of whether it concerns theory, methods, or politics. *Doubt* is an important counterweight to ideological, activist-driven zeal. Therefore, we think that all academics—and particularly those inclined towards activism—would benefit from now and then asking themselves important questions such as: Where do my ideas come from? Am I seduced by a particular discourse/set of ideas/demagogue? Are there contradictions, trade-offs, or goal conflicts which I have not been aware of or ignored? Do I have ideological blinders which affect my research and teaching? What do I do with empirical findings which contradict my ideological convictions?

Furthermore, and not elaborated by Gümüsay and Reinecke (2022), working as an imaginative scholar means that we have to develop our writing accordingly. Many scholars have argued for the need to write differently to develop the field of management and organisation and for not being constrained by current writing norms (Beavan et al., 2021; Gilmore et al., 2019; Grey & Sinclair, 2006; Kostera, 2022; see also Martin Holgersson (2024) in this book). Adopting imagination as the *leitmotif*, our writing will aim less for a realistic representation of "reality" and embrace a more fictional (Czarniawska, 1999) or pre-factual (Gümüsay & Reinecke, 2022) style. Beyond "writing up" data relating to the present (or rather the past, at the time of writing) which then must be interpreted—however creatively that might be done—imaginative writing needs to make the "not-yet but potential" come to life. The imaginations must be plausible, and the alternatives transparent so as not to risk being dogmatic. In "going visiting" (Arendt, 1989), different perspectives and possible implications for a variety of envisioned stakeholders need to be explored. Imaginative writing is more playful and less formulaic (Alvesson & Gabriel, 2013), and it seeks to engage the reader in collaborative acts of imagining alternative futures.

So far in this chapter, we have primarily talked about the practical implications of imaginative scholarship from a research perspective. As teachers, we also need to be less focused on "what is", whether from a normative or a critical perspective, and more focused on "what ifs" in terms of potential alternatives to existing norms, institutions, and behaviours. A good pedagogical approach would be to engage students in joint explorations of potentialities, their conditions, and possible implications, as well as what would be required for their realisation. Working collaboratively could help foster a teaching approach which is less dogmatic and more open to diverse perspectives and viewpoints. The aim of our teaching should not be to confine our students to believing that only one future is possible or undisputedly preferable, because it very seldom is. Instead, we should prepare our students for a future which is uncertain but undetermined and to develop their "future literacy" (Mangnus et al., 2021; Miller, 2007; Spanjol et al., 2023)—i.e., their capacity to engage productively and reflexively with the future in the present.

Discussion and Conclusion

Many scholars, including ourselves, struggle at times with balancing personal values and interests with professional ambitions and conceptions, as well as with trying to find ways to make our scholarly activities relevant and productive. These struggles often reflect deeper efforts of trying to figure out who we are, personally and professionally, and who we should be. Some scholars, profoundly passionate about their issues of concern but frustrated by the (in their view) lack of societal progress, respond to these struggles with activism, explicitly or implicitly mobilising their academic activities or affiliation to promote political aims. In some cases, it becomes who they are and think of themselves—i.e., academic activists. In this chapter, we problematise this inclination on two major fronts. First, we believe that being too invested in certain viewpoints or preferred outcomes can interfere with the scholarly necessity to be open to the unexpected, to engage with arguments and perspectives different from one's own, and, when justified, to change our minds about what we previously believed. Second, we think that engaging in activism as individual scholars or institutions might sometimes impair our public credibility and, consequently, our ability to contribute to society. As teachers and researchers, we all simultaneously lean on and are part of the reproduction of the credibility of academia and science as institutions. This credibility is currently being challenged, with unforeseen consequences (Nichols, 2017). We should be careful to not add to that negative development through our own actions.

However, this does not mean that in our scholarly work we should retract from engaging with societal challenges, nor from doing our best to broadly communicate the results of our efforts. But we should simply be less dogmatic when doing so, and openly explore alternative interpretations and solutions (Spicer et al., 2009; Wickert & Schaefer, 2015). To inspire such an approach, in this chapter we suggest the "Imaginative scholar" as a more productive self-understanding than the "academic activist". Drawing and elaborating on Gümüsay and Reinecke's (2022) initial suggestion, we outline what could characterise an imaginative scholar: a scholar engaged in disciplined imagination, carefully embracing its performative potential, and—in dialogue and collaboration with fellow researchers, students, and other stakeholders—exploring alternatives to the present.

After having made a case for productive imaginations rather than spectacular protests or actions, we might do well to end this chapter with some reflections and self-critical remarks. In this chapter, we the authors can be accused of defending higher education's classical and traditional values, virtues, assumptions, and positions, thereby defending the status quo and a conservative view of research and higher education (close to what Ericsson and Cinque (2024) in this book refer to as "*Homo moralis*"). To be sure, colleagues with a radical change agenda will probably find our suggested way of "voicing" (namely, developing and discussing imaginary futures) too quiet and ineffective in the current media and political landscape, where only the loud and the spectacular gain attention. Scholars in research traditions closely linked to social justice movements will probably also find our arguments secondary to their struggles (e.g., gender, class, race, etc.). Again, we are not arguing for the return of the idealised "*Homo academicus*" self-view of scholarship. Instead, we are arguing for an engaged scholarship which is less dogmatic and more playfully explorative—a scholarship which takes our task and institution seriously, but ourselves and our personal agendas a bit less so. We must sincerely ask ourselves if our scholarly pursuit for knowledge and truths is an end in itself, or just a means in support of some greater cause (e.g., the fight for the climate, social justice, gender equality, etc.). If action and quick real-life results are more important than the slow, systematic, and curious search for knowledge, one should perhaps think about leaving the scholarly profession and going "all in" as an activist. At least in our part of the world, this move seems rare. Partly, of course, due to the sacrifice of a privileged position (social status, decent pay, freedom, networks), but also since an explicit association with academia provides activist actions with valuable intellectual legitimacy.

Related to this is the question of whether we in academia attract activists more than other professions. The above-mentioned legitimacy, the generous conditions for side projects, and the significant degree of freedom when it comes to planning one's own time all constitute a solid platform for activist activities. Another question is whether higher education as an institution fosters and nurtures activism. Arguably, visionary and less conformist ideas/ideologies find more fertile ground in academia compared to society at large. Bold thinking, disputing ideas, and arguing are all vital elements of scholarly life, and the step of leaving the armchair to ensure the impact of one's pet ideas might for some not be that dramatic a move.

Again, the context of course looks different in different parts of the world; the conditions above are primarily derived from North America and Western Europe, and in particular the authors' own home country of Sweden.

To conclude, the importance of scholars' credibility is hard to overemphasise. If we publicly engage in activist actions and campaigns, our sincerity and zeal might be confirmed, but at some point, our public persona might be more associated with a particular cause or ideological position than with the virtues which (at least should, in our opinion) characterise a scholar: open-mindedness, curiosity, and a willingness to listen to and take one's challengers' best arguments seriously. If this scholarly integrity and academic credibility have been severely—and perhaps irreparably—compromised in the eyes of our one's stakeholders, it might be the right time to leave the armchair to someone else and truly get one's hands dirty.

References

Alvesson, M., & Blom, M. (2022). The hegemonic ambiguity of big concepts in organization studies. *Human Relations, 71*(1), 58–86. https://doi.org/10.1177/0018726720986847

Alvesson, M., & Gabriel, Y. (2013). Beyond formulaic research: In praise of greater diversity in organizational research and publications. *Academy of Management Learning and Education, 12*(2), 245–263. https://doi.org/10.5465/amle.2012.0327

Alvesson, M., Blom, M., & Sveningsson, S. (2017a). *Reflexive leadership: Organising in an imperfect world.* SAGE.

Alvesson, M., Gabriel, Y., & Paulsen, R. (2017b). *Return to meaning—A social science with something to say.* Oxford University Press.

Alvesson, M., & Sandberg, J. (2013). *Constructing research questions: Doing interesting research.* SAGE.

Alvesson, M., & Sköldberg, K. (2009). *Reflexive methodology: New vistas for qualitative research.* SAGE.

Antonakis, J. (2017). On doing better science: From thrill of discovery to policy implications. *The Leadership Quarterly, 28*(1), 5–21. https://doi.org/10.1016/j.leaqua.2017.01.006

Arendt, H. (1989). *Lectures on Kant's political philosophy*. University of Chicago Press.

Barnett, R. (2021). The activist university: Identities, profiles, conditions. *Policy Futures in Education, 19*(5), 513–526. https://doi.org/10.1177/14782103211003444

Beavan, K., Borgström, B., Helin, J., & Rhodes, C. (2021). Changing writing/writing for change. *Gender, Work & Organization, 28*(2), 449–455. https://doi.org/10.1111/gwao.12644

Bendix, R. (1956). *Work and authority in industry*. Wiley.

Bennis, W. G., & O'Toole, J. (2005). How business schools have lost their way. *Harvard Business Review, 83*(5), 96–104.

Chatterton, P., Hodkinson, S., & Pickerill, J. (2010). Beyond scholar activism: Making strategic interventions inside and outside the neoliberal university. *ACME: An International E-Journal for Critical Geographies, 9*(2), 245–275.

Contu, A. (2020). Answering the crisis with intellectual activism: Making a difference as business school scholars. *Human Relations, 73*(5), 737–757. https://doi.org/10.1177/0018726719827366

Cox, L. (2015). Scholarship and activism: A social movement perspective. *Studies in Social Justice, 9*(1), 34–53. https://doi.org/10.26522/ssj.v9i1.1153

Croog, R., Hayes-Conroy, A., Gutierrez-Velezs, V. H., & Montoya, A. S. (2018). Real world food justice and the enigma of the scholar-activist label: A reflection on research values. *ACME, 17*(4), 1024–1044.

Czarniawska, B. (1999). *Writing management: Organization theory as a literary genre*. Oxford University Press.

Davis, M. S. (1971). That's interesting! Towards a phenomenology of sociology and a sociology of phenomenology. *Philosophy of the Social Sciences, 1*(4), 309–344. https://doi.org/10.1177/004839317100100211

Delmestri, G. (2023). Are we all activists? *Organization Studies, 44*(1), 159–162. https://doi.org/10.1177/01708406221133507

Derickson, K. D., & Routledge, P. (2015). Resourcing scholar-activism: Collaboration, transformation, and the production of knowledge. *The Professional Geographer, 67*(1), 1–7. https://doi.org/10.1080/00330124.2014.883958

Diefenbach, T., & Sillince, J. A. A. (2011). Formal and informal hierarchy in different types of organization. *Organization Studies, 32*(11), 1515–1537. https://doi.org/10.1177/0170840611421254

Du Gay, P. (2000). *In praise of bureaucracy*. Sage.

Duch, B. J., Groh, S. E., & Allen, D. E. (Eds.). (2001). *The power of problem-based learning*. Stylus.

Duhamel, F., Niess, A., & De Geuser, F. (2023). Imagining aesthetic leadership. *Leadership, 19(5)*, 413–430. https://doi.org/10.1177/17427150231186000

Emirbayer, M., & Mische, A. (1998). What is agency? *American Journal of Sociology, 103*(4), 962–1023. https://doi.org/10.1086/231294

Ericsson, D., & Cinque, S. (2024). Debating *Homo academicus*: A maieutic quest for self-reflexivity. In S. Cinque & D. Ericsson (Eds.), *Debating Homo academicus in management and organization: Ontological assumptions and practical implications* (pp.1–22). Palgrave.

Etzioni, A., & Bowditch, A. (2006). *Public intellectuals—An endangered species?* Rowman & Littlefield Publishers.

Fernbach, P. M., & Bogard, J. E. (2023). Conspiracy theory as individual and group behavior: Observations from the Flat Earth International Conference. *Topics in Cognitive Science, 16(2)*, 187–205. https://doi.org/10.1111/tops.12662

Gee, K. (2017, March 1). Business schools face surge in activism. *Wall Street Journal*.

Ghoshal, S. (2005). Bad management theories are destroying good management practices. *Academy of Management Learning & Education, 4*(1), 75–91. https://doi.org/10.5465/amle.2005.16132558

Gilmore, S., Harding, N., Helin, J., & Pullen, A. (2019). Writing differently. *Management Learning, 50*(1), 3–10. https://doi.org/10.1177/1350507618811027

Greenhalgh, A. M. (2007). Case method teaching as science and art: A metaphoric approach and curricular application. *Journal of Management Education, 31*(2), 181–194. https://doi.org/10.1177/1052562906291306

Grey, C., & Sinclair, A. (2006). Writing differently. *Organization, 13*(3), 443–453. https://doi.org/10.1177/1350507618811027

Gümüsay, A. A., & Reinecke, J. (2022). Researching for desirable futures: From real utopias to imagining alternatives. *Journal of Management Studies, 59*(1), 236–242. https://doi.org/10.1111/joms.12709

Haidt, J. (2022). When truth and social justice collide, choose truth. *The Chronicle of Higher Education, 69*(6).

Hambrick, D. (1994). What if the academy actually mattered? *Academy of Management Review, 19*, 11–16. https://doi.org/10.5465/amr.1994.9410122006

Harley, B., & Fleming, P. (2021). Not even trying to change the world: Why do elite management journals ignore the major problems facing humanity? *The Journal of Applied Behavioral Science, 57*(2), 133–152. https://doi.org/10.1177/0021886321997189

Hoffman, A. J. (2021). Business education as if people and the planet really matter. *Strategic Organization, 19*(3), 513–525. https://doi.org/10.1177/1476127020967638

Holgersson, M. (2024). Homo scribens—Notes on writing management. In S. Cinque & D. Ericsson (Eds.), *Debating Homo academicus in management and organization: Ontological assumptions and practical implications* (pp. 93–116). Palgrave.

Kostera, M. (2020). *The imagined organization: Spaces, dreams and places.* Edward Elgar Publishing.

Kostera, M. (Ed.). (2022). *How to write differently: A quest for meaningful academic writing*. Edward Elgar Publishing.

Kotcher, J. E., Myers, T. A., Vraga, E. K., Stenhouse, N., & Maibach, E. W. (2017). Does engagement in advocacy hurt the credibility of scientists? Results from a randomized national survey experiment. *Environment Communication, 11*(3), 415–429. https://doi.org/10.1080/17524032.2016.1275736

Levitas, R. (2003). Introduction: The elusive idea of utopia. *History of the Human Sciences, 16*(1), 1–10. https://doi.org/10.1177/095269510301600 1002

Levitas, R. (2013). Some varieties of utopian methods. *Irish Journal of Sociology, 21*(2), 41–50. https://doi.org/10.7227/IJS.21.2.3

Lundholm, S. E., Rennstam, J., & Alvesson, M. (2012). Understanding hierarchy in contemporary work. *Research in the Sociology of Organizations, 35*, 113–140. https://doi.org/10.1108/S0733-558X(2012)0000035007

Lynn Jr, L. E. (1999). *Teaching & Learning with Cases.* Chatham House Publishers.

Malm, A. (2021). *How to blow up a pipeline: Learning to fight in a world on fire*. Verso Books.

Mangnus, A. C., Oomen, J., Vervoort, J. M., & Hajer, M. A. (2021). Futures literacy and the diversity of the future. *Futures, 132*(1), 1–9. https://doi.org/10.1016/j.futures.2021.102793

Meyer, R. E., & Quattrone, P. (2021). Living in a post-truth world? Research, doubt and organization studies. *Organization Studies, 42*(9), 1373–1383. https://doi.org/10.1177/01708406211039103

Mintzberg, H. (2004). Managers not MBSs. *Management Today, 20*(7), 10–13.

Miller, R. (2007). Futures literacy: A hybrid strategic scenario method. *Futures, 39*(4), 341–362. https://doi.org/10.1016/j.futures.2006.12.001

Mills, C. W. (1959). *The sociological imagination.* Oxford University Press.

Nelkin, D. (1977). Scientists and professional responsibility: The experience of American ecologists. *Social Studies of Science, 7*(1), ii. https://doi.org/10.1177/030631277700700110

Nelson, M. P., & Vucetich, J. A. (2009). On advocacy by environmental scientists: What, whether, why, and how. *Conservation Biology, 23*(5), 1090–1101.

Nichols, T. (2017). How America lost faith in expertise. And why that's a giant problem. *Foreign Affairs, 96*(March–April), 60–73.

Nicolai, A., & Seidl, D. (2010). That's Relevant! Different forms of practical relevance in management science. *Organization Studies, 31*(9&10), 1257–1285. https://doi.org/10.1177/0170840610374401

Oomen, J., Hoffaman, J., & Hajer, M. A. (2022). Techniques of futuring: On how imagined futures become socially performative. *European Journal of Social Theory, 25*(2), 252–270. https://doi.org/10.1177/1368431020988826

Parker, M. (2018). *Shut down the business school: What's wrong with management education.* Pluto Press.

Patriotta, G. (2019). Imagination, self-knowledge, and poise: Jim March's lessons for leadership. *Journal of Management Studies, 56*(8), 1753–1765. https://doi.org/10.1111/joms.12536

Pettigrew, A. M. (2001). Management research after modernism. *British Journal of Management, 12,* S61–S70. https://doi.org/10.1111/1467-8551.12.s1.8

Pielke, R. A., Jr. (2007). *The honest broker: Making sense of science in policy and politics.* Cambridge University Press.

Pfeffer, J., & Fong, C. T. (2002). The end of business schools? Less success than meets the eye. *Academy of Management Learning & Education, 1*(1), 78–95. https://doi.org/10.5465/amle.2002.7373679

Popper, K. R. (1986). Utopia and Violence. *World Affairs, 149*(1), 3–9.

Reedy, P. (2014). Impossible organisations: Anarchism and organisational praxis. *Ephemera, 14*(4), 639–658.

Sargent, L. T. (1982). Authority & Utopia: Utopianism in political thought. *Polity, 14*(4), 565–584. https://doi.org/10.2307/3234464

Spanjol, J., Rosa, A., Schirrmeister, W., Dahl, P., Domnik, D., Lindner, M., de la Cruz, M., & Kuhlmann, J.-F. (2023). The potential of futures literacy for impact-oriented business schools. *Futures, 146*(2), 1–15. https://doi.org/10.1016/j.futures.2022.103084

Spicer, A., Alvesson, M., & Kärreman, D. (2009). Critical performativity: The unfinished business of critical management studies. *Human Relations, 62*(4), 537–560. https://doi.org/10.1177/0018726708101984

Susman, G. I., & Evered, R. D. (1978). An assessment of the scientific merits of action research. *Administrative Science Quarterly, 23*(December), 582–603.

Sutherland, N., Land, C., & Böhm, S. (2014). Anti-leaders(hip) in social movement organizations: The case for autonomous grassroots groups. *Organization, 21*(6), 759–781. https://doi.org/10.1177/1350508413480254

Tallberg, L., Välikangas, L., & Hamilton, L. (2022). Animal activism in the business school: Using fierce compassion for teaching critical and positive perspectives. *Management Learning, 53*(1), 55–74. https://doi.org/10.1177/13505076211044612

Thompson, T. (2021). Scientist Rebellion: Researchers join protesters at COP26. *Nature, 599*, 357. https://doi.org/10.1038/d41586-021-03430-5

Tormos-Aponte, F., Ph., Brown, Dosemagen, S., Fisher, D. R., Frickel, S., Mackendrick, N., Meyer, D. S., & Parker, J. N. (2023). Pathways for diversifying and enhancing science advocacy. *Science Advances, 9*(20), 1–13. https://doi.org/10.1126/sciadv.abq4899

Tourish, D. (2019). *Management studies in crisis: Fraud, deception and meaningless research*. Cambridge University Press.

Tushman, M. L., O'Reilly, C., Fenollosa, A., Kleinbaum, A. M., & McGrath, D. (2017). Relevance *and* rigor: Executive education as a lever in shaping practice and research. *Academy of Management Learning & Education, 6*(3), 345–362. https://doi.org/10.5465/amle.2007.26361625

Vermeulen, F. (2005). On rigor and relevance: Fostering dialectic progress in management research. *Academy of Management Journal, 48*(6), 978–982. https://doi.org/10.5465/amj.2005.19573102

Warren, M. E. (1999). What is political? *Journal of Theoretical Politics, 11*(2), 207–231. https://doi.org/10.1177/0951692899011002004

Weber, M. (1947). *The theory of social and economic organisation*. The Free Press.

Weick, K. E. (1995). *Sensemaking in organizations*. SAGE.

Western, S. (2014). Autonomist leadership in leaderless movements: Anarchists leading the way. *Ephemera, 14*(4), 673–698.

Wickert, C., & Schaefer, S. M. (2015). Towards a progressive understanding of performativity in critical management studies. *Human Relations, 68*(1), 107–130. https://doi.org/10.1177/0018726713519279

Young, A. M., Battaglia, A., & Cloud, D. L. (2010). (UN)disciplining the scholar activist: Policing the boundaries of political engagement. *Quarterly Journal of Speech, 96*(4), 427–435. https://doi.org/10.1080/00335630.2010.521179

12

Homo academicus as Guild, Employment, and Attitude: The Academy in Transition

Alf Westelius

Introduction

Homo academicus, who are we, who do we want to be, and how do others view us? There are many alternative answers to these questions. In this chapter, I explore three different conceptions, conceptions that not only differ in outlook and underlying assumptions, but also on who counts as *Homo academicus*. The three are *Homo academicus* as guild, employment, and attitude to knowledge and learning. These three could appear anywhere in the academic world and to differing degrees also outside of it. I will therefore alternate between a more general perspective, and the specific context of organisation and management.

Entering a road towards *Homo academicus*-ship may be motivated by a range of desires and the basic assumption that these desires can be fulfilled by becoming a *Homo academicus*. The range of desires includes

A. Westelius (✉)
Department of Management and Engineering, Linköping University,
Linköping, Sweden
e-mail: alf.westelius@liu.se

S. Cinque and D. Ericsson (eds.), *Debating 'Homo Academicus' in Management and Organization*, Palgrave Debates in Business and Management,
https://doi.org/10.1007/978-3-031-58195-3_12

the search for truth or justified true belief; a longing for becoming an authority—or merely to be accepted into the circles where those one views as authorities reside and act; making a career in a structure with a seemingly clear hierarchy—or merely making a living; a passion for a topic; a wish for intellectual challenges—or merely intellectual conversations .... These desires can be met to differing degrees and in different forms depending on the conception of *Homo academicus*.

The chapter is organised as follows. Starting with the conception of *Homo academicus* as guild, I then move on to *Homo academicus* as employment and then to *Homo academicus* as an attitude characterised by a yearning for learning. Before continuing my exploration, I then sum up these three different conceptions of *Homo academicus*. Next, I look closer at ideas of what counts as valuable knowledge, how this is connected with management scholarship in academic and non-academic settings, and how channels and venues for learning have changed through advances in information and communication technologies—possibly enriching, possibly challenging business schools and other traditional organisations of higher education and learning. I conclude the chapter by taking a closer look at what counts as true or acceptable knowledge in different traditions, how this plays out in the field of organisation and management, how it relates to the guild and the yearning-for-learning attitude conceptions of *Homo academicus,* ending with the open-ended question of if current practices conform with how we want the academic discourse and search for knowledge to function.

Homo academicus as Guild

The guild conception considers only those who have been accepted by existing guild members as academics. An underlying assumption of a guild is that some topic circle—merchants, shoemakers, goldsmiths, or university teachers—can agree on some type of standardisation of their trade—participation, practices, output, pricing, etc.—and can be recognised as an entity by the surrounding community, especially those parts of the surrounding community with whom they interact commercially. This unity is assumed to serve as a foundation for power—power in negotiations with others, power against outside influence and control. To uphold such unity, we would expect some degree of self-disciplining in the guild—corrective action, or in the extreme case, expulsion. In the academic world, corrective action is exceedingly rare once you have achieved a prominent position. The guild-administered self-disciplining is rather one of fostering and selection on the way in and upwards, than one of exclusion of existing but increasingly deviant members.

Perhaps the guild conception really encompasses a host of guilds, each with their own cherished assumptions, traditions, and quality criteria, and with hierarchies and "families" of guilds of differing status. Rather than actively being expulsed from one guild, we see a migration of deviant members to related guilds where opposition to the exited guild is seen as laudable (for example labelling themselves Critical), or just to a similar but less prestigious guild, open to new members, sharing the basic assumptions. In business studies, the mainstream has served and developed business interests, embracing the basic assumption that shareholder value should be the overarching goal. Often, this is not even debated, but can at times, especially if challenged from outside of academia, become vehemently defended, as by Milton Friedman in 1970, where he invoked cold-war symbolism:

> The businessmen believe that they are defending free enterprise when they declaim that business is not concerned "merely" with profit but also with promoting desirable "social" ends; that business has a "social conscience" and takes seriously its responsibilities for providing employment, eliminating discrimination, avoiding pollution and whatever else may be the catchwords of the contemporary crop of reformers. In fact they are—or would be if they or any one else took them seriously— preaching pure and unadulterated socialism. Businessmen who talk this way are unwitting puppets of the intellectual forces that have been undermining the basis of a free society these past decades. (Friedman, 1970, p. 17)

Multi-stakeholderism is today more tolerated within the mainstream of organisation and management studies, as long as alternative concerns can still be construed as compatible with shareholder value. It is then comforting when prominent businessmen make statements of the type that Larry Fink, CEO of BlackRock, wrote in *The Power of Capitalism.*

"In today's globally interconnected world, a company must create value for and be valued by its full range of stakeholders in order to deliver long-term value for its shareholders" (Fink, 2022).

"Critical" scholars in business studies have tended to form guilds of their own, which tend not to, but can, share this fundamental shareholder-value assumption. Whether or not they share this central one, critiquing (other) assumptions of mainstream business research and practice becomes the central norm. The assumption of managers behaving rationally tends to be a favourite target for such critique. An example of a prominent Critical scholar is Mats Alvesson, critiquing the grandiosity and functional stupidity of managers on the assumption that leadership ought to be based on criticism and reflection (e.g., Alvesson & Spicer, 2016; Alvesson et al., 2017). This could be viewed as following in the footsteps of Nils Brunsson (e.g., *The Irrational Organization*, 1985; *The Organization of Hypocrisy*, 1989) in exposing traits that mainstream business scholars are less keen to notice, explore, and expose, as it clashes with the assumption that managers are rational and competent. But it could also be seen as following in footsteps more acceptable in mainstream circles, following Chris Argyris and Donald Schön in promoting how critical reflection can help managers improve (e.g., Argyris & Schön, 1974). This speaks to an assumption uniting the majority of business scholars' guilds, that business studies should contribute to management practice.

However, being on the critical side of the spectrum can generate opposition from the mainstream. Martin Parker (2020) describes the creation of a Critical Management Studies faculty at Leicester University, at first positively profiling business studies at Leicester by adhering to a critical, poststructuralist, increasingly guild-like community, diverging from the mainstream profile of business schools.

> This was work that developed a sophisticated critique of the language and ideology of managerialism, relying on Habermas, Foucault, Derrida and others in order to do so. As the growing business schools appointed new staff, so did CMS grow rapidly, and by the end of the decade had its own conference, a section at the American Academy of Management, and

> various sympathetic journals. CMS was gradually becoming institutionalised, with an increasing number of texts which constructed the canon []. (pp. 4–5)

This profiled business school grew, as business studies continued to grow in general. But eventually, the CMS faculty at Leicester succumbed to mainstream guild opposition, being expulsed from the university's business school on the assumption that Critical Management Studies scholars are less attractive to prospective business students than mainstream scholars.

Few *Homo academici* would talk of themselves as guild members, but the guild label has been used before. For example, Rashdall (1895) sees the origins of universities as guilds of students and masters,[1] and Macfarlane and Jefferson (2022) distinguish between "guild-route" academics, growing up in research universities, and "non-guild" academics, who either come from teaching universities or enter academia "from the professions or industry often without a PhD" (p. 36). Examining the traits of the conception I term *the guild conception*, certainly uncovers guild-like traits.

A guild rests on the assumption that knowledge and skill reside in people, rather than being clearly externalisable. In Polanyi's terms, important knowledge is to a large extent tacit rather than explicit (Polanyi, 1958). Thus, to acquire that knowledge, you need to associate with someone already possessing it, a master, learning directly from them in what Nonaka (1994) termed socialising, by working alongside the master in an apprenticeship. The road as apprentice from novice to *Gesell* status, and eventually to masterhood will be both guided and assessed by existing masters. Indeed, Huisman (2012) proposes that a lasting capability of universities, in our age of abundant digital access to sources, is this guild-like socialising into the craft of performing research.

---

[1] "'University' means merely a number, a plurality, an aggregate of persons. [] At the end of the twelfth and beginning of the thirteenth centuries, we find the word applied to corporations either of Masters or of students; but it long continues to be applied to other corporations as well, particularly to the then newly formed Guilds and to the Municipalities of towns [] It is a mere accident that the term has gradually come to be restricted to a particular kind of Guild or Corporation" (Rashdall, 1895, p. 7).

In the guild, legitimacy does not just derive from competence in the guild's subject matter; it also rests on constancy, on the assumption that change can be detrimental, and that not shifting governance model or quality criteria at will is beneficial for the guild. Upholding tradition thus becomes important, and outside interference (for example attempts at controlling or directing the guild, the inclusion and exclusion criteria, and the ideals and processes [or rites] of the guild) is strongly opposed by the guild members (Ogilvie, 2004). A basic assumption is that the strength of the guild rests on its ability to project an image of unity to its surroundings. Internal critique and renewal could thus also be problematic, since it could threaten the tradition. Collegiality is a cherished idea in the guild, both in the sense that we, as guild members, should stick together and support each other, but also in the sense that control should be exercised from within the guild, the collegium (Rashdall, 1895, pp. 153 ff.). That it is still cherished—or longed for—not least by some organisation and management scholars is attested by business studies professors Kerstin Sahlin and Ulla Eriksson-Zetterquist's *Revitalizing Collegiality: Restoring Faculty Authority in Universities* (2023).

If we scrape a bit at this visible guild surface, underlying assumptions about negotiating power begin to appear. The lone one is not strong—strength lies in numbers, in being a group acting together, looking to the good of the guild, rather than just to an individual member of it. But for the group to be strong, there is also an underlying assumption that the group members must possess something valuable that is exclusive to them. If too many possess this competence that the guild possesses and guards, it will no longer be as valuable. So numbers, yes, but not "the larger, the better". There must be a far larger "them" than "us" to make the guild important and guild membership valuable. So the assumption is that power lies both in the knowledge possessed by the masters, and by the ability of the guild, the ingroup, the we, to define what counts as knowledge, skill, and quality. The customer is not always right, the guild is. And if masses flock to the guild to learn its secrets and be admitted, guild membership needs somehow to be restricted. To the early-modern guild, this could mean seeking, and attempting to enforce, exclusive privileges to work in the guild's occupation and to set strict rules for apprenticeship and acceptance into the guild (Ogilvie, 2004). For universities and current organisation and management guild members, it is also a market issue. The product is knowledge, learning, or certification signalling some valuable qualification regarding knowledge or learning. To keep the guild from ballooning until membership loses its exclusivity, it becomes important to identify some knowledge, skill, or competence to be made a product to sell to customers, rather than an intellectual or embodied asset that unlocks access to guild membership. (I will return to this issue in connection with the growth in popularity and size of business studies.)

The ideal that control should be exercised from within the guild, the collegium, is not to be confused with the office of rector (chancellor, president) of universities. Rectorship is an official organisational position at a specific university (related to the next conception that I will treat: employment), not a signal of authority in academy viewed as a guild. Indeed, rectorship is often even looked down upon, if that position has been actively striven for by its incumbent, in line with Plato's stance that a ruler should not wish to rule, but, if qualified, may reluctantly accept the position (Plato, 2000, p. 26). However, the collegium is not devoid of hierarchy, it does not rest on an assumption of desirability of equal and absolute democracy. Rather, there is a clear sense of hierarchy among *Homo academici* viewed as guild members; Professors holding prestigious chairs certainly rank higher than other Professors, followed by Readers or Associate Professors and mere holders of research degrees. Degrees are proxies for insight and knowledge, not absolute. Those who are perceived as truly knowledgeable by others in the guild gain status through their knowledge, but if someone's actual intellectual capacity and learning are not known to others, the status of the degree and from where it stems serve as status indicators and help establish the internal influence ranking.

The guild could, but need not, include PhD candidates, and possibly even those with graduate and undergraduate degrees. However, in much of the developed world, university enrolment is now at a level where university degrees are commonplace, and business studies is now the most popular subject in, for example, the UK (16.3%)[2] and the

[2] 16.3% of students in UK higher education in 2019–2020 (The British Academy, 2021).

USA (19%).[3] With rising numbers attending university and university colleges,[4] it would, however, be uncommon to count undergraduate students, and often even graduate students, as guild members in guilds where high-status members reside. Huisman (2012) talks of the PhD as the guild entry level, while Macfarlane and Jefferson (2022) suggest that the PhD is still only a journeyman, the level before being accepted as master. As noted above, for a guild to function as a guild, it requires some degree of exclusivity. Thus today, the guild masters in business studies, the professors, do not view the early stages of the academic ladder as really legitimating guild membership.[5] However, those who hold a Master's or Bachelor's degree may view themselves as legitimate members of a *Homo-academicus* guild (cf. Macfarlane & Jefferson, 2022), and be viewed and treated as such by people who do not hold degrees. In Sweden, for example, the Swedish Confederation of Professional Associations gathers almost one million members with a university or college degree in its 21 unions. Thus, around 13% of the Swedish workforce are members. The Swedish name is *Svenska Akademikers Centralorganisation*, where *Akademiker* refers to having a university or college degree. In some sense, these members could thus be said to self-identify as *Homo academici*.

All of this deflates the value of more junior degrees; the Master (for example of business administration) is no longer a master in the *Homo-academicus* guilds as viewed by those holding research degrees; the Master degree has become a product to sell to the market, albeit the possession of that product is a prerequisite for entry into the exclusive guilds where professors are Masters. The exclusivity of the guild is kept up by requiring a long path to qualify for entry. The MBA may suffice for working practically, applying insights gained to a practice outside of academia, but the *Gesell* certification is now the PhD, and the master certification is at

[3] 19% of bachelor's degrees awarded in 2020–2021 (National Center for Education Statistics, 2023) 19% in the US (NCES) 2021 https://nces.ed.gov/fastfacts/display.asp?id=37.

[4] At a global level, tertiary school enrolment started to rise substantially in 1990 (12% in 1970, 14% in 1990, 42% in 2022). UNESCO reports tertiary enrolment rates in Western countries of around 70% in Poland and France, 75% in Germany and the UK, 85% in Sweden and the US, to 100% in South Korea and Finland (World Bank/UNESCO, 2024).

[5] "it may be well to point out that the three titles, Master, Doctor, Professor, were in the Middle Ages absolutely synonymous" (Rashdall, 1895, p. 21).

least the Reader, Associate Professor, and *Habilitation* degrees (awarded by the academic guild), possibly even the Professorship level. Partly, this path provides for an enculturation into the norms and assumptions of the guild. The path also provides opportunity for acquiring knowledge and absorbing the skills the masters hold (as suggested by Huisman [2012]). Although ostensibly assumed to promote and protect the quality of the masters and the guild output, it possibly importantly actually is imposed as a filter, controlled by the masters, to protect the privileges of guild membership, through criteria set by the masters, even when different (or lower) qualifications could suffice to create desirable output, akin to Ogilvie's (2004) case of early-modern guilds.

Although some entrepreneurs and successful business managers proudly state that they did not finish their university degree, or did not even start on one, the MBA has today become a standard entry ticket for a business career. Whether it signals useful knowledge and skills, or merely ambition, is outside the scope of this chapter to explore. What is interesting from the guild perspective, is that employers assume that the MBA is valuable. It thus serves as a qualification for entering a less rigid guild, one of the business practitioners, where performance gradually becomes more important than the formal prescribed route for entry. This flexible guild practice parallels some of the more successful guilds in Ogilvie's (2004) study, although it violates the assumptions of what a guild should be. The professor-led academic guilds, on the other hand, so far successfully protect their privileged status in "producing" and certifying MBAs, even though academic status in these guilds is far more connected with academic research that is largely tailored to the academic research community, rather than to "commercial" product university education. This seems to indicate a difference between these two types of guilds in assumptions of what is worth striving for. In the professor-led guilds, the internally designed status criteria trump economic success, while in the loosely operated and controlled "practitioner" *Homo-academicus* guilds, it is the other way round; the more economically successful, the less important the academic qualification becomes.

Homo academicus as Employed

The second conception of *Homo academicus, the employment conception* is based on universities and university colleges as workplaces. But everyone working or having worked there would not be counted as a *Homo academicus*; only teachers and researchers would be included. Administrators who are not, or have not been, university or university college teachers or researchers, do not qualify as belonging to the tribe. An underlying assumption is that employment contracts are the bases of our society. It is your (paid) work that defines and legitimates you. Note that we ask others (and about others) what their work is (and where) as early and foundational points of orientation when trying to sort a new acquaintance into our mental maps. We assume that place and type of (paid) work, and organisational position there, are important aspects of "knowing" who someone is and in determining our relation to them. Assumptions underlying the employment conception include that official titles and employment positions confer status.

However, employment also has consequences. Employment builds on the assumption that an employer hires employees for tasks and goals the employer decides on. All other concerns that the employee may have are his individual ones and should not influence him as an employee if they clash with his employee mission, as famously argued by Milton Friedman in 1970 (Friedman, 1970). Friedman does not preclude the option to *suggest* alternative courses of action, but rules out *pursuing* them at will; "[t]he individual may have a vote and a say in what is to be done, but if he is overruled, he must conform" (p. 17). However, this is not the only view on the matter. For example, Albert Hirschman simultaneously argued that dissent is a central option, not a marginal one. When the organisation is moving in a direction contrary to employees' basic assumptions of what is good and desirable, the three avenues open to them are exit, voice, and loyalty (Hirschman, 1970). Exiting or remaining loyal conforms with Friedman's position. Voice, however, may seem not to. Painting speaking up and trying to influence the course taken as one of three courses of action, on par with the other two, affords it a prominent place.

Sardais et al. (2021) go even further, claiming that disobedience is a fourth option, and demonstrate in the case of Renault executive Pierre Lefaucheux how disobedience, while disloyal, dissonant with the assumptions of a direct agent-theory conception of employment, can be loyal, consonant with the assumptions of a stewardship-theory conception of employment. In the case of Lefaucheux, they even view his disobedience to the directives of his principals as a type of enlightened agent loyalty; through his disobedient actions he does what is actually in the long-term best interests of his principal(s mission). (This is akin to Brünhilde's loyal disobedience to Wotan's direct command in Wagner's *Der Ring des Nibelungen*, doing what he would actually want, rather than what he orders.)

However, voicing and disobedience as options are still operating within the basic assumption that the employer has the last call, including the possibility to terminate the employment (tempered, but not revoked, by legislation). Thus, if the employment is the main defining feature, then the employer holds the main source of power, not *Homo academici* themselves. Consequently, within academia, the employment conception makes it easier to apply control or give directives to *Homo academici* than the guild conception does, but such attempts can still meet resistance relating to the guild conception. By tradition, these institutions were self-governing, whether they (like Paris and Oxford) arose as teacher unions to increase bargaining power versus students, or (like Bologna) as student unions to increase bargaining power versus teachers and serve as a home away from home (Rashdall, 1895, pp. 19 ff.). In the Middle Ages, they typically even had jurisdiction over teachers and students (who could not be tried according to the laws of the surrounding society) (pp. 150 ff.).

Some sense of being special, and not to be run as just any corporation, lingers. However, the employment conception of *Homo Academicus* only provides a rather weak sense of identity, receiving prestige—or scorn—based on the views held in the society of which they form a part. It certainly has neither the self-sufficiency nor the self-determinacy that the guild conception has. Being employed at a prestigious university could help open doors, and can lend weight to your views, but in our money- and business-focused society, general managers and other high-earners tend to be strong(er) authority figures, especially concerning "real" issues;

"academic" can convey a sense of devoid of usefulness or practical value, an assumption possibly even growing stronger regarding people having advanced higher on the university-title ladder.

Like organisations in many other industries, universities and university colleges form groups and coalitions, both for knowledge exchange and to strengthen their bargaining power in relation to the surrounding society. As the prestige and privileges in society once attaching to universities and the scholars working there, now has mainly dissipated, and more readily associates with (successful) businesspeople and people amassing wealth, the employment conception assumes—and confers—a business and service perspective; scholars are just workers, employed by someone and supposed to perform the tasks those providing the money assign to them. There is no particular assumption of what knowledge is, or should be, underlying the employment conception. Instead of possessing valuable insights that you can allow others to access on terms that you postulate, academics according to the employment conception try to sell what(ever) someone is willing to buy from them. The employment conception thus placing academics as just any trade is the one I find the least interesting, and will in the rest of the chapter mainly refer to in relation to the other conceptions.

Homo academicus as Attitude

The third one, *the attitude conception*, is based on personal traits, on a yearning for learning: the (preferably unbiased) search for knowledge and insight. This corresponds with *Bildung*, the classical Humboldtian learning ideal that Wilhelm von Humboldt formulated in 1809 to revitalise the defeated Prussia with its strict teaching focus (Günther, 1988). Humboldt's visions were instantiated through the founding of the University of Berlin. The driver of education should be the individual, not a standardised plan or programme dictated by the state, professors, or some other authority.

> Just as primary instruction makes the teacher possible, so he renders himself dispensable through schooling at the secondary level. The university teacher is thus no longer a teacher and the student is no longer a pupil. Instead the student conducts research on his own behalf and the professor supervises his research and supports him in it. (von Humboldt as quoted by Clark (2007), p. 333)

Problem-based learning could be said to be drawing on this ideal. But those who have tried it, know that neither the attitude such learning builds on nor the process through which it is enacted, come easily or quickly to those who are not used to it.

Although individualistic, the *Bildung*-pursuit of the yearning for learning is not inherently selfish; the search for knowledge and insight helps shape the individual as a constructive member of society, with integrity, an ability to learn and communicate, and a willingness to rethink and reconsider in the face of new input or challenges (Günther, 1988; Sjöström & Eilks, 2020), a reflecting, critical mind, if you will. Humboldt considered this to be of primary concern, based on the assumption that a society foremost needs good, upstanding, and well-informed human beings. On that foundation, skills can be acquired, and vocational training undertaken at will, on an as needs basis, catering to possibly shifting vocational needs over a lifetime. Anyone could be a *Homo academicus* in this sense, regardless of attending university or not. Indeed, according to Humboldt, everyone should be, but looking at our fellow humans, it is easy to note that not everyone is. Current debates about (higher) education tend to rest on different assumptions; education should provide commercial competitiveness (of individuals, enterprises, and nations), and competitiveness rests on practically applicable skills, on being valuable human capital, rather than on being a good and generally well-informed human being. Looking at ranking lists of universities and business schools, criteria build more on the fame and title-based status of faculty and employability of students (and salary increase through getting a degree) than on a *Bildung* ideal.

Not surprisingly, several studies have found that US students tend to value course completion and good grades over actual learning and development (Miley & Gonsalves, 2004; Arum & Roksa, 2011; Pascarella et al., 2011). In line with this, and contrary to the *Bildung* ideal, many students do not improve their higher-order academic skills during their first years at university (Arum & Roksa, 2011; Pascarella et al., 2011). This is in line with the higher-education explosion—that a majority, or indeed everyone, should attend higher education, and that having done so becomes a prerequisite for employment. Although Humboldt saw a quest for learning as desirable and felt that a society populated by people who follow a *Bildung* ideal would be a good and capable society, if university studies are driven by an external expectation rather than by internal yearning for learning, the population at large will not turn into *Bildung*-type *Homo academici*.

This does not just hold for the population at large. Certainly, not all *Homo academici* according to the previous two conceptions could be considered *Homo academici* based on this third conception. As noted above, a widespread assumption in society is that what really matters is earning potential. A *Bildung*-penchant tends to be viewed as a laudable attitude, although not necessarily monetarily profitable. To people outside of university circles, and who value universities, the *Bildung*-penchant may be what they believe characterises university people in general. At one end of the spectrum, the Ivory-tower ideal of knowledge for knowledge's sake, regardless of its potential or present practical applicability, is followed by some and may be ascribed by people outside of academia also to others who actually have more of an employability-usefulness perspective on their knowledge-seeking. At the other end, we would expect to find those who have a clear wish for knowledge to be practically useful and can be willing to let potential usability direct their search. Less common today is to encounter the Platonian view of true philosophers (lovers of wisdom), where the knowledge sought should benefit both society and individuals; *arete*, the excellence or virtue, should also be morally good, a view that seems to have resonated with von Humboldt. For quite some time, the pursuit of knowledge has often been considered to be divorced from its potential uses; the basic assumption then is that knowledge in itself is not good or evil, only the uses to which it is put, and those uses, if harmful to someone, can not be blamed on the academic who developed the knowledge. Although people now and then question if academics should be allowed to pursue knowledge that could potentially be harmful, the idea of basic research—research for the sake of developing knowledge, regardless of its usability (and thus regardless of its potential uses)—tends to work as a defence for ivory-tower attitudes that divorce the development of knowledge from its potential uses.

In the mainstream field of organisation and management, there is little discussion of harmfulness of applying the cherished assumptions. The Friedman quotation above rests solidly on the assumption that economic success builds (the good and desirable) society. In such a view, organisation and management is intimately tied with economic benefit and progress. Accordingly, a yearning for learning that does not serve those interests, and could even prove detrimental to them. This could be seen as biased. But so could a critical stance: for example, posing societal benefits against owner benefits. Any stance takes a position, has to overtly or tacitly assume something as desirable. We will never find a position that everyone agrees on, and thus achieve unanimity on what is to be considered harmful and what is considered beneficial or desirable. But what is mainstream and what is viewed as critical may change—as von Humboldt was well aware, living through the social upheavals of revolutions and the Napoleonic wars. The *Bildung* ideal has from various critical perspectives been viewed as bourgeois, Western-imperialistic, racist, sexistic, and even by some viewed as speciesistic—often based on assumptions characterising specific instantiations of the ideal in university settings (Taylor, 2017). However, von Humboldt's original vision is compatible even with a posthuman interpretation, which pluralises

> what and who counts as those 'others' with whom we (humans) live our lives, thus erasing the differences that Humanism installed at the heart of relations. It replaces difference as alterity with different with/in entanglement, thereby reconstituting *Bildung* as a postanthropocentric ethic of encounter which moves beyond speciesism and hierarchy towards modes of interbeing, interspeciesbeing and worlding [ ]. These new modes of contact generate new responsibilities, accountabilities and commitments, which emerge in the embodied specificity of incarnate relations, not in universalist codes. (p. 432)

When Carol Taylor wrote this in 2016, it may have seemed rather far from mainstream, challenging assumptions of what we should care about. This is rather far from a shareholder-value-centric world. However, with global warming an increasingly palpable challenge, and sustainability a term that is now entering all fields, including mainstream organisation and management, the appeal to an interest in and concern for not only different aspects of our human societies, but also our interactions and interrelations with the biological and inanimate realms, appears far less niche. Had Plato been alive today, it seems plausible that he, too, would have adopted Taylor's view of what should morally concern us. But do organisation and management scholars, in a naturally curious *Homo-academicus* manner, try to reassess their assumptions in light of input like Taylor's, or do they, rather more guild-like, attempt to protect their assumptions, akin to Larry Fink's argumentation:

> I believe the decarbonizing of the global economy is going to create the greatest investment opportunity of our lifetime. It will also leave behind the companies that don't adapt, regardless of what industry they are in. [ ] We focus on sustainability not because we're environmentalists, but because we are capitalists and fiduciaries to our clients. (Fink, 2022)

He does not want to view the reorientation as moving away from the basic shareholder-value-supremacy assumption. Instead, he tries hard to consolidate these new concerns with classical economic reasoning where the wider range of concerns are not important in their own right, but because they make business sense: will contribute to long-term shareholder value.

Summing Up the Three Types of *Homo academicus*

So far, I have painted a picture of the guild conception as one where the basic assumption of what constitutes a *Homo academicus* is belonging to a guild. The main concern of a guild is the ability to stake out a turf, defend dominion over it, create a hierarchy—a structure of status—for peripheral participation and gradual adoption into the guild, where becoming a master is the stage of being fully adopted into the guild, and from then on being able to participate in its further governance, in the delimitation of the turf and the design and operation of the criteria for acceptance into the guild and the output of the guild. For an academic guild, the turf is a subject, complete with assumptions of how that subject should be treated. The path of entry into the guild is the sequence of academic degrees and titles to obtain, in order to finally be accepted as a full member. I have broadly painted the area of organisation and management as a set of related guilds, largely divided into mainstream and critical ones, where mainstream tends to rest more firmly on the assumption that the objective is to help improve business practice, especially with regard to the creation of shareholder value, and that business practitioners, especially managers, behave, or strive to behave in line with principles of economic rationality. Critical guilds tend to question the assumption of (economic) rationality and possibly also the primacy of stakeholders, among the potential range of stakeholders.

This stylised description of academic guilds could of course be substantially elaborated, with more groups and more both complementing and contrasting assumptions. And as I have exemplified, the division into mainstream and critical is not in practice necessarily this clearcut. However, for the purpose of this chapter, it will suffice. I also question the assumption that the output of the academic guilds of organisation and management is learning. Increasingly, under the pressure of dramatically increasing demand for higher education, degrees may become more important than whatever learning has taken place before being awarded a degree. Also, the path of entry into a professor-controlled guild in organisation and management does not really start with undergraduate or graduate degrees. They are products controlled and produced by the guild for a market of business and other organisational practices. This in turn has led to the growth of less stringent *Homo-academicus* guilds of practitioners, outside the universities, where part of identity lies in having obtained a higher-education degree, but where the practice track record rather than the academic credentials take precedence as the career progresses. Research publications are more products internal to the guilds than ones aimed at its markets. Much of the research-publication output may even appear inconsequential to the surrounding society. For the markets, the teaching and practice-oriented publications are the important channels for research results, channels that are of little importance for internal status in the guilds.

According to *Homo academicus* as employment, focus rests on assumptions of relations between employer and employed. Whereas the guild conception promotes the assumption that the *Homo academici* themselves are in control (and that universities or business schools are the tools and preserves of the guilds), the "as employment" conception exposes the underlying assumption that it is the employer, not the *Homo academici*, that has the ultimate control. The academic employees serve their employers. If they do not agree with the directives given by the employer, they could possibly exercise exit, voice, or disobedience, but then at the peril of losing their jobs. Or they could show loyalty and follow the directives, regardless of how these resonate with their own convictions and judgement. This simple picture could be somewhat complicated by replacing underlying assumptions of agency theory (with the employee as the agent of the employer) with the assumptions of stewardship theory, where the employees are foremost stewards of the organisation, the university, or commonly for organisation and management scholars, specifically the business school. Sentiments in the surrounding society, and laws and regulations, could temper the employer's dominance, but ultimately, the power lies with the employer, and *Homo academici* are employed to do their bidding.

The third conception, that of *Homo academicus*-ship as an attitude of yearning for learning, is based on the assumption that *academicus* stands for someone striving towards a fuller understanding of the world in which they live; striving for a capacity to learn, including relearning and challenging previously held assumptions; and learning in order to be a constructive part of society—or of an even more encompassing world—possibly even non-anthropocentric. This conception is not organisation-based, as the previous two; it is individual-trait-based. Thus here, there is no obvious connection between *Homo academicus*-ship and universities and business schools. A business school could serve as a source of input or as a place for acquiring *Homo-academicus* skills and learning how to learn. But that rests on the assumption that the business school operates in a way that promotes, or at least can support, a mode of learning that caters to the individually motivated yearning for learning. Neither the guild nor the employment conception builds on assumptions that specifically cater to individualised yearning for learning, nor are they specifically opposed to it. Above, I have brought up examples of when the assumption of universities and business schools as places for individualised learning is not fulfilled. Part of such clashes could be traced back to the growing numbers of students and the assumption that standardisation is *the* road to cost efficiency. Individualised learning opportunities then increase with the progression to higher degree levels, when student cohorts thin out and faculty/student ratios increase. Another consequence of the growing numbers is that academic degrees are assumed to be proxies for employability. The attitude of yearning for learning, and its possibly resulting level of *Bildung*, is poorly captured by degrees, and difficult for a job applicant to adequately signal. Thus, our current society, though possibly as much in need of *Bildung* as in the time of von Humboldt, is not well-rigged to deal with it. I will return to societal developments outside of universities that *are* rigged to cater to this type of *Homo academicus*. But here, I will finish by looking at the possible connection between the *Bildung* ideal and faculty positions.

I am not trying to say that university and business school employment is antithetical to the conception of *Homo academicus* as attitude of yearning for learning. The growth of organisation and management as an academic field, and the growth of the higher-education sector, on the one hand fuel standardised mass production and output, but can also provide room for specialisation and niches. Creating new guilds to provide a *raison d'être* can cater to curiosity within that area, not just define boundaries that close the interest in. Trying to find new angles within existing areas can also lead to interesting opportunities for learning. And in general, the higher-education sector builds on the assumption that careers should encompass increased learning and competence. Although many forces and practices restrict the freedom of pursuing individualistically designed paths of learning, university and business school employment offers opportunities for such pursuit to those who learn to navigate the environment.

One challenge facing academics is to what end they are academics—for self-serving guild reasons? For subservient employment reasons—working to make a living, working at an employer that can hold some social prestige? Out of curiosity, and possibly in search of learning (in service of the world?)?

Valuable Knowledge, Management Scholarship, and Channels for Learning

Since the time of Aristotle, philosophy has been a profession, often associated with academies. Churches and religious institutions have housed, nurtured, and sometimes restricted them, and from the rise of the university as an institution, philosophy has been a core discipline within universities, largely concerned with logic and reasoning. Among the ancient Greeks, philosophy could relate to any subject, and even today, the degree Doctor of Philosophy can be awarded in many subjects, management, and organisation, among them, that by neither the general public nor by the holders of the degrees would be thought of as philosophy, which has become more related to sophism and detachment from practical topics. A reason for this is the growing connection between the term philosophy and the pursuit of logic reasoning. The original meaning of love (and pursuit) of knowledge is no longer the obvious loading of the term. But already Plato questioned those sophists who would practice and teach the art of reasoning and argumentation for the winning of arguments, regardless of the (societal or moral) merit of the line of reasoning, rather than use logic to develop valuable knowledge (Adamson, 2014). (Could those sophists perhaps be considered early management scholars?).

What, then, is valuable knowledge? An assumption underlying Plato's position is that value lies in the enabling of *arete*, of achieving one's full potential, but in a morally good way. The value of winning an argument, although it could be great in monetary or political sense, would not be the type of value Plato was looking for, if it did not contribute to *arete*. That assumption was perhaps not held by a majority in antiquity, and it certainly is not the linchpin of current societies. In the part of academia targeted in this book, organisation and management, the mainstream is geared towards the commercial, towards profitability and employability. Shareholder value is an unquestioned goal. And people have, and continue to argue like Friedman, that this is actually good, this is what builds and maintains a good society. Certainly, there are critical streams, but they are not mainstream, and tend to have little influence on the mainstream. Even in areas such as business ethics or sustainability, there is a strong tendency to look for the confluence of ethical and profitable behaviour, sustainability, and business success, rather than focus on clashes and trade-offs. Perhaps, the increasing physical threats posed by global warming are about to lead to sustainability issues (economic and social, not just environmental) forcing a critical strain into the mainstream; are perhaps many of the mainstream teachings harmful, after all? Is a strict shareholder-value focus sustainable from a societal perspective? Might Plato's insistence on a more encompassing *arete* get renewed relevance?

Today, much research with practical goals is carried out in commercial companies, and the resulting knowledge is typically guarded (by patents or secrecy) to provide a return on investment. By contrast, the ideal of university research has been to disseminate the findings as freely as possible. This is increasingly meeting two obstacles. One is that research published in academic journals has become big business, where highly profitable publishers are trying to profit from the process of publishing, charging high fees for accessing the publications and in practice restricting the readership to those with library access to universities who deem they can afford subscriptions (Puehringer et al., 2021). "Open publishing", providing the publications to readers, free of charge, typically moves the cost (including publishers' profits) from libraries and readers to the authors and those who fund the published research. The other obstacle is that university management increasingly promote the assumption that universities are entities engaged in (commercial) competition, and we should thus view research and other knowledge development as a means of generating commercially profitable operations (with concomitant restricting effects for the dissemination of the findings).

But just as all knowledge developed at universities is not made widely and freely available, not all knowledge developed in commercial companies is kept secret and beyond paywalls. Especially results that may form a (new) platform for products (like the cassette tape, developed by Phillips, or the PC standards developed by IBM) are sometimes made freely available in the hope that this will lead to their rapid and widespread adoption, thus increasing the potential market that can be built on that platform. This reasoning is still commercial, but with a different practical result for the dissemination of knowledge. The objective is a collaboration on the assumption that this collaboration will increase the share of a pie that can then be divided, rather than holding a more singular competition perspective, where knowledge sharing without compensation is to be avoided.

So what about the role of universities for knowledge development? Obviously, universities and the academics active at universities, do not have a monopoly on knowledge development, and never have had. Leonardo da Vinci, the polymath, never worked at a university. Niccolò Machiavelli, diplomat, author, philosopher, and historian, who is still taught in leadership classes, didn't either. Nor did Edward Gibbon, in researching and developing his history of the rise and fall of the Roman empire, the six volumes which he published between 1776 and 1788 with their influential investigation of organisational issues. Friedrich Engels, acting independently, interviewed workers in Manchester to develop his *Die Lage der arbeitenden Klasse in England* (*The Condition of the Working Class in England*) in 1844–1845, and Karl Marx famously frequented the British Library to develop *Das Kapital*, first volume published in 1867. These are just some prominent, historical examples forming foundations for much current thinking in the field of organisation and management. Many more have contributed to the growth of the body of knowledge in society over the years, since time immemorial, and with an increasing range following information-technology innovations: writing, inexpensive paper, printing presses and publishing houses, innovations decreasing the physical transportation of people and printed material, the telephone, radio, and television, making communication and dissemination possible at low cost without the need to move people or material. Whereas the telephone facilitated communication at individuals' initiative, radio and television mainly centralised dissemination, from few senders to many recipients. However, universities rarely started radio and television channels to systematically disseminate insights.

Since the advent of the Internet for public use, the assumption of universities as the sources of knowledge and the places for knowledge-seeking has been further challenged by individuals, increasingly able to access material and discussion partners at will, and publishing the results of their knowledge-seeking on the Web and on commercial but free-access platforms. High-quality blogs, forums, video channels, and podcasts now form part of the knowledge-dissemination scene, and the communities forming around them also serve knowledge-development functions. Certainly, organisational actors like Harvard Business Review have long used the format. Their HBR IdeaCast has since 2006 published close to 1,000 episodes. But the wide availability of material, low cost of communication, and low cost and potential worldwide-reach dissemination and interactivity now provide historically unparalleled possibilities for philosophers in the sense of knowledge-lovers and—seekers to act. This also leads to a mass of entrants and an unparalleled supply, where the success in terms of really large audiences or communities is very skewed, but where a long tail of actors may find it worthwhile to dive into knowledge-seeking and broadcasting and sustain it even with a modest classroom-sized following.

Educational podcast communities, the Intelligent Speech Conference and similar public events for the podcasting community, TED talks, knowledge-focused YouTube channels, university-independent MOOCs, and similar ICT-facilitated venues could be viewed as today's counterparts of the Bolognas and Oxfords of a millennium ago, linking those who have knowledge to share with those who seek to acquire such knowledge. So far, these venues mostly operate along the *attitude* conception, based on the love of, and search for knowledge, a yearning for learning. But in the marketing and gaining adherents to a specific channel, podcast, or course, it being an experience good, difficult to assess until you have experienced it, generally recognisable merits from *the guild* or even *the employment* conception of *Homo academicus* may serve as useful signals, proxies for quality that attracts listeners—and collaborators—to the venue, until adherents have sampled the form and content and formed an experience-based view of the merits of the venue.

Like in other parts of society, success breeds success, so a podcast or channel that has attracted a large following will attract new users and collaborators who take popularity as a signal of quality, thus lessening the need for, for example, *Homo-academicus* credentials to attract people and grow the community. But as with the growth and spread of universities in the previous millennium, the typical institutionalising processes of genre construction and aggregation have led to the formation of "educational" podcast and YouTube-channel formats, with subgenres based on content or form; the building of communities of communities (for example Intelligent Speech, political science podcasts, ancient history, ...) to some extent forming proto-guilds—associations who set entrance rules and start to shape competence-development venues and processes, although so far not systematised and formalised. Inclusion is open to those who seem to qualify, regardless of how they achieved those qualifications. (Like the weak, lax, or flexible early-modern guilds.)

Perhaps the institutionalisation processes will give rise to new guilds, but so far, these IT-mediated—and ICT-enabled—knowledge seekers and disseminators have partly chosen these non-academic platforms because of restrictions that the *guild conception* or the *employment conception* place on the choice of topics, both in terms of what may be included, and the depth to which a topic can be covered, but also in terms of who is allowed to design and "send", and who can listen and interact. Some hold traditional academic credentials and positions in academia, but either want to go deeper into the subject than the traditional academic setting would allow them, or move outside of the topic or audience delimitations that their academic position imposes on them. An example is *Talking about organizations*, run by organisation researchers with academic credentials and backed by established academics at business schools and journals. Others have chosen other careers than academic ones, and find that their search for knowledge, or will to share their insights, although of a *Homo-academicus attitude conception*, is not met by current academic institutions, but fits some of the new, ICT-enabled forms. However, drawing on academic sources and interacting with professional academics tends to be an important component—as is interaction with listeners and viewers, building a community rather than an anonymous broadcasting audience. Some certainly lean heavily towards an entertainment side of what to draw on, present, and how to present. I leave them aside and focus on those who profess or appear to search for high-quality knowledge, carefully evaluating sources and declaring the reasoning that lead them to conclude what they believe and present. What is knowledge, and what are the criteria by which it is assessed? I will now turn to that issue and its connections with the three *Homo-academicus* conceptions.

What Counts as True or Acceptable Knowledge?

In many systems, be they legal, religious, or academic, we tend to get alternative ways of determining what counts as true or acceptable knowledge, with different versions of authorities and rational reasoning. These alternative ways, and their underlying assumptions, appear similar across systems. For example, Islamic law and Islamic orthodoxy (to a large degree intertwined) hold the divine revelations transmitted via the Book, the Quran, to be central and in some sense supreme, in most versions of Islam supplemented by Sunnah, the traditions and practices of the prophet Muhammad (Adamson, 2016). The underlying assumption seems to be that there is some source of truth or acceptable knowledge, and the order of preference among ways of ascertaining it is based on the assumed directness to that source. There are authorised versions of the Quran, established by secular and religious authorities in the centuries following the death of the prophet, just as there are authorised versions of what texts are to be considered the true Bible in various variants of Christianity, established by religious and secular authorities over the centuries. These are assumed to be direct revelations of divine truth (Neuwirth, 2003). Sunnah is more difficult, as it builds on verbal accounts handed down, or supposedly handed down as examples, hadiths, by the prophet's direct followers, those who could observe his actions and ways of reasoning. At different points in time, people have attempted to distinguish between reliable hadiths and those that have more tenuous claims of authenticity. Assuming that the prophet was in direct contact with God, a seemingly reliable trace back to the prophet would make the hadith a valid indication of divine will and judgement (Adamson, 2016).

For legal issues not explicitly covered in the Quran or the Sunnah, there are additional ways of determining what is right and not. Ijmā, consensus among jurisprudent, consisting of *al qawl* (explicit), *al fi'l* (according to praxis), or *al sukut* (tacit acceptance—those who do not explicitly disagree are seen as agreeing) is one way. Here, the assumption seems to be that the jurisprudent have a good understanding of the divine will, and, although not as clear as the direct word through the Quran, or the divinely inspired and directed actions of the prophet, consensus among the jurisprudent would be a reliable indication of the divine position of the issue in question. If such consensus is not available—or not reached—independent reasoning or judgement, *ijtihad*, but only by someone deemed qualified to think or reason in such matters, is a next step, where *Dalil al-'aql*—rational proof or logic—is a specific version of reasoning not just based on general thinking or conviction. Another type is Qiays, analogy from explicit Quran text. This may seem very similar to independent reasoning, but is lent extra weight by its explicit connection to the foundational text, the Quran (However, analogy obviously rests on an interpretation, and this interpretation depends on who is making it. What seems like a clear analogy to someone, may not have been thought of by another Quran reader, and could perhaps even be viewed as debatable by others [Hallaq, 2009]).

Note that all these versions of reasoning and interpretation are not left up to anyone, but restricted to those specifically awarded authority by a guild-like structure: those who are recognised by others in that structure, and recognise each other, as qualified. However, exceptional people may come to hold authority, arising via self-appointment as an authority, and then demonstrating through the merit (clear reasoning or persuasiveness) of the form and content of one's judgement as worth listening and adhering to, for example Ibn-Sīnā (known in the West as Avicenna). But they are definitely the exception (Adamson, 2016).

Do you as a reader find this to be a farfetched example, too removed from your academic setting? Or do you, as I do, see remarkable similarities? Is it not extremely rare to be taken seriously when speaking on academic matters to a guild audience if you do not belong to an accepted guild—have the traditional education and background of people in your branch of academia? Don't we as academics award great importance to acknowledged foundational texts (for example, work by Aristotle, Foucault, Herbert Simon, Robert Anthony, Karl Weick, Wanda Orlikowski, or whatever counts as key references in your specific discipline), and collections of texts, lending credence to specific items in those texts because of the status of the collection (Accounting, Organizations and Society; Academy of Management Journal; Organization Science; etc.)?

Even if we ascribe to basic assumptions of knowledge as the best current explanation or description of a phenomenon, one that can be improved on, or even outcompeted by observations and arguments based on their inherent merits, is this ascribing really a case of theory-in-use, or just an espoused theory (Argyris & Schön, 1974) seldom put into practice? To what extent do we actually weigh an argument just based on its inherent merits (which would be in line with the assumptions underlying the yearning-for-learning attitude conception of *Homo Academicus*), rather than largely on the basis of the status of its references and its author (more in line with the basic assumptions of the guild conception)? Although this protects the guild from free competition from just any direction, and it also may be viewed (inside the guild, and perhaps by those outside who put trust in academia just because it is academia) as a convenient heuristic for judging quality, is this really how we would want the academic discourse and search for knowledge to function? Or does it give us pause, and cause to consider whether we have become entrapped in habits turned rituals? Have our traditions become our Iron cage (DiMaggio & Powell, 1983)?

References

Adamson, P. (2014). *Classical philosophy: A history of philosophy without any gaps,* (Vol. 1). Oxford University Press.

Adamson, P. (2016). *Philosophy in the Islamic World: A history of philosophy without any gaps,* (Vol. 3). Oxford University Press.

Alvesson, M., Blom, M., & Sveningsson, S. (2017). *Reflexive leadership: Organising in an imperfect world*. SAGE Publications.

Alvesson, M., & Spicer, A. (2016). *The stupidity paradox: The power and pitfalls of functional stupidity at work*. Profile Books Ltd.

Argyris, C., & Schön, D. (1974). *Theory in practice: Increasing professional effectiveness*. Jossey-Bass.

Arum, R., & Roksa, J. (2011). *Academically adrift: Limited learning on college campuses*. The University of Chicago Press.

The British Academy. (2021). *Business and management provision in UK higher education*. https://www.thebritishacademy.ac.uk/publications/business-and-management-provision-in-uk-higher-education/ (accessed online on January 28th, 2024).

Brunsson, N. (1985). *The irrational organization*. Wiley.

Brunsson, N. (1989). *The organization of hypocrisy: Talk, decisions and actions in organizations*. Wiley.

Clark, C. (2007). *Iron kingdom: The rise and downfall of Prussia, 1600–1947*. Penguin Books.

DiMaggio, P. J., & Powell, W. W. (1983). The iron cage revisited: Institutional isomorphism and collective rationality in organizational fields. *American Sociological Review, 48*(2), 147–160. https://doi.org/10.2307/2095101

Engels, F. (1845). *Die Lage der arbeitenden Klasse in England*. Otto Wigand.

Fink, L. (2022) *The power of capitalism: Larry Fink's 2022 letter to CEOs*. https://www.blackrock.com/corporate/investor-relations/larry-fink-ceo-letter

Friedman, M. (1970, September 13). The social responsibility of business is to increase its profits. *New York Times Magazine*. https://nyti.ms/1LSi5ZD

Gibbon, E. (1776–1788). *The history of the decline and fall of the Roman empire. I-VI*. W. Strahan/A. Strahan and T Cadell.

Günther, K.-H. (1988). Profiles of educators: Wilhelm von Humboldt (1767–1835). *Prospects, 18*, 127–136. https://doi.org/10.1007/BF02192965

Hallaq, W. B. (2009). *An introduction to Islamic law*. Cambridge University Press.

Huisman, T. J. (2012). Universities: Challenges to the last guild in a new information age. *NJAS: Wageningen Journal of Life Sciences, 59*, 1–2, 3–5. https://doi.org/10.1016/j.njas.2012.01.005
Macfarlane, B. J., & Jefferson, A. E. (2022). The closed academy? Guild power and academic social class. *Higher Education Quarterly, 1–12*,. https://doi.org/10.1111/hequ.12305
Marx, K. (1867). *Das Kapital. Kritik der politischen Oekonomie. Buch 1.* Otto Meissner.
Miley, W. M., & Gonsalves, S. (2004). Grade expectations: Redux. *College Student Journal, 53*(3), 327–332.
National Center for Education Statistics (2023). *Fast facts*. https://nces.ed.gov/fastfacts/display.asp?id=37 (accessed online on January 30th, 2024).
Neuwirth, A. (2003). Qur'an and history—A disputed relationship. Some reflections on Qur'anic history and history in the Qur'an. *Journal of Qur'anic Studies, 5*(1), 1–18.
Nonaka, I. (1994). A dynamic theory of organizational knowledge creation. *Organization Science, 5*(1), 14–37. http://www.jstor.com/stable/2635068
Ogilvie, S. (2004). Guilds, efficiency, and social capital: Evidence from German proto-industry. *The Economic History Review, 57*(2) 286–333. https://www.jstor.org/stable/3698609
Parker, M. (2020). The critical business school and the university: A case study of resistance and co-optation. *Critical Sociology, 47*(7–8), 1111–1124. https://doi.org/10.1177/0896920520950387
Pascarella, E. T., Blaich, C., Martin, G. L., & Hanson, J. M. (2011). How robust are the findings of *Academically Adrift*? *Change: The Magazine of Higher Learning, 43*(3), 20–24. https://doi.org/10.1080/00091383.2011.568898
Plato. (2000). *The Republic*. G. R. F. Ferrari (Ed.); translated by Tom Griffith. Cambridge texts in the history of political thought.
Polanyi, M. (1958). *Personal knowledge: Towards a post-critical philosophy*. University of Chicago Press.
Puehringer, S., Rath, J., & Griesebner, T. (2021). The political economy of academic publishing: On the commodification of a public good. *PLoS ONE*. https://doi.org/10.1371/journal.pone.025322
Rashdall, H. (1895). *The universities of Europe in the middle ages* (vol. 1). Clarendon Press.
Sahlin, K., & Eriksson-Zetterquist, U. (Eds.). (2023). *Revitalizing collegiality: Restoring faculty authority in universities*. Emerald Publishing Limited. https://doi.org/10.1108/S0733-558X202387

Sardais, C., Blom, M., & Lortie, J. (2021). Exit, voice, loyalty, and … disobedience: When a CEO opposes his principal. *Corporate Governance: An International Review, 29*(2), 188–207. https://doi.org/10.1111/corg.12352
Sjöström, J., & Eilks, I. (2020). The Bildung theory—From von Humboldt to Klafki and beyond. In B. Akpan & T. J. Kennedy (Eds.), *Science education in theory and practice. Springer texts in education* (pp. 54–67). https://doi.org/10.1007/978-3-030-43620-9_5
Taylor, C. A. (2017). Is a posthumanist *Bildung* possible? Reclaiming the promise of *Bildung* for contemporary higher education. *Higher Education, 74*, 419–435. https://doi.org/10.1007/s10734-016-9994-y
World Bank/UNESCO. (2024). *School enrolment, tertiary (% gross).* https://data.worldbank.org/indicator/SE.TER.ENRR?most_recent_value_desc=false (accessed online on January 1st, 2024).

The manufacturer's authorised representative in the EU is Springer Nature Customer Service Centre GmbH, Europaplatz 3, 69115 Heidelberg, Germany. If you have any concerns regarding our products, please contact ProductSafety@springernature.com

Printed and bound by CPI Group (UK) Ltd, Croydon, CR0 4YY
28/09/2026
02224072-0013